Africa and the New World Order

Society and Politics in Africa

Yakubu Saaka
General Editor

Vol. 7

PETER LANG
New York • Washington, D.C./Baltimore • Boston • Bern
Frankfurt am Main • Berlin • Brussels • Vienna • Canterbury

Julius O. Ihonvbere

Africa and the
New World Order

PETER LANG
New York • Washington, D.C./Baltimore • Boston • Bern
Frankfurt am Main • Berlin • Brussels • Vienna • Canterbury

Library of Congress Cataloging-in-Publication Data

Ihonvbere, Julius Omozuanvbo.
Africa and the new world order / Julius O. Ihonvbere.
    p. cm. — (Society and politics in Africa; vol. 7)
    Includes bibliographical references (p.   ) and index.
  1. Africa—Economic conditions—1960– 2. Democracy—Africa.
    3. Africa—Foreign economic relations. I. Title. II. Series.
        HC800.I35   337.6—dc21   97-48672
              ISBN 0-8204-3889-8
              ISSN 1083-3323

Die Deutsche Bibliothek-CIP-Einheitsaufnahme

Ihonvbere, Julius O.:
Africa and the new world order / Julius O. Ihonvbere.
–New York; Washington, D.C./Baltimore; Boston; Bern;
Frankfurt am Main; Berlin; Vienna; Paris: Lang.
    (Society and politics in Africa; Vol. 7)
              ISBN 0-8204-3889-8

Cover design by Nona Reuter

The paper in this book meets the guidelines for permanence and durability
of the Committee on Production Guidelines for Book Longevity
of the Council of Library Resources.

© 2000 Peter Lang Publishing, Inc., New York

Printed in the United States of America

To Grace, my very best friend, confidante, colleague,
comrade, and partner.

Contents

Acknowledgments

This book is the product of my thinking and writings in the last decade. My views have been informed by experiences in the field of popular politics, research, and teaching in and outside Africa. It is therefore an opportune moment to thank all those who have, in one way or the other, shaped my ideas over the years. This includes, in particular, those with whom I have had and continue to have intellectual, especially ideological, disagreements. I have always maintained that no scholarship is neutral, in spite of the efforts by some of my colleagues in the West to pretend that their themes, interpretations, conclusions, and projections are value- free or neutral. I would like to begin by thanking my teachers at the University of Ife (now Obafemi Awolowo University) in Nigeria for imparting in me the desire to avoid the bureaucracy and embrace the academy. At Carleton University, Ottawa, Canada, Dr. Lynn Mytelka, who (with Andrew Axline of the University of Ottawa) supervised my master's thesis, stands out as a major source of inspiration. She convinced me that it could be fun to be an academic. At the University of Toronto, my three years there were full of fun with wonderful teachers, many of whom I still call "teacher" to this day: Richard Sandbrook my dissertation supervisor, Jonathan Baker, Richard Stren, Bob Matthews, Cranford Pratt, and the late C.B. Macpherson. I would also like to thank Jose Nun, who convinced me that theory is actually the strength of scholarship anywhere in the world. I have found this to be very true. Of course, Macpherson, "the grandfather of political theory in Canada," not only made political theory look interesting, he also made it look very easy. I would also like to thank some scholars who were not my teachers but from whom I have gained a lot: Timothy M. Shaw, Linda Freeman, Ralph Onwuka, Bade Onimode, Okwudiba Nnoli, Festus Iyayi, Claude Ake, Yusuf Bala Usman, Mahmood Mamdani, Issa Shivji, Adebayo Adedeji, Peter Anyang Nyongo, Terisa Turner, Bill Graf, James Mittleman, George Shephard, Jr., Ngugi Wa Tiongo, and Ali Mazrui. Of course, this list is not exhaustive. My academic family in the United States, Pita Agbese, Femi Vaughan, Femi Taiwo, Kelechi Kalu, Ike Udogu, Bolaji Aluko, Sam Atteh, George Kieh, Gloria Thomas, Bolaji Aluko, Kunirum Osia, and Okon Akiba, have supported my work over the years with research materials. Suzanne Colwell and Joe Tenbarge of the Government Department at the University of Texas have rescued me several times from my problems with the computer! My Research Assistants, Fran Buntman and friends, Prosper Bani, Rose Tamfuh, Krysta Lyons, and Caroline Shaw assisted in immeasurable ways. Many of my friends and relatives have supported me with materials over the years: George Najomo, Daniel Ihonvbere, Nancy Najomo, Athan Ogoh, Kehinde Ofunrein, Edward Najomo, Eddie Akpaka, Adamu Sule, Florence Ngonga, Sunny and Rosemary Uzuh and Boniface Nnaji. My thanks also go to Audrey Robinson of the Ford Foundation, New York who worked on the final version of the manuscript. I would like to thank Owen Lancer of Peter Lang Publishing and the anonymous readers for their support and encouragement. A version of chapter two was published in *In-Depth: A Journal for Values and Public Policy* (Winter 1994). A version of chapter four appeared in *Current World Leaders* (August 1994); and a version of chapter seven was published in *International Politics* (September 1996). I thank these journals for allowing me to re-use these works and for providing initial outlets for them. Of course, I alone take full responsibility for the contents of this work.

Julius O. Ihonvbere
Austin, Texas
October 1996

Preface

In setting out to write this book, I called my longtime friend and colleague, Femi Taiwo, who teaches philosophy at Loyola University in Chicago. I wanted his advice on how to title the book: "Africa *in* the New World Order," or "Africa *and* the New World Order." He hardly allowed me to complete my question before he opted for the latter. His reason was that Africa was **not** *in* the new world order. Femi reasoned that if Africa was *in* the new world order how come it has remained an almost irrelevant actor, weak, dominated, exploited, and marginalized as usual. No one can fault this line of reasoning though at times, it is mischievously confused with "Afro-pessimism." Afro-pessimism is that line of thinking which has given up on Africa: nothing positive is happening, and nothing positive could happen. Africa is simply a lost cause.

Dr. Taiwo's line of reasoning simply admits the terrible state of Africa's political economy. It acknowledges the weaknesses of institutions, communities, and social forces. However, it does not write off the continent. By avoiding undue romanticization of the African reality, it is possible to draw inspiration from the current state of decay and dislocation, and generate the necessary political will, alliances, and consciousness required for Africa's genuine liberation. Over three decades of political independence have witnessed the impoverishment of Africans. On all indicators of growth and development Africa is doing so badly that most Africans can no longer imagine that things could be better. If nothing else, no one can accuse African leaders of having tried to promote development or democracy. To be sure, the political elites in Africa have done very well for themselves. The vaults of foreign banks are bursting with their loot. Yet, the continent remains the "sick child" of the global system. This condition is not natural. It is not the consequence of poverty or the lack of skills. Africa remains one of the most resource-endowed regions of the world. With some 54-odd countries and over 600 million people, it is a huge market of growing urban centers and an ebullient population. Yet, all economic and political models have failed to work in Africa: indigenization, one-party rule, one-person rule, military juntas, nationalization, African socialism, humanism, basic needs, growth-pole development strategy, even structural adjustment have all failed to redefine internal economic and power relations just as they have failed to restructure Africa's peripheral location and role in the global division of labor and power. If this is the long-awaited *uhuru*, many Africans are beginning to wonder when it would come to an end because "*Uhuru*" has only brought poverty, hunger, pain, disease, marginalization, and brutal exploitation and repression.

In spite of the record of repression, waste, corruption, mismanagement, and the suffocation of civil society, there are new pressures for change in the region. This new process of change has been greatly aided by the changes in the global system. Of course, it is too early to be definitive on where the current changes will take the world. It is equally early to predict what Africa will benefit from the unprecedented changes in the global system. We can however, make tentative guesses that the on-going changes will only benefit Africa indirectly, and minimally. This is because the changes have been initiated, constructed, and programmed by non-African interests. They reflect the problems, interests, and aspirations of the West and Japan. Africa does not possess the resources, institutions, technology, and other qualities that will enable it take advantage of new revolutions and carry out the required restructuring for the next century. However, this should not dampen our enthusiasm to see Africa liberated from the shackles of backwardness, underdevelopment, and foreign domination. The end of the cold war does not mean the end of imperialism. It is interesting to note that in the current milieu, even radical scholars are joining the mainstream, afraid to call a spade a spade. Africa is still dominated and exploited by powerful transnationals and financial institutions. Africa is still powerless in the United Nations. In a global order dominated by American and Western interests, Africa is still at the very bottom of their economic and geostrategic calculations. It is so easy to forget that most of the predicaments of Africa today are precipitates of Western imperialism. The most brutal dictators were put in power, nurtured and subsidized by Western governments- Zaire, Kenya, Liberia, the Sudan, Nigeria, Somalia, and so on. With the end of the cold war, it is the African people who are bearing the brunt of decades of support for maniacal repression and unbridled corruption. Even in the so-called new global order, there is yet to emerge a special program or package to respond to the peculiar and particularly daunting problems of Africa.

The marginalization and powerlessness of Africa provide ample opportunity to look inward and design an internally generated agenda for change, growth, development, and self-reliance. Rather than complain about marginalization, this is the opportunity for Africa to exploit increasing disinterest and to drastically alter internal relations of power, politics, production, and exchange. This is an opportunity to map out alternative platforms for dealing with external interests and other nations, especially the Western nations. And this is the time to exercise full control over local resources, mobilize the people, focus on the problems of the people, and design programs for empowering the people and the communities.

Will ongoing movements for change achieve these goals? The answer is a definitive no. Politics is still elitist. The same repressive and unaccountable state is still around to domesticate and encapsulate programs dedicated to change. The elites have not changed a bit in their consciousness, alliances, and politics. In spite of this, however, they need to be monitored, encouraged, supported, and used to deepen the struggle for a more genuine and popular agenda for transforming the society.

In this volume, we examine some of the critical issues in Africa's predicament. It has not been possible to cover all the themes. Mostly, the goal is to provide information and ideas that will generate discussions and debates around the various themes: the nature and causes of the African crisis, the state and its custodians, structural adjustment, the debt crisis, democracy and democratization, regionalism, and Africa and the new globalization. The common theme that seems to run through the chapters is that the predicaments of Africa are not new. To expect the global system or the Western nations to solve the problems would be the height of naivety. As well, unmediated integration into the global market will be a big mistake irrespective of the rosy picture sometimes painted by the Western powers and Japan, and by the World Bank in its 1995 report. However, the recomposition of the sites of politics, power, and production *internally* will empower Africans and Africa to seek changes in the global system. This will take quite a while, but in the context of the emerging global order that is dominated by the United States, Africans have no alternative to a genuine agenda for internal mobilization and democratization. The end of the cold war and the elimination of the "iron curtain" has not meant the end of the "poverty war" and the elimination of gross inequality, exploitation, domination, racism, and other forms of socioeconomic and cultural discrimination in the global system. Given that the developed nations have so far made only cosmetic and selective responses to Africa's predicament, only a genuine restructuring of internal socioeconomic and political relations to reflect the interests of the majority can empower the region to effectively participate in an increasingly competitive global division of labor and power. For Africans, the establishment of a new national and regional order must precede the establishment of a new world order.

Chapter One

Africa's Contemporary Crisis: Depth, Dimensions, and Implications

It is a crisis of unprecedented and unacceptable proportions manifested not only in abysmal declines in economic indicators and trends, but more tragically and glaringly in the suffering, hardship and impoverishment of the vast majority of African people.[1]

...the reality, and severity of our more recent set-backs are undeniable; I believe that they are more shocking because of their contrast with the earlier advances, and because they are nullifying years of great effort by Africa's peoples and leaders...Virtually every African country is now suffering from the effects of foreign exchange strangulation; that is, it is unable to import enough goods to keep its economy running efficiently, much less to develop it.[2]

The depth of the current crisis in sub-Saharan Africa is, to put it mildly, alarming. Data from the World Bank, the Organization of African Unity (OAU), the United Nations Economic Commission for Africa (ECA), and other international organizations show very clearly the general socioeconomic and political decay, dislocation and deterioration, in practically all African countries. Though there is now a high degree of agreement on the depth, dimensions, even the implications of the crisis for both Africa and the global community, there are still some disagreements on the origins of the crisis. Broadly, there are those who argue that the crisis is the precipitate of external forces: falling prices of primary exports, exploitation by transnational corporations, declining investment and foreign aid, failure of the West to transfer technology, and a generally hostile international environment for poor, dependent, and underdeveloped economies.

On the other hand, there are those who contend that the crisis has become more internal in origin and pattern of reproduction. They argue that personal rule, human rights abuses, marginalization of the majority from decision-making processes, corruption, mismanagement of the economy, failure to make radical restructuring of the respective economies, inefficiency, and the general disregard for democratic values, popular participation, and self-reliance are, among other factors, the main causes of the crisis. The real point is that both positions are essentially correct in that they address different points of the issue. Beyond both positions, however, is a fundamental weakness which is prevalent in the literature and discourse: the tendency to look at the symptoms or *manifestations* of the crisis as against the fundamental *causes* and the ways in which it has been reproduced since the early years of political independence. The World Bank is particularly guilty of this approach which downplays issues of power, class, social contradictions, and more importantly, history and historical experience. After all, it is these factors and how they interact at various levels that determine and condition the nature and relations of exchange which the Bank and the International Monetary Fund (IMF) tend to focus on exclusively. In this chapter, we shall argue that it is the reproduction of these fundamental historically determined causes that have combined with other developments to deepen the African crisis. The first section, therefore, looks at the origins of the crisis. In the second part, we examine the data and debates on the crisis. The third part of the chapter focuses on prescriptions mainly by the World Bank, the OAU and the ECA. In the final section, we identify obstacles to the implementation of some, if not all, the recommendations advanced to the crisis.

The African Crisis: The Real Causes

In recent debates on the African crisis, attention has focused on the fragility of states, corruption, mismanagement, and the inability of governments and dominant social classes to promote an appreciable level of growth and accumulation. These factors, along with low industrialization, technological backwardness, and stagnant agricultural production as well as rising external indebtedness, have continued to contribute to the continent's marginalization in the international division of labor. The question often neglected is: Why is this the situation? To be sure, the present crisis is not a natural state of affairs. Yet, the recent tendency, especially in North American scholarship, is to isolate the contradictions and conflicts, in fact, atomize them and make prescriptions which have continued to either deepen the crisis or lead to waste, instability, and social tensions. This occurs when the impacts of critical historical issues are overlooked and the victims of current predicaments and conditions are blamed or presented as hapless and willing actors in the process of reproducing underdevelopment and dependence. Unfortunately, many African scholars have joined in this game of blaming the victims, ignoring history, overlooking structural contradictions, and emphasizing the manifestations of the African predicament. What then are the main causes of the crisis?

It is essential that we do not lose sight of the continent's historical experience. In fact, it is impossible to make a serious and holistic analysis of the African predicament without acknowledging and being duly aware of the historical contacts between the precapitalist and relatively self-sufficient communities of Africa and the forces of Western imperialism. While we do not subscribe to the attempt to explain every problem in the continent as the precipitate of the colonial experience, it is our view that no serious discussion of the crisis can fail to take due cognizance of this experience, the distortions and structural deformations it caused in Africa. To be sure, there have been numerous important postcolonial developments in Africa. Even then, these developments have continued to be influenced and determined by the inherited situations of instability, poverty, structural distortions, unproductive and repressive institutions, foreign domination, and the marginalization of the underdeveloped formations in a hostile and exploitative international system.

This line of argument is not intended to paint a helpless and hopeless situation: that because African states were colonized and underdeveloped, nothing can be done about reversing the conditions of backwardness. On the contrary, our contention is that the colonial experience generated specific structures, interests, social relations, and contradictions. The experience also established specific patterns of power, politics and accumulation as well as institutions which have not only survived, almost intact to this day, but have continued to condition the nature of state and class formation, as well as relations with the outside world. It is these precipitates of the historical experience that have continued to promote the crisis in the continent. Consequently, it is impossible to make prescriptions which do not in the first instance address these critical situations which affect class relations, the nature of civil society, the stability and capacity of the state, the productive disposition of the local bourgeois classes, the role of foreign capital in the local economy, and the place of the masses in the process of change, growth, and development.

Thus as background explanation of the African crisis, we isolate seven main factors: 1) the experience of slavery, which not only drained Africa of some of its most productive peoples but also increased inter and intracommunity violence and for a long time redirected the nature and pattern of trade and accumulation; 2) the termination of the endogenously driven patterns of state and class formation through the imposition of colonial rule, the balkanization of the continent, and the imposition of alien values, tastes, and institutions; 3) the creation of a repressive, corrupt, unproductive, nonhegemonic, unstable, and illegitimate state; 4) the creation of a highly fractionalized, factionalized, dependent, corrupt, and weak elite; 5) the domination of the African economy by profit-and hegemony-seeking transnational corporations dedicated to the profit motive, which stultified the emergence or growth of a viable and productive local elite and market; 6) the total denigration of local cultures, values, and institutions, and the introduction and promotion of primordial differences and suspicions; and 7) the structured incorporation of the African economy into the periphery of the global division of labor and power as a vulnerable, dependent, underdeveloped, weak, and largely raw material-producing region. Without doubt, these factors and more laid the foundation for the African crisis.

In their submission to the Special Session of the United Nations General Assembly on "Africa's Economic and Social Crisis" on 13 May 1986, Ministers for Foreign Affairs and Economic Development and Planning in African states took the position that the crisis is caused by "insufficient structural transformation, widespread low level productivity and a lack of the economic diversification that is required to move the continent away from inherited colonial economic structures."[3] Thus, the ministers were quite clear on the fact that African economies had, since political independence, only in the 1960s, not carried out any serious structural transformation needed to promote growth, accumulation, and development. Class balances and social relations of power, production, and exchange were preserved and the colonial modes of surplus extraction, repression, and openness to external interests were also more or less preserved. Without a proper understanding of these issues, how can we understand or appreciate the contemporary manifestations of these legacies?[4]

In contrast to this recognition by African leaders is the World Bank's position, which sees the problem from more recent manifestations of balance of payment deficits, declining exports, mounting foreign debts, inability to meet external financial obligations especially in the area of debt-servicing, and the general inability of African states to maintain an open economy for foreign investment. Robert S. McNamara in his 1985 Sir John Crawford Memorial Lecture argued that the "major cause of the distorted policy environment in many of the African nations has been the encroachment of the state into almost every sphere of economic activity. The politicization of economic life has proceeded further in Africa than in other region of the developing world."[5] This position is echoed by the World Bank in its 1989 report on Africa, where the central thesis is that "Africa needs not just less government but better government—government that concentrates its efforts less on direct (economic) interventions and more on enabling others to be productive."[6] The Bank and its officers never really try to explain or further our appreciation of the nature or composition of the state in Africa. At the very least, such a project would enable us understand, not just its level of solidity, but the extent to which its history has facilitated its composition in a manner that would enable the state to promote growth, development, and accumulation. Yet, as Robert Jackson and Carl Roseberg have noted, in "Tropical Africa, many so-called states are seriously lacking in the essentials of statehood. They are ramshackle regimes of highly personal rule that are severely deficient in institutional authority and organizational capability. The writ of government often does not extend to all parts of the country, and where it does is observed irregularly and without obligation or fear in many quarters, including even state agencies themselves."[7] If this assessment is correct, how can such state structures be blamed for the failings of African economies? Were these states ever structured or composed to perform efficiently, effectively, and productively?

It is not enough to argue, as Richard Sandbrook does, that "what characterizes most states today is a bloated, overextended state of limited capacity that is often given to disorder, capricious management, and faulty policies."[8] One would get the impression that these features which are attributed to the African state are not only peculiar to the region, but also that those obviously negative characteristics were deliberately evolved after political independence. Such assumptions lead to the conclusion that "the Leviathan must be tamed and redirected."[9] By whom? In what context? In what direction? The truth of the matter is that the state in Africa was never structured or composed by imperialism to promote growth, development, peace, stability, harmony, or law and order. It was structured to continue the imperialist project of class domination, exploitation, and elite collaboration with foreign capital as part of the international capitalist order. In this project the African state has been a huge success. As well, the state in Africa, in the final analysis, is not different from the state in the developed formations: a capitalist force designed to dominate and exploit nonbourgeois forces. Yet, its history, environment, activities, and ability to mediate contradictions and organize the extraction of surplus differ as these have been informed by its marginal location in the global system and its fractured economic base.

The World Bank, as well as external donors and lenders, has unanimously prescribed a rolling back of the state in Africa as a major reform path that must be followed. As the Bank clearly articulated in its 1991 World Development Report, the "agenda for reform calls for governments to intervene less in certain areas and more in others—for the state to let the markets work where they can, and to step in promptly and effectively where they cannot."[10] As the Bank itself has admitted, "economic policy cannot be implemented in laboratories; it has to be made to work in the real world."[11] The state in Africa has not been able to operate with the license of the colonial state. It cannot use violence without moral censure. Forced taxation and labor is no longer possible. It has to respond to primordial, economic, social and other pressures and demands. If the market was there, and if there was a viable, responsible and productive bourgeois class in the first place, the state would not have emerged as the largest employer, investor, exporter, and importer. The unmediated prescription of less government or rolling back the state, outside the historical environment and dynamics of the state, can be quite misleading, especially if taken at face value. In the first place, it fails to explain why the state is so important to the accumulation process in Africa. Second, it does not tell us if state intervention or participation in the economy is peculiar to Africa. Third, the World Bank concentrates on the pattern of state intervention rather than on the character of the state, the character of its intervention, and the implications of its pattern of participation in African economies. Finally, the Bank creates the impression that the capitalist state in the developed countries is not interventionist, when in reality it is even more interventionist than most states in Africa! In advanced capitalist formations, aside from helping private capital to seek and guarantee markets abroad, the state subsidizes a variety of social and economic activities.

The dominant role of the state is a colonial creation. The colonized economy moved from a pre-capitalist stage to a monopoly stage without experiencing any form of capitalist development or competition. The colonial state was the judiciary, executive, and legislature all rolled into one. It was corrupt, irresponsible. violent, manipulative, undemocratic, and biased in favor of expatriates, foreign investors, and minority elements who served its purposes of divide-and-rule and exploitation. Hence, given the underdevelopment of the colonial economy, the weaknesses of the dominant elites, the domination of the economy by foreign capital, and the general conditions of sectoral disarticulation, the state easily emerged as the most powerful, the most organized, and the most resource-endowed force and structure in the neocolonial society. The experiences of Europe and the newly industrializing countries show very clearly that it is unrealistic to talk about an unmediated rolling back of the state in the process of development, even capitalist development.[12] Thus, rather than try to understand the critical issues of the character of state, class, politics, production, and exchange relations, and the sort of political restructuring needed to redirect the pattern of production and exchange, the World Bank has concentrated on the manipulation of statistics, the prescription of monetarist measures, and an attack on structures which are invaluable to the accumulation process in Africa.

In sum therefore, our analysis of the African crisis must take due cognizance of the colonial experiences which underdeveloped the continent: the neocolonial inheritance of instability, poverty, and vulnerability to foreign penetration, manipulation, pressures, and exploitation; and the general conditions of alienation, antagonism, backwardness, illiteracy, low industrialization, and dependence on metropolitan countries. As Julius Nyerere notes, at political independence in 1961, "the whole of Africa was poor, undeveloped, and technically backward...Africa was so poor, backward and undeveloped that the majority of our people did not even realise that it could be different."[13]

As indicated above, it would have been a miracle if Africa's condition had turned out differently. In every sector of politics and society, the region was virtually predesigned to run into crisis and instability and to be confined to the margins of the global system. The inheritance at independence included a weak, unstable and nonhegemonic state; a weak and unproductive bourgeois class; foreign domination of the economies; an inefficient and ineffective bureaucracy; ethnic, regional, and other forms of suspicions, antagonisms and conflicts; a premium on politics, political power, and access to the state and its resources for accumulation; rural-urban inequities; class factionalization and fractionalization; the limited commodification of production factors; limited state autonomization and a weak and very marginal location and role in the international division of labor. The colonial experience also culminated in the excessive concentration of the local economy on the production and exportation of a narrow range of cash crops to markets in the metropole; the domination of the productive, even commercial sectors of the economy by expatriate capital; science and technology backwardness; a neocolonial educational system which served to reproduce ignorance, inferiority complex, and a shallow understanding and appreciation of Africa's history; elite reliance on the state for accumulation; and cultural and ideological dependence on the metropole. These points must be borne in mind in any discussion of the African predicament, with particular attention paid to the fact that the contemporary manifestations of the crisis, which we shall discuss shortly, are influenced and determined largely by these consequences of the African experience.[14]

Given Africa's colonial experiences, which had been preceded by the era of informal empire and the trans-Atlantic slave trade, it would have been a miracle for the region to have succeeded in reversing the constraints of underdevelopment after *political* independence was granted in the 1960s. The real point is that *political* independence, like the OAU and ECA have recognized recently, was not accompanied by economic, social, and cultural independence. Africa has remained essentially a market for the mass produced goods of Europe, North America, and Japan as well as a source of cheap raw materials. The region lacked any capacity to influence the prices of its raw materials on which it depended for foreign exchange earnings. It lacked any influence over the prices of finished goods produced from its raw materials. Furthermore, the region lacked the scientific and technological capacity to preserve, store, and process its raw materials, and this increased its vulnerability to foreign manipulation and exploitation. To make its conditions worse, those who captured political power at independence had been steadily incorporated into the economic orbits of the profit and hegemony-seeking transnational corporations in the 1940s and 1950s as agents, representatives, political consultants, shareholders, board members, and legal advisers. It is in this context that we can understand why political power was used following political independence, to depoliticize, terrorize, intimidate, and eliminate popular organizations and nonbourgeois elements.

The new elites inherited a distorted, foreign-dominated, and poverty-stricken economy and found that the alliances they had struck with powerful foreign interests constrained their efforts at fundamental restructurings. Thus they became defensive, repressive, and exploitative and began to rely on propaganda, rhetoric, and the establishment of special security networks to preserve their political positions. In this context, scarce resources were diverted from development to security and politically expedient projects. The politics of religion, region, ethnicity, and manipulation took on new dimensions. Defensive radicalism and ideological posturings became the order of the day and within a short time, the conditions of dependence, underdevelopment, and marginalization in the global system were consolidated within the broad political and economic context of neocolonialism.

The Contemporary Depths and Dimensions of the Crisis

There is now sufficient information to show how alarming the rate of economic and social decline in Africa is. The rate is so fast and the implications so glaring that the ECA has argued that by the year A.D. 2000, the present will sound like a golden age.[15] Claude Ake was likewise forced to reach the conclusion that in view of the recent economic and political declines, the only choice for Africa was between socialism and barbarism.[16] In fact, the depth of decline and decay in Africa forced V.S. Naipaul to declare that "Africa has no future."[17] The signs of crisis had been there all along. The early years of political independence showed very clearly that the path to growth, development, and self-reliance was not going to be easy and that unless drastic restructuring took place within African economies, the path to disaster would be wide open and very steep.

The contradictions and inequalities inherited at political independence were quickly legitimized and concretized in the 1960s through unequal "terms of trade, corporate activities and the impact of technology."[18] Summarizing the achievements of the first two decades of political independence, Timothy Shaw noted that:

> The continent's long-time role in the world system-to export raw materials and to import manufactured goods-has served to define its position and its orientation. Its position at the periphery is largely a function of its relationship to the centre. And its orientation-outward-looking, towards external exchange and criteria-is an aspect of this incorporation. African states have engaged in foreign trade rather than domestic development, in satisfying 'international demand' rather than internal basic human needs. This inheritance of extroversion has profound implications for the present performance and future potential of the continent.[19]

Yet, while the "extroversion" of Africa's trade relations has profoundly affected its accumulation and production patterns, internal socioeconomic and political arrangements, characterized by waste, misplaced priorities, repression, the asphyxiation of civil society, corruption, mismanagement, and accumulation by the elites through lucrative but unproductive economic activities, have served to reinforce the "extroversion." The ECA had cause to alert Africa to the implications of this debilitating pattern of accumulation in the mid-1970s:

> If past trends persist and if there are no fundamental changes in the mix of economic policies that African governments have pursued during the last decade and a half, and if current efforts to fundamentally change the international economic system fail to yield concrete positive results, the Africa region as a whole will be worse off compared to the rest of the world at the end of this century than it was in 1960.[20]

The ECA also noted with great concern that there had been "no marked improvement in many African economies since 1960. The African economy today still exhibits all the characteristics of underdevelopment. The implications are clear and, of course, somber."[21] In the same period, the Food and Agriculture Organization (FAO) delivered a disappointing verdict on the achievements of the region in over one decade of political independence: "of all the developing regions, Africa is the only one where food production has grown less than population in the 1970s. The average annual rate of growth in 1970–76 was only 1.2%, or less than half the population growth of 2.7%."[22] Obviously, therefore, the steady decline, decay, and deterioration of the African economy did not begin in the 1980s.

In its *Economic Report on Africa 1990* the ECA was to confirm its earlier fears and warnings when it declared the 1980s as "Africa's Lost Decade".[23] This was not an alarmist declaration. Rather, it reflected the realities of the African predicament and drew global attention to the urgent need for action. In his 1985 Sir John Crawford Memorial Lecture, Robert McNamara was clear about the fact that:

> No set of statistics, however dramatic, can convey the level of human misery that exists and is increasing throughout the continent. The most helpless victims are the children. It is they who reflect most quickly in physical terms the fact that tens of millions of human beings are living, literally, on the margin of life...the continent has not been able to escape the turbulence of the international economic environment of recent years: the persistent recessions; the severe decline in commodity prices; increasing protectionism (which has been particularly damaging to two of Africa's major exports: sugar and livestock); the high real interest rates; and the decreasing net capital flows.[24]

McNamara also identified "inadequate trade and pricing policies, especially in agriculture; overvalued exchange rates that discriminate against exports; mounting fiscal deficits; and a variety of burdensome government interventions and controls in the production process"[25] as factors which have continued to contribute to the reproduction of the African crisis.

Reflecting on the African crisis in 1983, the North-South Institute noted that the crisis was as political and social as it was economic. This observation agreed with that of the ECA, which had consistently drawn attention to the political dimension of the African crisis since the 1970s. The North-South Institute reported that in sub-Saharan Africa "as a whole, political instability is reflected in the frequency of abrupt changes in government (often by military coups), the widespread use of political power for individual gain, the abuse of human rights and, in extreme cases, either civil war (as in Chad), or wars between neighboring states (as in the horn of Africa). In many countries there is an increasing incidence of corruption, violent crime and a loss of confidence in government generally."[26] The Institute then went on to identify high population growth rates; poor growth of total output in most sectors; fall in Gross Domestic Product (GDP) growth from 3.7 percent per year in the 1960s to 1.7 percent per year in the 1970s; the neglect of agriculture, particularly food production; growing unemployment; an increase in food imports; urban unemployment; scarcity of skilled workforce, rising external debts, and a general inability to "finance recurrent expenditure, investment programs and the necessary maintenance of infrastructure,"[27] as part of the African predicament. This was over a decade ago. Since then things have become worse in the continent:

> Tropical Africa now has the world's lowest rate of economic growth. Whereas per-capita incomes increased at a robust rate of 1.4 percent in the 1960s, this rate declined to 0.2 percent in the 1970s and to *negative* 2.4 percent in the 1980s. Consequently, the number of Africans enduring absolute poverty grew by two-thirds in the first half of the 1980s; in the remainder of the Third World the number rose by a fifth.

Drastic reductions in social expenditures during the past decade have made the situation of Africa's poor even worse...Literacy rates, life expectancy, and employment in the official economy have remained stagnant or declined. Rising food imports, declining terms of trade, and other problems have resulted in a massive jump in Africa's external debt.[28]

Africa's foreign debt is perhaps one of its greatest problems today (see Chapter Two). Since 1970, the continent's "debt has risen 19-fold" and is now equal to "its gross national product (GNP), making the region the most heavily indebted of all."[29] Today, most African countries have become classified as "debt distressed."[30] The importance of this point can be better appreciated when we consider the conditions of declining foreign exchange earnings, declining agricultural productivity, increasing prices of imports and military supplies, rising consumption, falling savings and investment levels, drastic reductions in the level of capital inflow into Africa, rising real interest rates, and stagnant or declining aid flows. The debt burden has subverted possibilities for growth and accumulation, mortgaged the future of African economies, and increased the vulnerability and powerlessness of African states in global economic relations.[31]

The situation is not different at the level of foreign assistance. For the financial year 1991, the Bush administration earmarked only "$616 million for the 47 nations of sub-Saharan Africa, declining from 14 percent of all U.S aid in 1984 to 11 percent in 1991. This compares with $1.6 billion for Egypt, $900 million for Eastern Europe, $720 million for Panama and Nicaragua, and $3.5 billion for Israel (plus the supplements for the Iraqi war and Soviet Jewish immigrants in 1991)."[32] Declining assistance and investments in Africa are a reflection of both Western frustrations at the very limited economic achievements since political independence and of the new interest in redeploying capital to other regions, even if these new locations are not necessarily more politically stable. A typical example is the increased investments in the Soviet Union and Eastern Europe, which are perhaps more unstable, unpredictable, and uncertain than Africa. To be sure, the need to ensure that the spirit of socialism is buried permanently might be the underlying reason for this unparalleled interest. Yet, countries like Ethiopia, Angola, Mozambique, Somalia, Benin, and Guinea which have also abandoned socialism have not received support similar to that given the East European nations. The deepening crisis of Africa is bound to worsen the situation on all fronts:

> ...aside from the occasional rock concert, nothing approaching a serious rescue effort has been mounted for Africa by the West, and none seems likely in the future. (Africa) is moving to the margins of the geopolitical field of attention in the developed world.[33]

As David Wiley has rightly observed,

> Economically, most U.S. corporations are disinterested in a continent they believe to offer only poverty, small markets, chaos and uncertain returns on investments. Indeed, only corporations with a very long-term perspective on profits retain an interest in the continent due to the relative insignificance of U.S. trade and investment in Africa as compared with the "Asian tigers." Many Western governments are disillusioned with the pace of socio-economic development in Africa and perceive Africa as intransigent in the Non-Aligned Movement and the United Nations System.[34]

It is unlikely that this perception of Africa as "intransigent" will continue in the context of the current domination of global security and political relations by the United States and its rather large influence over the United Nations (UN) Security Council, the UN system, and global economic and military relations. In any case, the argument that Africa is unstable is mere rationalization to abandon the region for other parts of the world. After all, the same Western corporations continue to invest in unstable and unpredictable regions of the Middle East and Eastern Europe.

While the debt burden has placed considerable pressures on African governments, compelling them to borrow more to service their debts and import essential commodities, it has also forced many of them to surrender their sovereignty to international financial institutions and other creditors and transnational corporations. In the context of the new globalization (see Chapter Seven), possibilities for recovery get dimmer by the day as the new revolutions in science and technology, like the industrial revolution, once again, bypasses Africa. The adoption of harsh monetarist measures in the name of structural adjustment is equally part of the struggle to keep credit lines open by satisfying the requirements of the IMF and the World Bank. The ECA noted the very disastrous economic and social conditions in the continent in its 1990 report when it stated that:

> The 1980s was a period of general economic and social retrogression. During this period, Africa moved from one social and economic crisis to another. On a yearly basis between 1980 and 1989, per capita income fell by 1.7 per cent, gross fixed capital formation by 1.9 per cent; export volumes by 2.7 per cent, import volumes by 3 per cent, commodity prices by 3.1 per cent, while unemployment increased four times faster than in the 1970s. Indeed, many other socio-economic indicators have continued to worsen. The stock of debt almost doubled to US$256.9 billion between 1982 and 1989, amounting to 328.4 per cent of exports of goods and services. Also, during the 1980s, the number of African least developed countries rose from 17 to 28.[35]

The ECA report should sound alarming enough especially with more African countries becoming classified as "least developed." By mid 1992, of the forty-seven least developed countries in the world, thirty-two were in Africa. Countries like Nigeria and Ghana moved from being classified as "middle-income" to being classified as "low-income" by the World Bank. In fact, Ghana declined the invitation to join the unfortunate club of "least developed countries."[36] Coups and countercoups continued to disrupt political programs and generate tensions as economic deterioration created deeper class and primordial divisions, the state lost its legitimacy, elites lost the ability to provide leadership, and several negative political openings emerged in the system.

Civil wars continued to waste lives and resources, destroying achievements of the past thirty years. In Rwanda, Burundi, and Somalia, ethnic, clan, and other conflicts and violence found their most gruesome expressions as hundreds of thousands of women, children, the old and weak were massacred. The Laurent Kabila military operation which saw the ouster of Mobutu Sese Seko in Zaire also cost thousands of human lives. At a time when East and West Germany are coming together and North and South Korea are establishing more contacts and negotiating the possibility of unification, African states are breaking up into smaller units. In Somalia, Ethiopia, Senegal, Togo, Nigeria, and Tanzania, issues of creating new political units largely to satisfy the hunger of a few elites for power continue to be major obstacles to progress. Eritrea has finally seceded from Ethiopia after three decades of violent and costly war. The Somaliland Republic which seceded from Somalia in 1991, has practically no standing structure and no international recognition. In Southern Sudan, Casamance (Senegal), Tuareg Mali, western Cameroon, Southern

Mauritania, Northern Mozambique, Northern Malawi, and Zanzibar, separatist movements continue to tax the scarce resources of central governments and continue a tradition of waste, carnage, massacres, and instability. With over 500 million people, Africa has more countries than any other region in the world. Of course, it also has more refugees than any other region of the world.

Corruption reached outrageous proportions, especially in countries like Zaire and Nigeria where the national debt profiles allegedly equaled the amount of known savings in private foreign bank vaults.[37] While corruption is not peculiar to Africa, the impact is often more severe because of the gross inequality in the distribution of income, limited national resources, and widespread poverty. Under the cover of structural adjustment, regimes like the now deposed Babangida military junta in Nigeria diverted millions of dollars into private accounts all over Europe, North America, and the Middle East. The Nigerian situation is so serious that private investors now build corruption into their annual budgets and it has almost become a way of life as most Nigerians are compelled to voluntarily and/or involuntarily participate in a neatly woven culture of bribes, kickbacks, and frauds. Internally, widespread corruption in public and private organizations eliminates merit and replaces it with mediocrity, sycophancy, and waste. Moreover, it encourages the rise of powerful, unproductive, and highly undisciplined elites who contribute to the instability and delegitimization of the state. Since public resources are cornered by a tiny minority, corruption increases inequality, the arrogance of power, and the failure of discipline, and it encourages violence and crime. Given the largely unproductive disposition of the African bourgeoisie, looted funds are put away in private banks abroad while small portions are used to penetrate the political process, buy political support, influence the judiciary, eliminate opposition, and promote a culture of decadence.

Several major cities all over the continent have been practically taken over by armed gangs, drug pushers and other criminals as unemployed youths roam the cities in the struggle for survival. It is not unusual in a country like Nigeria to hear armed robbers address or "lecture" their victims in perfect English including strong ideological statements on the wasteful and irresponsible character of the African elite. In Robert Kaplan's recent graphic, though largely a historical and selectively exaggerated report on the decay and dislocation in Africa, he reached the conclusion that:

The cities of West Africa at night are some of the unsafest places in the world. Streets are unlit: the police often lack gasoline for their vehicles; armed burglars, carjackers, and muggers proliferate...In Abidjan, effectively the capital of the Cote d'Ivoire, or Ivory Coast, restaurants have stick- and gun-wielding guards who walk you the fifteen feet or so between your car and the entrance, giving you an eerie taste of what American cities might be like in the future.[38]

Kaplan's widely discussed piece presents us with a gruesome catalogue of decay, instability, disorder, fear, uncertainty, violence, and the almost total return to a "nasty" and "brutish" state of nature in Africa and other parts of the globe. To him,

West Africa is becoming *the* symbol of worldwide demographic, environmental, and societal stress, in which criminal anarchy emerges as the real 'strategic' danger. Disease, overpopulation, unprovoked crime, scarcity of resources, refugee migrations, the increasing erosion of nation states and international borders, and the empowerment of private armies, security firms, and international drug cartels are now most tellingly demonstrated through a West African prism. [39]

However, we do not see in Kaplan's work any deep or serious attention to issues of historical experience; coalitions and contradictions arising from unequal and exploitative relations of politics, power, production, and exchange; the role of imperialism and neocolonialism in the consolidation and reproduction of unequal relations and the marginalization of crisis-ridden formations in the international division of labor. And we do not see any appreciation of the real stuff of politics and political change in these societies. Has Africa been always crisis-ridden? In what ways did the geopolitics of imperialism, especially during the cold war, deepen or accentuate the African predicament? In what ways did the policies and programs of the World Bank, the International Monetary Fund, donors, non-governmental organizations, transnational corporations, and other lenders contribute to the arrogance of power, the delegitimization of the state, corruption and misplaced priorities, and the unprecedented debt profile of Africa?

In fact, Kaplan has presented us with a journalistic description of the sensational and stereotypical *manifestations* of crises without accounting for the dynamics of politics and change at deeper levels. The greatest weakness of Kaplan's work is the inexcusable neglect of the forces of democracy and accountability, popular organizations, pro-democracy movements, human rights associations, trade and students' unions, environmental movements, and the like. In the last decade and in all the nations covered by Kaplan these movements have grown in number, challenged the state and its custodians, mobilized popular forces for political action and defeated incumbents in the open field of politics, forced democratic political concessions from the military and presidents-for-life, and presented Africans with an alternative agenda for recovery, growth, accountability, environmental protection, respect for human rights, strengthening of civil society, and the steady empowerment of the people, their organizations and communities. The net effect of writings like Kaplan's is to blame the victim, reify conditions which are clearly historically determined, and leave us with prescriptions which are not rooted in a holistic appreciation and understanding of the African reality. If one overlooks these very important developments, the focus will be will be misplaced on issues of crime, violence, and poverty. In many cases, the breakdown of law and order in reality is evidence of increasing popular challenges to the state. This is not to deny that there is decline and disorder in Africa.

Of course, such conditions as described above by the ECA, Kaplan, and the North South Institute are unlikely to attract tourists, investors or researchers. At a time when many countries are doing everything to attract tourists and foreign exchange, the growing conditions of violence and insecurity are chasing away visitors. Only the most daring tourist world want to spend time in Somalia, Liberia, Burundi, Togo, Rwanda, The Sudan, even Nigeria today, given the unprecedented dislocation of political processes and the clear conditions of insecurity. The urban and rural unemployed have had their ranks swelled by hundreds of thousands of workers who were retrenched as part of the IMF/World Bank-inspired adjustment programs. Riots, religious conflicts, and political violence have spread to virtually all parts of Africa. Further, as the process of state delegitimization increased, politics took an atavistic form as social forces confronted each other in the struggle for state power and opportunities to accumulate capital.

These conditions were made worse by the wanton violation of human rights.[40] Academic institutions which were once famous for the quality of their staff and students have declined to unbelievable levels as research facilities have disappeared, academic staff have deserted the institutions, the best libraries are five to ten years behind in the relevant literature, and the quality of teaching and administration are at an all-time low. Social critics, intellectuals, journalists, lawyers, and students became the targets of state violence, and the judiciary virtually became an arm of the executive. Incidents of coups, real and/or imagined, became excuses for the governments to execute opposition elements and settle old political scores. In 1995 for instance, reminiscent of the Gaffer Nimeiri style in the Sudan, General Abacha of Nigeria used the excuse of a planned coup to arrest prominent politicians, former political leaders, pro-democracy activists, journalists, and union leaders. In a recent pronouncement, Adebayo Adedeji, the then Executive Secretary of the ECA, pointed out that "basic rights, individual freedom, and democratic participation by the majority of the population have become increasingly lacking in Africa. This pervasive lack of democracy has also made popular mobilization and effective accountability difficult."[41]

The adoption of IMF/World Bank-inspired structural adjustment programs have not helped the situation in any way. International organizations including the World Bank, but excluding the IMF, have now come to realize that adjustment under conditions of mass poverty, structural weaknesses, marginalization of the masses, human rights abuses, the absence of democracy, and continuing vulnerability to more powerful international interests is unlikely to yield positive results. All over the continent, where about two-thirds of the countries are implementing these harsh policies, sociopolitical and economic conditions have worsened. Policies of deregulation, desubsidization, privatization, debt-equity swap, imposition of user-fees on social services, retrenchment of workers, embargo on appointments, massive debt servicing, external borrowing, and containment of popular forces have not encouraged the inflow of foreign investment, promoted growth, stability, respect for human rights, or social and political harmony, or reduced the national debt profile.[42] While Richard Sandbrook has noted that "today most Africans are as poor or poorer than at independence three decades ago,"[43] the World Bank makes the same point when it notes that "Sub-Saharan Africa as a whole has now witnessed almost a decade of falling per capita incomes, increasing hunger, and accelerating ecological degradation. The earlier progress made in social development is now being eroded. Overall, Africans are almost as poor today as they were 30 years ago."[44] In the same vein, the ECA has reached the conclusion that the "policy prescriptions widely adopted during the decade, based on conventional adjustment programmes, have failed to address the fundamental structural issues in Africa's development; hence their failure to arrest the downward trend, less reverse it and bring about a sustainable process of development and transformation."[45] Finally, Carol Lancaster, in a recent review of Africa's reform programs reached the conclusion that the promises and hopes that stabilization from the IMF and adjustment from the World Bank would be the key to recovery and growth have not come to pass:

The anticipation proved to be false. Balance-of-payments gaps were often narrowed, but by less than expected and only temporarily. The benefits of reforms were often overwhelmed by the effects of adverse external shocks-like the collapse of export prices. New investment failed to appear. Indeed, the demand-restraint policies encouraged by the IMF depressed investment instead of increasing it, and many African economies continued to stagnate in the 1980s.

...private investment—the key element in the long-term success of these economic reform programs and the anticipated engine of future economic growth—remained limited throughout the region.[46]

This is not necessarily an argument against the need for adjustment. Nor is this to argue that some gains have not been made. However, orthodox structural adjustment programs have eroded all the gains of the postindependence era, seriously eroded the legitimacy of the state, deepened contradictions within and between social constituencies, and further marginalized Africa in the global order (see Chapter Three).

The situation in Africa today is still critical. In his 1994 end of year report on Africa, Layashi Yaker, the Executive Secretary of the ECA recounted the steady march to disaster in the region:

...in 1994, African economic output has grown by 2.8 per cent, up from 1.1 per cent in 1993 and -0.3 percent in 1992. This means that incomes per head is still declining and that the region is continuing to lose ground both in absolute and relative terms. Over the period 1990–1994 GDP has in fact declined at a rate of nearly 1.5 percent per annum. Over this period, the proportion of the population living under conditions of poverty has increased at even a faster rate. This applies to both the rural areas where the economy continued to decline and the cities where there has been a lack of dynamism in fostering growth and job creation in the industrial and service sectors.[47]

The ECA noted that "Africa's share of aggregate world economic output has continued to shrink, in spite of the fact that its population growth rate is roughly twice that of the world. Africa has also continued to fall behind the other developing regions which are now accepted as important engines of world economic growth."[48] Thus, clearly, the continent is approaching the twenty-first century in a much weaker, more vulnerable, unstable, poverty-stricken, and marginal condition than it did at the beginning of the twentieth century. In the next section we look as *some* of the numerous responses to the African crisis.

OAU, ECA, and World Bank Responses to the African Crisis

There have been numerous responses to the African crisis from sub-regional organizations, the OAU, the ECA, the IMF, the World Bank and other international bodies. Some of the prescriptions have focused on external issues: better terms of trade, more foreign aid and foreign investment, reduced protectionism by the developed countries, and definitive responses to the debt crisis. Yet, others have looked at internal issues: less corruption, better management of resources, structural adjustment, and the liberalization of the economies. Whatever the focus of the responses, there is agreement that policies should be adopted at the internal and external levels to redress mismanagement of the economy, the neglect of agriculture, and capital flight. There is an urgent need to initiate viable programs to restore investor confidence, check the neglect of the rural areas and the conditions of the poor, and to effect the drastic reorganization of national priorities.

The OAU has responded to the African crisis through the *Lagos Plan of Action (LPA) and the Final Act of Lagos (FAL)*; the ECA through the *African Alternative Framework to Structural Adjustment Programmes (AAF-SAP)*; and the *African Charter for Popular Participation in Development and Transformation*. The World Bank has responded through its 1981 *Accelerated Development in Sub-Saharan Africa: An Agenda for Action* and its 1989 report, *Sub-Saharan Africa: From Crisis to Sustainable Growth: A Long-Term Perspective Study*.[49] To be sure, there are other major responses to the African crisis like the Abuja Declaration; the Khartoum Declaration; African Priority Programme for Economic Recovery (APPER) adopted at the twenty-first ordinary session of the OAU's assembly of heads of state and government and later presented to the United Nations General Assembly, and the United Nations Programme of Action for African Economic Recovery and Development (UNPAAERD) adopted in 1986.[50] There are also special responses from the G-7, the Non-Aligned nations, the Commonwealth of Nations, the Scandinavian nations, and the United Nation's (UN) *Agenda for Africa*, which replaced the UNPAAERD.

The LPA and the FAL were adopted in April 1980 by African leaders as blueprints for the socioeconomic and political transformation and emancipation of Africa. At that time, it had become obvious even to the most optimistic of African leaders that the continent was fast sliding down the road to disaster. The Plan was therefore an attempt by African leaders to reexamine the crisis of the continent, achievements since political independence, obstacles to growth and development, and possibilities for self-reliant and self-sustaining development. Overall, this meant a drastic re-evaluation of the location and role of the continent in the world capitalist system. As LPA proudly announced, it was "the instrument which African countries through their heads of state and government have fashioned to attack their economic, social and technological problems so that they may not only initiate and nurture internally-generated and self-sustaining development and economic growth process but also attain national and collective self-reliance albeit overtime, in various economic, social, technological and even cultural areas."[51] Thus collective self-reliance was the fundamental objective of the Plan with the hope that by A.D. 2000, Africa would have set up a "viable common market." The document therefore made recommendations on industrialization, intraregional trade, agriculture, rural development, the preservation of the environment, communications, and the general reorientation of the direction of growth and development.

The LPA failed to make much of a difference in the battle against economic, political, and social decline for several reasons. Preoccupation with debt, drought and internal decay, and destabilization soon diverted the attention of African leaders to nationalistic programs for survival. More importantly, African leaders demonstrated the usual lethargic attitude to such matters: they signed the document and went back to their respective capitals to pursue alternative and divergent policies. The LPA itself was flawed in its attempt to put the blame for the African crisis entirely on imperialism, foreign exploitation, and neo-colonialism. In doing this, it was silent on the gross mismanagement of the economies, massive corruption, political intolerance, human rights abuses, the marginalization of women and the poor, squandermania, and misplaced priorities. African leaders were completely silent on the suffocation of civil society which meant the closure of all democratic openings, and the frequent rehabilitation and repackaging of discredited leaders and useless models of "development."

The LPA believed that continued reliance on the same forces and interests it blamed for Africa's predicament, in the absence of critical internal reforms, would promote Africa's quest for self-reliance and self-sustainment. Not only did the document remain silent on the critical issues of human rights and democratization, it also had no program for political, social, and economic restructuring at levels capable of promoting internal mobilization, accountability, and direct attacks on structures of dependence, inequalities, and underdevelopment. Finally, the LPA overlooked, even underestimated, the numerous internal and external obstacles to regional integration in the continent, an area where achievements, whether in the Economic Community of West African States (ECOWAS), the now dissolved West African Economic Community (CEAO), the Economic and Customs Union of Central African States (UDEAC), the Southern Africa Development Community

(SADC), the Economic Community of Central African States (ECCAS), or even the OAU itself, have shown that the majority of African leaders and governments prefer to retain their unequal and exploitative relations with metropolitan interests to the promotion of collective self-reliant policies. Thus over the decades, petty-jealousies, the lack of political will, politicization of integration policies, domination of decision-making bodies by politicians and ignorant leaders rather than by experts, lack of resources, the absence of programs to attack economic dependence, political instability and reliance on foreign aid to name a few, have continued to militate against the survival and effectiveness of regional integration schemes in Africa (see Chapter Five). Yet, the OAU, in its misplaced optimism, was confident that Africa could become a Common Market between 1980 and A.D. 2000! As the ECA noted in its 1990 economic report on Africa, "the share of recorded intra-African trade in the total trade of Africa declined from an average of 6.1 per cent in the 1960s to 5.2 per cent in the 1970s and further to 4.9 per cent during the 1980s."[52]

The LPA was abandoned by 1986 when African leaders came up with the APPER a somewhat more realistic document that paid attention to internal failings and external obstacles to growth and development. In explaining why the LPA had failed, the APPER identified "the widespread, severe and persistent drought; the acceleration of the desertification process; persistent and destructive cyclones in the Indian Ocean; and the intensification of destabilization attempts from South Africa on neighboring African countries."[53] It also argued that if "most of the measures recommended in the LPA had been implemented, the ravaging effects of the current world recession and drought on African economies would have certainly been minimized."[54] This realization that the nonimplementation of the programs of the LPA increased Africa's vulnerability to internal and external pressures is important. It shows clearly that one of the major problems of Africa is not the absence or scarcity of prescriptions for economic and political recovery, but internal *political obstacles* arising mostly from the nature of internal power balances, extant ideological discourses, character of regimes, depth of political spaces, and entrenched class interests.

The ECA has done much more than any other organization in the effort to identify the real causes and obstacles to growth and development in Africa. Unlike the OAU, the ECA is not dominated or controlled by the same military and civilian despots and corrupt leaders who are responsible for the desperate African condition in the first place. In fact, without the ECA, the OAU would probably have been an onlooker to efforts by the

IMF and the World Bank as well as credit clubs to unilaterally set the political and economic agenda for Africa's recovery and survival. A year after the adoption of the LPA, the World Bank, in an attempt to ensure that Africa did not move away from the path of monetarism that was dominant in Britain and the United States, came up with its own orthodox monetarist prescriptions in *Accelerated Development in Sub-Saharan Africa: An Agenda for Action*: the "Berg Report".[55] The Berg Report practically spelt the death knell of the LPA and pushed African countries along the lines of desubsidization, deregulation, trade liberalization, devaluation, privatization, retrenchment, and other market-oriented policies: the stabilization and structural adjustment package.[56] It moved African states away from the path of collective responses to the crisis through emphasis on self-reliance and basic needs for the people. Rather, it placed before African governments an agenda based on market reforms and left the leaders in no doubt as to the economic philosophy that was to condition foreign aid and economic relations in the 1980s and beyond.

It was to this World Bank package that the ECA responded by producing the AAF-SAP, which was adopted in April 1989 by the assembly of heads of state and government of the OAU at its twenty-fifth meeting, and by the UN General Assembly at its forty-fourth meeting as a credible blueprint for economic recovery in Africa and an alternative to IMF\World Bank-inspired adjustment programs which have "almost never worked in sub-Saharan Africa."[57] In its own alternative response to the African crisis, the ECA proposed a "structural transformation" in place of "structural adjustment." In addition, the ECA proposed a "human centred strategy of recovery," emphasized the internal dimensions of the recovery process, and stressed the need for a new partnership with external interests. Also the ECA alternative argued that the "process of formulation of these programmes should avoid the mistake of excluding the people from full participation in the formulation, implementation and monitoring of adjustment programmes."[58] The ECA defined the crisis as both political and economic in nature, a significant departure from World Bank and IMF perspectives and interpretations. It emphasized the place of democratization, the role of "popular forces," the need for popular participation, and the indispensability of an enabling environment with democratic participation in order to mobilize the people for the costs, pains and benefits of structural transformation towards self-reliance, growth, and development. The ECA did not mince words in noting that adjustment at the expense of the poor and vulnerable was doomed to failure and would be resisted by popular communities and constituencies. Finally, the ECA was emphatic on the need to transform "the real and material structures and relations of production, consumption and technology; the socio-economic institutional structures; the domestic financial structures; and international trade and finance structures."[59]

To achieve the goals spelt out above, the ECA made specific recommendations: the elimination of subsidies except those for the social sector and basic industries; reduction of military expenditure; reduction of government spending on the nonproductive public sector; guaranteed minimum prices for food crops on the basis of managed food stocks; a "natural" depreciation of local currencies, and the establishment of two exchange rate systems as a temporary measure: one for essential imports and the other for nonessential imports. The AAF-SAP also prescribed a lowering of interest rates and the determination of priority programs with guidelines to the banks for credit allocation; the avoidance of blanket trade liberalization in view of the increasing protectionism in the international economy; a selective export promotion strategy, in view of the decline in demand for Africa's exports; deficit financing for productive and infrastructural investments gradually reduced in order to maintain fiscal balance; land reform to increase production and employment opportunities; the allocation of 20–25 percent of public investment to agriculture; increased foreign exchange allocation for agricultural inputs and for essential imports for industry; the rationalization and rehabilitation of productive and infrastructural capacity through the promotion of an effective maintenance culture; and the centrality of popular participation in the attainment of these objectives. For the first time, the rights of students, disadvantaged groups, professionals, workers, peasants, and women were given equal weight and built into the transformation package in Africa.[60] The ECA made it clear that its alternative framework which was "being regarded as a confrontational...paper by the IMF and World Bank,"[61] was "essentially a working document whose objective is to supply a theoretical basis for designing programmes for Africa's recovery. The document is not ideological in the narrow sense of the word. It is an attempt to generate an African nationalist approach against the ongoing process of re-colonising Africa...it represents a consensus in Africa."[62] The ECA, in order to publicize the document and make it available to popular communities, printed a shorter "popular version" in 1991 and organized several workshops around the prescriptions of the AAF-SAP. This is in sharp contract to the LPA, which was printed and distributed abroad and is hardly available to researchers, not to mention ordinary people.

The World Bank, in a dramatic move in 1989, came up with a report that distanced it not only from its earlier postures and prescriptions but also from the more insensitive and conservative positions of the IMF. First, the Bank admitted that "fundamental structural change is needed to transform African economies and make them competitive in an increasingly competitive world."[63] Second, it recognized not only that adjustment programs should continue, but that they needed to be "broadened and deepened" with "special measures...to alleviate poverty and protect the vulnerable."[64] Third, the Bank subscribed to the need to provide an *enabling environment* for the productive use of resources and that development strategy must be "human centered" in line with calls already made by the ECA and UNICEF. Fourth, the Bank's report called for "good governance," a reliable judicial system, public accountability, and a "better balance...between the government and the governed." Fifth, in a surprising move and certainly as a direct response to criticisms from the OAU, the ECA, African governments, intellectuals, and the Organization of African Trade Union Unity (OATUU), the World Bank's report set out "a range of proposals aimed at empowering ordinary people, and especially women, to take greater responsibility for improving their lives-measures to foster grassroots organization, that nurture rather than obstruct informal sector enterprises, and that promote nongovernmental and intermediary organizations."[65] Finally, sixth, the Bank admitted that, given the current situation in Africa and the power balances in the global system, the "difficulties facing Africa are formidable. The margin for manoeuvre is slim indeed. The risks of failure are devastating in human terms." In fact, the Bank went to the extent of admitting that in many respects it has been part of the problem in Africa:

> Responsibility for Africa's economic crisis is shared. Donor agencies and foreign advisers have been heavily involved in past development efforts along with the African governments themselves. Governments and donors alike must be prepared to change their thinking fundamentally in order to revive Africa's fortunes.[66]

The Bank also conceded that a 1987 evaluation of completed rural development projects it had supported in Africa showed that half of them had failed and emphasized the point that "Africa's future can only be decided by Africans. External agencies can play at most a supportive role."[67] To be sure, the concerns and confessions above are significant deviations from traditional preoccupations with financial matters, debt negotiations, balance of payments, export promotion, and trade liberalization. True, the Bank has not abandoned its traditional prescriptions and preferences for structural adjustment which, it sees as critical to economic recovery. But, beyond adjustment, the Bank recommended better governance, improved health delivery, more access to education especially for women, food security, the involvement of women in the process of change, a stable economic and political environment in order to attract investors, and the establishment of "a well functioning judicial system that can be relied upon to protect property and to enforce contracts." As well, the World Bank recommended that more attention to environmental protection, diversification of external markets away from inherited ties to former colonial powers, population control, and policies to promote democracy, accountability, and political stability. Of course, the Bank equally paid attention to problems of corruption at all levels of government and in the society at large and to the urgent need to reverse the growing alienation of the poor from the state and check growing pessimism about the future.

Perhaps the most important contribution of the Bank's report was the cautious reformulation of its position on the role of the state. Contrary to its traditional unmediated advocacy of privatization and the "rolling back" of the state, the new report, while insisting that the "State would no longer be an entrepreneur, but a promoter of private producers," and that "Africa needs not just less government but better government–government that concentrates its efforts less on direct interventions and more on enabling others to be productive,"[68] also noted that "state-owned enterprises will still be appropriate in many cases, especially in providing utilities and some public goods. In some cases the private sector lacks the capacity to take over, but in time and with imagination privatization can still work."[69] This is precisely one of the major reasons for the attacks on adjustment programs in the past: the blanket attacks on the state and the handing over of the economy to corrupt, highly fractionalized and factionalized, largely unproductive, and very weak local elites who merely front for foreign investors, thus increasing the fear of re-colonization.[70] Finally, the Bank recommended a 4 percent annual growth rate for agriculture; a 5–8 percent growth rate per annum for industry; inflow of foreign assistance at a minimum of 4 percent per annum in real terms to a level of $22 billion a year by A.D. 2000; higher levels of domestic savings and a 1–2 percent per annum increase in the productivity of labour, and special attention to the conditions of women and vulnerable groups.

It is following this renewed and different interest in Africa's recovery that the ECA came out with a new document: *African Charter for Popular Participation in Development and Transformation*. This document emerged out of an international conference held in Arusha, Tanzania, in February 1990 as a collaborative effort of African governments, non-governmental organizations, and the United Nations agencies. Its main goal was to operationalize the Alternative Framework, the UNPAAERD, the outcome of the 1987 Abuja International Conference on the "Challenge of Economic Recovery and Accelerated Development," and the 1988 Khartoum International Conference on the "Human Dimensions of Africa's Economic Recovery and Development." The *Charter* was the product of a realization that:

> ...what Africa needs is a fundamental change and transformation, not adjustment, and that the change and transformation required are not just narrow, economistic and mechanical ones but those that will foster and internalize, in every country and at every level of our society, the democratization of the development process and the evolution of an enabling environment that promotes initiative and enterprise, guarantees the dignity of each human being and accelerates the process of the empowerment of the people. These are the broader and fundamental changes that will bring about over time the new Africa...where there is development and economic justice, not just growth; where there is democracy and accountability not despotism, authoritarianism and kleptocracy; and where the governed and their governments are moving hand-in-hand in the promotion of the common good.[71]

Thus the fundamental program on which the *Charter* was anchored was the mobilization and participation of popular forces-workers and their trade unions, peasants, women, professionals, students, intellectuals in their mass organizations and as individuals. Along the lines of this recognition, the *Charter* attacked "all economic programmes, such as orthodox structural adjustment programmes, which undermine the human condition and disregard the potential and role of popular participation in self-sustaining development."[72] The document then outlined what was to be done and how the identified goals could be achieved. Perhaps more importantly, the document outlined how the implementation of its recommendations can be monitored. At the level of program identification, the document, like the World Bank, advocated the "imperative of establishing an enabling environment with all its ramifications;" the promotion of political freedoms; the broadening of decision-making bodies; encouragement of more entrepreneurship, individual initiative and private enterprise; the democratization of the development process through the empowerment of the people; the promotion of social justice; and respect for human rights. The *Charter* is emphatic that the empowerment of the people as well as their mobilization and involvement "in decision-making, in implementation and monitoring processes–is a *conditio sine qua non* for socio-economic recovery and transformation."[73] According to the ECA, this was because "previous development strategies have never really put the people first as the centres of development. Since development is in the first instance about people; the people should be the active agents of change and not just "passive beneficiaries."

The *Charter* then outlined what various interest groups and organizations must do in order to ensure and sustain this new approach to economic recovery, growth, and development. The people themselves have to be "fully involved, committed and indeed seize the initiative...it is essential that they establish independent organizations at various levels that are genuinely grass-root, voluntary, democratically administered and self-reliant and that are rooted in the tradition and culture of the society so as to ensure community empowerment and self-development." These peoples' organizations must ensure the "survival, protection and development of children," full participation in decision-making by women, and popular participation beginning at the family level. African governments must move away from their traditional roles of dictating to the people. Governments must realize that "popular participation is dependent on the nature of the state itself and ability of government to respond to popular demand." So governments must "yield space to the people," broaden decision-making bodies, promote political accountability by the state to the people, and ensure women's involvement in the processes of change at all levels of decision-making. African governments were also enjoined to assure the basic human rights of the people by vigorously implementing the *African Charter of Human and People's Rights* and the *Universal Declaration of Human Rights*, the *Convention on the Rights of the Child*, and other international conventions dealing with human rights and basic human needs.

The *Charter* called on the international community to "examine its own record on popular participation, and hereafter to support indigenous efforts which promote the emergence of a democratic environment and facilitate the people's effective participation and empowerment in the political life of their countries." The United Nations is called upon to "intensify its effort to promote the application of justice in international economic relations, the defence of human rights, the maintenance of peace...and to assist African countries and people's organizations with the development of human and economic resources." While emphasizing the importance of socioeconomic and political transformations within Africa, the document acknowledged that the global environment has been hostile to African initiatives. Unless changes occurred at both ends, local initiatives would be negated by international conditions and vice versa.

In the struggle to ensure popular participation in development, African governments, according to the *Charter,* must initiate and implement programs "in line with the interest and aspirations of the people" and aim at the "transformation of African economies to achieve self-reliant and self-sustaining people-centered development based on popular participation and democratic consensus." In doing this, more economic power must be extended to the people, mass literacy and skills training must be promoted, greater participation and *consensus building* in the formulation and implementation of policies must be ensured, and employment opportunities must be generated. In addition, small-scale indigenous enterprises must be encouraged and the communication capacities of community organizations strengthened. Finally, the document spelt out specific roles for popular organizations, nongovernmental organizations (NGOs), the media, women's organizations, organized labour organizations, and of youth and students. In all cases, the emphasis is on ensuring that the human dimension is central to adjustment programmes which must be compatible with the objectives and aspirations of the African people and with the African realities and must be conceived and designed internally by African countries as part and parcel of the long-term objectives and framework of development and transformation.[74]

The *Charter* concludes with an outline of how its implementation is to be monitored through some identifiable indicators: literacy rate, freedom of association, (especially political association), representation of the people and their organizations in national bodies, and the extent of the rule of law and economic and social justice. Other indicators included the degree of protection of the ecological, human and legal environment; press and media freedom; number and scope of grassroots organizations with effective participation in development activities; political accountability of leadership at all levels; decentralization of decisionmaking processes and institutions; and finally, the extent of implementation of previous agreements and declarations on structural change, self-reliance, and self-sustenance

It is obvious from the discussion of the *Charter* thus far that it goes beyond previous declarations in its recognition of political dimensions of the African crisis. Moreover, its prescriptions on the need to empower the people, restructure and expand political spaces, and promote mobilization and accountability within an enabling environment put it somewhat ahead of previous African initiatives like the LPA. While the NGO community has embraced the document and its prescriptions, African states and their custodians, as usual, have largely distanced themselves from it. This is because the implementation of the *Charter* has far-reaching implications for power, politics, production, and accumulation patterns and relations. Without doubt, its implementation will drastically restructure power bases and the control of the state in favor of nonbourgeois and popular communities.

Conclusion

African governments have limited options, in the face of ongoing changes in the world economy, other than to carry out fundamental changes within their respective economies. The situation in the continent right now, is alarming and disastrous to say the least. Between 1991 and 1993, "when most of Asia and much of Latin America was booming, GDP per person shrank by 2.3% a year. The continent attracts less than 5% of the direct investment going to the developing world, an estimated $2.5 billion or so in 1994."[75] These figures and more do not speak too well for a region of 54 nations and a population of over 500 million. The new position adopted by the World Bank, donors, and lenders, which now recognizes political dimensions of the crisis and emphasizes some degree of political conditionality for assistance, must be supported in spite of the opposition from some African leaders. Three or more decades of political independence and experimentation with a variety of economic and political options have only led to a mounting debt profile, mass poverty, the exploitation and marginalization of the people, human rights violations and massive corruption, mismanagement, and abuse of power and office. It is certainly no exaggeration to say that African governments and elites can no longer be trusted with the future of the continent or with carrying out reforms based solely on their narrow and often conservative agendas. In the area of mobilizing the people, promoting self-reliance, stimulating agriculture, encouraging science and technology, and resisting foreign domination and exploitation, African governments since the 1960s have, without exception, failed woefully. Thus political conditionality and the indicators of empowerment outlined in the *Charter* must be taken as the new basis for promoting change in the African continent. Though the West has its own agenda, at least, political conditionality has forced elections in repressive nations like Kenya, Ghana, and Malawi. It has opened up the political terrain to the recomposition of political interests and constituencies. Political conditionality has opened up some breathing space for civil society and enabled previously suppressed communities and constituencies to challenge the status quo. The ultimate challenge is for the new constituencies to seize the initiative and dictate the content and context of politics rather than weave new and complex patterns of subservience to foreign dictates.[76]

In spite of the crises, contradictions, and conflicts discussed above, how have communities and constituencies responded? What sort of new initiatives and struggles are emerging? What changes have taken place at the levels of organization, politics, and praxis in and outside the African continent? How have the impacts and implications of these problems and contradictions changed or reconstructed the organization of politics, power, production, and exchange? What are the viable solutions that will move Africa forward into the twenty-first century and beyond? What obstacles and opportunities will Africa face in the context of a post-cold war global order dominated by the United States? What is Africa's future in the new globalization?

Endnotes

1. Economic Commission for Africa, *African Charter for Popular Participation in Development* (ECA: Addis Ababa, 1990), p. 17.

2. Mwalimu Julius K. Nyerere, *Reflections on Africa and Its Future*, (Lagos: Nigerian Institute of International Affairs, Lecture Series No.41, 1987), p.6.

3. Organization of African Unity, *Submission to the Special Session of the UNGA on Africa's Economic and Social Crisis by Ministers for Foreign Affairs and Economic Development and Planning, 13 May 1986.*

4. See Walter Rodney, *How Europe Underdeveloped Africa* (Washington, D.C.: Howard University Press, 1981); Frantz Fanon, *The Wretched of the Earth*, (London: Grove Press, 1966); Claude Ake, *Political Economy of Africa*, (London: Longman, 1981); and his "Explaining Political Instability in New States," *The Journal of Modern African Studies* Vol. 11 (3) (1973); and Toyin Falola, (ed.), *Britain and Nigeria: Exploitation or Development?* (London: Zed Books, 1988).

5. Robert S. McNamara, *The Challenges for Sub-Saharan Africa* (Washington, D.C: Sir John Crawford Memorial Lecture, November 1, 1985), p. 5.

6. World Bank, *Sub-Saharan Africa: From Crisis to Sustainable Growth- A Long-Term Perspective Study* (Washington, D.C: World Bank 1989), p. 5.

7. Robert H. Jackson and Carl G. Roseberg, "Sovereignty and Underdevelopment: Juridical Statehood in the African Crisis," *Journal of Modern African Studies* Vol.24, (1) (1986), pp. 1–2.

8. Richard Sandbrook, "Taming the African Leviathan," *World Policy Journal* (Fall 1990), p. 674.

9. Ibid.

10. World Bank, *World Development Report 1991* (Washington, D.C.: World Bank, 1991), p. 128.

11. Ibid.

12. For an interesting discussion of this issue, see Richard Sandbrook, "Taming the African Leviathan," *World Policy Journal* (Fall, 1990) and Julius O. Ihonvbere, "Making Structural Adjustment Programs Work in Africa: Towards a Research and Policy Agenda," Unpublished Manuscript, Department of Government, The University of Texas at Austin, November 1994.

13. Julius K. Nyerere, *Reflections on Africa*...op. cit. p. 4.

14. See Julius O. Ihonvbere (ed.), *The Political Economy of Crisis and Underdevelopment in Africa: Selected Works of Claude Ake* (Lagos: JAD Publishers, 1989); Claude Ake, *Political Economy of Africa* (London: Longman, 1981); and Toyin Falola (ed.) *Britain and Nigeria: Exploitation or Development?* (London: Zed Press, 1986).

15. ECA, *The Revised Framework of Principles for the Implementation of the New International Economic Order in Africa, 1976–1981/82* (Addis Ababa: ECA,1983).

16. Claude Ake, *Political Economy of Africa*, .p. 189.

17. V.S. Naipaul, *New York Times Book Review* (15 May 1979).

18. Timothy M. Shaw, "Discontinuities and Inequalities in African International Politics," *International Journal* Vol. 30 (3) (Summer 1975), p. 387.

19. Ibid, p. 832.

20. Adebayo Adedeji, "Africa: The Crisis of Development and the Challenge of a New Economic Order," Address to the Fourth Meeting of the Conference of Ministers and Twentieth Session of the Economic Commission for Africa, Kinshasa, February–March 1977, p.9.

21. Ibid, pp.7 and 9.

22. "Africa" in FAO, *The State of Food and Agriculture, 1977* (Rome: FAO 1978), pp. 2–3.

23. ECA, *Economic Report on Africa 1990* (Addis Ababa: ECA: April 1990).

24. Robert S. McNamara, *The Challenges for Sub-Saharan Africa*, p. 4.

25. Ibid, pp. 4–5.

26. North-South Institute of Canada, *Africa's Economic Crisis-Briefing Paper*, February, 1983, p. 1.

27. Ibid, p. 3.

28. Richard Sandbrook, "Taming the African Leviathan," pp. 674–675.

29. World Bank, *From Crisis to Sustainable Growth*, p. 2.

30. See Tony Killick and Matthew Martin, "African Debt: The Search for Solutions," UN Africa Recovery Programme, Briefing Paper, No.1, June, 1989 and the World Bank, *From Crisis to Sustainable Growth*, pp. 18–20. See also Stephany Griffith-Jones (ed.), *Third World Debt: Managing the Consequences* (London: IFR Publishers, 1989).

31. ECA, *Economic Report on Africa 1990*, p. 3.

32. David S. Wiley, "Academic Analysis and U.S. Policy-Making on Africa: Reflections and Conclusions," *Issue* Vol. XIX (2) (1991), p.40.

33. Ibid.

34. Ibid.

35. ECA, *Economic Report on Africa 1990*, p. VII.

36. Ernest Harsch, "More African States Are 'Least Developed'," *Africa Recovery* (April 1992), p. 11.

37. See Pita Agbese and Julius Ihonvbere, *The State and Structural Adjustment in Nigeria* (Washington, D.C.: Howard University Press, forthcoming 1997).

38. Robert D. Kaplan, "The Coming Anarchy," *Atlantic Monthly* (February 1994), p. 45. Kaplan must be joking to say that the feeling in Abidjan was like what an American city "might be like in the future," when the entire world knows that conditions are worse in Washington, D.C. (popularly known in the media as the "murder capital of the world"), Miami, where several tourists have been carjacked and killed, New York, and Chicago, to mention some of the very dangerous cities in America. There are over 200 million handguns in private hands in America, and someone is hurt with a weapon every ten seconds or so. With over 2 million Americans in jail, this is more than the population of many African countries like Cape Verde (359,000), The Gambia (840,000), Guinea-Bisau (932,000), Mauritania (1,804,000), and Equatorial Guinea (370,000). In the inner cities in virtually all American states, insecurity, fear, and uncertainty continue to affect the patterns of life.

39. Ibid, p. 46.

40. See Julius K. Nyerere, *Reflections on Africa and its Future*.

41. Adebayo Adedeji, *Putting the People First*, opening statement delivered at the International Conference on Popular Participation in the Recovery and Development Process in Africa (Arusha, Tanzania, 12 February 1990), p. 2.

42. See Adebayo Adedeji, *The African Alternative: Putting the People First* (Addis Ababa: ECA,1990); ECA, *The African Alternative Framework to Structural Adjustment Programmes for Socio-Economic Recovery and Transformation* (Addis Ababa: ECA, 1989); and Carol Lancaster, "Economic Restructuring in Sub-Saharan Africa," *Current History* Vol.88 (538) (May 1989).

43. Richard Sandbrook, "Taming the African Leviathan," p. 675.

44. World Bank, *From Crisis to Sustainable Growth*, p. 1.

45. ECA, *Economic Report on Africa 1990*, p. VII.

46. Carol Lancaster, *United States and Africa: Into the Twenty-First Century*, (Washington, D.C.: Overseas Development Council, 1993), p. 16.

47. Layashi Yaker, "Preliminary Assessment of the Performance of the African Economy in 1994 and Prospects for 1995; End of Year Statement," Addis Ababa: ECA Secretariat, 15 December 1994.

48. Ibid

49. See OAU, *Lagos Plan of Action for the Economic Development of Africa 1980–2000 and the Final Act od Lagos* (Geneva: Institute for Labour Studies, 1981); ECA, *African Alternative Framework to Structural Adjustment Programmes for Socio-Economic Recovery and Transformation (AAF-SAP)* (Addis Ababa: ECA, 1989); ECA, *African Charter for Popular Participation in Development* (Addis Ababa: ECA, 1990); and the World Bank,*Sub-Saharan Africa: From Crisis to Sustainable Growth-A Long-Term Perspective Study* (Washington D.C.: 1989).

50. For discussions see Adebayo Adedeji, "Economic Progress: What Africa Needs," *Transafrica Forum* Vol.7 (2) (Summer 1990); Timothy M. Shaw, "Popular Participation in Non-Governmental Structures in Africa: Implications for Democratic Development," *Africa Today*, Vol.37 (3) (3rd Quarter, 1990), pp. 5–22; and his "Africa in the 1990s: From Economic Crisis to Structural Readjustment," *Dalhousie Review* Vol. 68 (1–2) (Spring\Summer 1988), pp. 37–69.

51. OAU, *The Lagos Plan of Action*, p. 6.

52. ECA, *Economic Report on Africa 1990*, p. 30.

53. OAU, *Lagos Plan of Action*, p. 13.

54. Ibid, p. 12.

55. World Bank, *Accelerated Development in Sub-Saharan Africa: An Agenda for Action* (Washington, D.C.: The World Bank, 1981).

56. See Timothy M. Shaw, "Debates about Africa's Future: The Brandt, World Bank and Lagos Plan Blueprints," *Third World Quarterly* Vol.5 (2), (April 1983), pp. 330–344; and his "Africa's Crisis: Debate and Dialectics over Alternative Development Strategies for the Continent," *Alternatives* Vol.9 (1), (Summer 1983), pp. 111–127.

57. Carol Lancaster, "Economic Restructuring in Sub-Saharan Africa," p. 213.

58. ECA, *The African Alternative*, p. 49.

59. Ibid, pp. 4–7.

60. See Institute for African Alternatives (I.F.A.A.), *Alternative Development Strategies for Africa: Report on IFAA\IDS Conference* (London: IFAA, 1989); Trevor W. Parfitt, "Lies, Damned Lies and Statistics: The World Bank\ECA Structural Adjustment Controversy" *Review of African Political Economy* (47) (Spring 1990), pp. 128–141; and Adebayo Adedeji, *The African Alternative*...op. cit.

61. Bade Onimode, "African Alternatives to World Bank and IMF Programmes," keynote address at the IFAA conference on "Alternative Development Strategies for Africa," (Dar es Salaam, 12–14 December 1989).

62. Ibid.

63. World Bank, *Sub-Saharan Africa: From Crisis to Sustainable Growth*, p. XI.

64. Ibid.

65. Ibid, p. XII.

66. World Bank, *From Crisis to Sustainable Growth*, p. 2.

67. Ibid.

68. Ibid, p. 5.

69. Ibid, p. 55.

70. See John Ohiorenuan, "Re-Colonising Nigerian Industry: The First Year of the Structural Adjustment Programme," in Phillips Adeotun and E.C. Ndekwu (eds.), *Structural Adjustment in a Developing Economy: The Nigerian Case* (Ibadan: NISER, 1987).

71. ECA, *Economic Report on Africa 1990*, p. VIII.

72. ECA, *African Charter for Popular Participation*, p. 19.

73. Adebayo Adedeji, *Putting the People First*, p. 3

74. ECA, *African Charter for Popular Participation*, p. 26.

75. "Investing in Africa: A New Scramble," *The Economist* (August 12th, 1995), p. 128.

76. See Eboe Hutchful, "Structural Adjustment and Political Regimes in Africa," mimeo, University of Toronto, 1990.

Chapter Two

Between Debt and Disaster: The Politics of Africa's Debt Crisis

The dramatic increase in the volume of Africa's debt, and the heavy debt service burden is another source of our profound concern, especially since it represents a heavy drain on the meager foreign exchange resources of our Member States...We are fully aware of the fact that shortcomings in development policies have contributed to the present debt crisis.[1]

It is simply not possible for African countries to develop with their debt burden exceeding $270 billion.[2]

External debt is a millstone around the neck of Africa...It is a major obstacle to the return of private investment to Africa.[3]

The debt crisis is certainly one of the fundamental obstacles to growth, democratization, and economic recovery in Africa today. The continent's foreign debt and debt-servicing obligations have more than doubled in the last decade. In the context of deepening economic, political, and social crisis, as well as declining foreign aid and declining investor and donor interest in the continent, the impact and implications of the debt crisis cannot be overstated.[4] It has become a case of declining foreign exchange earnings, increasing expenditures, declining savings, declining inflow of resources from abroad, and rapidly rising repayments on existing loan obligations. As Adbou Diouf, the president of Senegal rightly noted in his address to the UN General Assembly, "Africa is confronted by old problems, some of which have even become worse. Such is the case with Africa's external debt payments, to which the continent devotes the bulk of the meager financial resources left by its deteriorating terms of trade."[5] Rising interest rates, growing debt-servicing obligations, and demands arising from constraints generated by huge external debts have recently cast a dark shadow on the prospects for development, democratization, and recovery in the continent. The chairman of the Organization of African Unity (OAU), in a 1991 address to the UN General Assembly, noted that "Africa's indebtedness is the single major obstacle to development in the continent. The debt problem is a central element of Africa's critical economic situation. Africa's debt is crippling."[6]

While Africa is not the most indebted region in the world in terms of the size of its total debt stock, it is the most "debt-distressed" region in the world. This is largely because of the very weak structural base of the African economy, declining output, and increasing inability to meet debt-servicing obligations. The size of Africa's debt has become a major problem with deep-rooted political and economic implications because of the distorted and disarticulated productive base of the economy as well as the increasing marginalization of the continent in the international division of labor and power. To be sure, internal economic and political policies continue to militate against effective policy responses to the debt and other crises. Yet, declining commodity prices, capital flight, increasing cost of imports, and higher costs of borrowing have contributed significantly to the deepening crisis in an increasingly hostile world economic system.[7] The debt crisis has, without doubt, complicated the possibilities for reform and recovery in Africa. As the North-South Roundtable rightly notes, the "overhang of African debt now constitutes a significant extra drag upon the prospects for African development. The constant pressure of debt-related financial negotiations deflect decision-makers from the necessary and more socially productive activities of development-oriented economic decision-making."[8]

It is in the context of the deepening crisis of the region (see Chapter One), which complicates and negates possibilities for viable political and economic restructuring, that we must locate the nature and impacts, as well as the politics, of the debt crisis. The OAU and the Economic Commission for Africa (ECA) have acknowledged this trend by pointing at the ways in which the debt crises has steadily eroded the stability and potentials for growth and development while making it completely impossible for governments to sustain the momentum of reform and recovery. According to Michael Holman and Edward Balls, the debt crisis is probably "more burdensome and debilitating" than "all the problems in Africa's post-independence legacy."[9] The United Nations Information, Cultural and Educational Fund (UNICEF) was even more sarcastic and accusatory in its view on the debt crisis when it noted in its 1991 *State of the World's Children Report* that the impact of debt is "a new slavery that has shackled the continent." It contended at that time that annual debt repayments of $28 billion were much more than what African governments, put together, spend on education and health.[10]

Numerous international and continental responses have failed to stem the tide of decline. Yet, the debt crisis must be addressed as part of the general crisis of the continent if it is to be resolved. In this chapter we discuss the origins and depth of the debt crisis, make a brief review of the responses to the crisis, and make prescriptions towards its resolution. Our basic argument is that the debt crisis can only be resolved as a political problem and as part of the overall crisis of the continent. True, the roots of the debt crisis can be traced to a mixture of internal and external policies, but the reproduction of the crisis and the inability to implement prescriptions for effective debt management are intrinsically linked to internal structures of power, politics, production, and exchange. We also contend that a solution to the crisis can only be found in a combined response from the global system which must be matched by visible evidence of internal political and economic restructuring so as to avoid the mistakes of the past while building a viable capacity to withstand unfavorable pressures from the international system. Finally, we contend that the debt crisis cannot be separated from deepening political contradictions and conflicts and is to a very large extent responsible for the increasing suffocation of civil society, political repression, human rights abuses, and political instability in the continent. It is our argument that this environment of political instability, uncertainty, and tension erode possibilities for generating internal capacities for responding to the debt crisis.

The African Crisis and the Origins of the Debt Crisis

Africa entered the 1990s as the "poorest, most troubled, least developed and hungriest" region in the world.[11] According to Layashi Yaker, Executive Secretary of the ECA, "Africa ended the 1980s with more misery and underdevelopment than it started with. Africa was the only continent where all the critical indicators of development showed unacceptable retrogression, and where all the socio-economic and political ills that were so overwhelmingly glaring in the 1980s, and which are still very much around us today," continue unabated.[12] True, Africa's current predicaments are precipitates of its historical experiences, which distorted, disarticulated, and underdeveloped the region. Its historical experience also ensured a marginal location and role in the global division of labor.[13] However, the truth is that decades of *political* independence have witnessed the alignment and realignment of forces within the African region in a direction which consolidated, legitimized, and reproduced inherited contradictions, conflicts, inequalities, and patterns of accumulation.

That the global economy, dominated by Japan, the United States, other Western economies and the Newly Industrializing Countries (NICs) is hostile to African economic interests is not new. That international financial institutions have little or no special provisions for Africa's special conditions as evidenced in the blanket imposition of orthodox stabilization and adjustment programs is by now quite obvious. That the World Bank and the IMF were not set up for Africa and were not designed to address African realities is well known. That transnational corporations would not bring in new capital, transfer skills, and technology, would not use local raw materials, and would repatriate huge profits to the metropole is part of the African experience. In fact, that Africa has no control over the prices of its exports and imports and that interest rates have continued to rise in the global financial markets are equally part of the numerous obstacles the continent confronts in its international economic relations. It follows, therefore, that all complaints by the OAU and African leaders in these directions are largely escapist, diversionary, and opportunistic. They know the conditions of global economic relations, and they are aware of the implications of underdevelopment, dependence, and vulnerability. They are not unaware of the unequal, hostile, and exploitative nature of the post-cold war international division of labor. Why have they done almost nothing serious about these conditions? Why has the region's debt profile continued to deteriorate?

This steady decline towards crisis is not a recent development in the continent. As far back as November 1983, the Executive Secretary of the ECA had noted that:

> Today, Africa faces a plethora of crises—the food crisis, the energy crisis, the debt crisis, and the crisis of economic management. We may also add to the list the climatic and ecological crisis resulting in the growing desertification of the continent, persistent droughts, and consequent crop failures, hunger and famine.[14]

Several years later, the ECA had cause to make the same pronouncement on the increasing marginalization of the continent as a precipitate of deepening internal crisis and worsening conditions of living;

> A diagnosis of the African situation—social, political and economic—has been attempted on many occasions by many eminent Africans. The assessment, in all cases, has been unanimous: the African region is most seriously affected by the burden of underdevelopment. In spite of its vast human and natural resources...the region is unable to boast of any significant achievement of well being.[15]

By the end of 1989, the World Bank had reached the conclusion that Africans were generally worse off than they were three decades ago.[16] The ECA and the OAU are now agreed that Africa has squandered its opportunity for growth and development, that the present, which by any rational standards is appalling, would be a golden age compared to what the future has in stock if present trends are not contained.

It is obvious, therefore, that the debt crisis is only a portion of the monumental and "unprecedented" crises confronting the African region today. It is quite possible that beyond the historically determined distortions and disarticulations of the social formations in the region, the debt crisis poses the most fundamental challenge to possibilities for growth and development in contemporary Africa. Ironically, most Africans, preoccupied with the exigencies of survival on a daily basis, are unaware of the size and implications of the continent's debt. Many are unaware of how much their respective nations owe and of what responses have been advanced internally and internationally. This is largely the result of illiteracy, limited information, and the deliberate manipulation and control of debates and information dissemination by desperate African regimes. As the South Commission has rightly noted, "debt has become a form of bondage, and the indebted economies have become indentured economies—a clear manifestation of neo-colonialism."[17] While this is true, the real issue is how Africa became such a heavily indebted region.

A combination of internal and external factors and forces have combined to weaken the African economy and contribute to its debt crisis. The literature from within the continent has tended to focus on the external factors: declining prices of exports, rising interest rates, the oil crisis of the 1970s, increasing cost of imports and services, and higher debt-servicing ratios. For instance, Ibrahim Babangida, as Chairman of the OAU, had argued that the causes of Africa's predicament could be found "mainly in the debt burden, the collapse of commodity prices, the low-levels of resource-flows from the developed countries, as well as natural calamities."[18]

Analyses of Africa's debt situation from outside the continent have tended to place more emphasis on the internal factors. As the World Bank—a typical body representative of this perspective—has noted, these internal issues include a "weak growth in the productive sectors, poor export performance...deteriorating social conditions...decay of institutional capacity," corruption, mismanagement, and the general inability to build a strong and viable economic base.[19]

It is obvious that a combination of a hostile external economic environment and widespread internal contradictions, mismanagement, and corruption have been responsible for the mounting debt problems of the continent. By global standards, Africa's foreign debt is small and of no major threat to the international financial system. In fact, between Brazil and Mexico, the two countries can match the region's debt dollar for dollar. At the end of 1992, Africa's total external debt was $290 billion. This was two and a half times greater than it was just ten years earlier. For sub-Saharan Africa, the debt profile had increased threefold from $56 billion in 1980 to $173.7 billion in 1990 in spite of foreign aid and the implementation of difficult austerity measures.

It would appear, therefore, that while the ongoing liberalization agenda certainly opens up political spaces for increased political activity, such spaces are in danger of being closed up again because the state structure in charge of this political renewal is exactly the same structure which had closed it up for decades. The custodians of the state have learnt almost nothing and seem to be very unhappy at being unable to repress and intimidate the people with state power because of the new political conditionalities imposed by donors and lenders. Africa is also in a bind over its debt relations with the multilaterals. In 1980 Africa owed only 14 percent of its total debt stock to the multilaterals. By the end of 1991, this had increased to 25 percent. Since multilateral debts cannot be rescheduled and have to be paid back before other creditors, this has "meant that multilaterals loom large in Africa's debt servicing bill—despite the occasional nature of some facilities, such as IDA." These figures notwithstanding, African regimes, as pointed out earlier, are not new to these conditions of marginalization and discrimination. The reality is that African leaders and governments have done very little to respond to developments in the global system, mobilize local resources, maximize existing opportunities, and promote viable conditions for growth, accumulation, and development. The debt crisis must, therefore, be seen as just a part of the larger crisis of power, politics, production, growth, and development in Africa.

Effects of Africa's Deepening Debt Crisis

The debt burden has virtually ruined the African economy, leaving very little room for recovery and contributing to the continent's further marginalization in the global system. As the South Commission noted in its recent report, "debt and its service must be reduced to a level that allows growth to proceed at an acceptable pace."[20] Without doubt, the debt situation in the region has led to a "grave deterioration in per capita income and consumption in Africa during the 1980s."[21] The mounting size of Africa's debt and the increasing inability to service these debts have led creditors and suppliers to impose severe conditionalities on African countries. They have been forced to go to the IMF and the World Bank to reach all sorts of loan and restructuring agreements in order to qualify for assistance and credit.[22] With inability to service foreign debts, creditors simply shut off supply lines to African countries. This response to Africa's increasing insolvency in itself has led to hunger, inflation, so-called black-marketeering, political protests and instability, and in several cases to the overthrow of regimes. The entire phenomenon of state collapse or disintegration as evidenced in Somalia, Liberia, even in states like Sierra Leone, Togo, and Rwanda, is not unrelated to the inability of the state to meet the needs of the people, the withdrawal of loyalties, and the creation of alternative networks of patron-client relations and survival. As nations spend their limited foreign exchange earnings on meeting debt and debt-servicing obligations, they increasingly have almost nothing left to meet the needs of the elites, not to mention those of the poor majority.

The African predicament was made worse with the imposition of policies of desubsidization, deregulation, privatization, devaluation, and the general rolling back of the state by the IMF and the World Bank through their stabilization and structural adjustment packages (see Chapter Three). Imposed on a sea of corruption, mismanagement and insecurity, presided over by a state that had limited legitimacy and hegemony, and operated by elites with only a tenuous linkage to production, these policies failed to stem the tide of deterioration.[23] Adjustment, rather than providing some relief, furthered the delegitimization of the state and the intensification of expenditure on security and stability by beleaguered power elites who had to contend with the rising frustrations of the people.

With rising interest rates, shortened maturity and grace periods on new credit and loans, and generally declining inflow of private and official investments and assistance, the size of the region's debts simply rose to unmanageable proportions. Between 1970 and 1987 interest rates rose from 3.7% to 10%—about 172%. The region's arrears in interest payments to creditors rose from about $1 billion in 1982 to about $11 billion in 1990.[24] The maturity period for loans shortened from 6.7 years to 4 years—about 35%, and the grace period was reduced by 36%. The overall grant element in the period under question was also down by 86%. These unfavorable conditions for loan transactions made it impossible for weak African economies to exercise effective control over the management of their debt profiles.

Debt-servicing obligations have become a fundamental obstacle to economic recovery in Africa. They have become an avenue for exercising control over the respective economies and a mechanism for the net transfer of resources out of the continent. In 1987, Michael Camdessus of the IMF confessed that the IMF was withdrawing more resources from Africa than it is providing.[25] While net transfer of resources to Africa declined from $20 billion in 1978 to $3 billion in 1985 and to $1.1 billion in 1990, the net outflow of resources from the continent between 1983 and 1990 was a staggering $30 billion.[26] In fact, net transfers from sub-Saharan Africa to the IMF rose from $426 million in 1985 to $895 million in 1986 and to $894 million in 1987. Debt-servicing continued to be one major way of depriving African economies of foreign exchange. Between 1983 and 1990 total debt service amounted to $77,332 billion. According to the United Nations (UN), debt-servicing costs Africa about $14 billion a year. In 1990 alone Africa paid out a staggering sum of $25 billion in debt-servicing. In 1991 debt service increased to $26 billion dollars in spite of the region's terrible economic situation.[27] This amount "accounts for 30 per cent of the continent's export earnings—an extremely high level for countries with acute development challenges. Yet, this level of debt-servicing represents only 60 per cent of the original obligation due, a result of rescheduled payments and the buildup of arrears."[28] The UN has estimated that "Africa as a whole can only meet about two-thirds (and sub-Saharan Africa less than half) of its originally-scheduled debt-servicing obligations, with the balance having had to be rescheduled or having built up as arrears. These arrears amounted to a massive $14 billion (in 1992), up from only $1 billion in 1980."[29]

The Organization of African Unity (OAU) has argued that "several African countries have a debt-service coefficient which is higher than that of Brazil, one of the most indebted countries of the Group of 77." The organization's survey revealed that debt-service payments accounted for 12% of the annual budget of Kenya, 15% for Egypt, 20% for Madagascar, 34% for Zaire, 50% for Guinea Bissau, 52% for Senegal, 59% for Togo, 84% for the Sudan, and 280% for Burundi. In addition, debt-service payments as a percentage of export earnings accounted for 240% for the Sudan, 205% for Comoro, 100% for Zambia, 87% for Madagascar, 50% for Malawi, Uganda, and Ghana, and 29% for Ethiopia, Zaire, Kenya, and Zimbabwe.[30] These figures were for 1987, and in spite of structural adjustment programs and several rescheduling arrangements, figures from the UN show that by 1991 the debt situation had worsened considerably.

Without doubt, debt-service obligations have "severely limited the ability of the region's countries to finance critical imports and development projects. Moreover, arrears on debt service have already interrupted some aid flows."[31] There is no doubt, therefore, that the debt crisis has mortgaged the autonomy of African states as their economies are handed over to creditors and international finance agencies who set up a form of informal government, a situation that erodes the political gains of the last three decades. Most central banks are under the control and direction of World Bank and IMF officials, in many instances such officials invite themselves or are invited to cabinet meetings, and national budgets and development plans first receive the approval of lenders and creditors before they are made known to nationals. The experiences of Zambia and Ghana, where IMF and World Bank officials enjoy unprecedented influence and power over public policies, are typical examples. Therese Sevigny provides a graphic illustration of the Zambian case:

> Let me give you a simple example of the havoc developing country debt plays with people's lives. Zambia had a growing economy in the 1960s and early 1970s, based on income from its major export, copper. Then, copper prices plummeted. Zambia borrowed, and the international community lent, money to make up the shortfalls in revenue, thinking the price collapse to be temporary. But it wasn't temporary: copper prices continued to fall, and Zambia's debt mushroomed from 40 percent of GDP in 1975 to 400 percent of GDP by 1986, or about $6 billion.
>
> By that time, Zambia's annual scheduled debt service payment had gone up to $900 million-equivalent to 95 percent of all its export earnings. That meant that if it paid its obligations, it would have no money at all for its vital imports, which are the basis of much of its economy, and which also include essentials like food, fertilizer, and medicines. So the government was in a position neither to adequately service its debt, nor to provide the variety of essential services for health, education, agriculture etc...[32]

In addition, policies which have been initiated as responses to the pressures from creditors have "reduced the amount of foreign exchange available to purchase imports, leading to a very severe import strangulation—depriving industry and agriculture of needed inputs; holding back new investment and even the maintenance of the existing capital stock; further reducing consumption standards and the incentives for greater work efforts. Debt servicing has also absorbed resources which could otherwise have been devoted to investment."[33] This has been the experience of Uganda, a country still trying to recover from the disastrous regimes of Idi Amin and Milton Obote, years of civil war, and the scourge of decay, dislocation, and AIDS. In spite of some debt cancellations, reschedulings, and soft loans, including "an 88 percent write-down of its commercial debt" which lowered its debt servicing bill to between $20 and $40 million a year, the country still had to pay out about $130 million in the 1993/94 fiscal year.[34] Inability to pay arrears, among other factors, is expected to push Uganda's foreign debt stock from $2.6 billion in 1993 to $3.2 billion in 1996, despite a 48 percent (about $280 million) reduction in Uganda's debt arrears in 1992/93. The country is expected to continue to devote close to 50 percent of its export earnings to debt-servicing.[35] Under such conditions, finding the money, especially in foreign exchange, to promote development of any sort, will require more borrowing, imposition of painful cost-cutting measures on an already impoverished populace, and listening to the dictates of lenders and donors.

Finally, the mounting debt crisis has now led to a situation where African states are constantly making pleas for concessions and breaks in their economic relations with the rest of the world. The helplessness is evidenced in the frequent, almost endless travels to world capitals, offices of international banks, and to the IMF and World Bank, as well as to countless seminars and meetings dedicated to finding solutions to the debt problem. Between 1980 and 1988, twenty-five countries in sub-Saharan Africa had their debts rescheduled 105 times.[36] The situation today is that the structure of the African economy is so weak and crisis-ridden that it is incapable of supporting the continued net drain of resources to the developed countries, nor can it continue to service its debts without significant international responses to externally generated constraints on the continent's recovery process. Yet, it must be added that only a carefully worked out program of internal restructuring at the levels of power, politics, production, and exchange will make external responses useful to the African debt crisis. What then is the way out for Africa?

Responses to the Debt Crisis

The deepening crisis of the African continent has not been short of responses and prescriptions from both the international community and regional organizations. From the OAU's 1980 *Lagos Plan of Action*, and the 1986 *African Priority Programme for Economic Recovery 1986–1990*, through other responses from the Commonwealth, the Scandinavian nations, American secretaries of state and the treasury, Western leaders, the ECA, and other international organizations, prescriptions towards resolving the continent's deteriorating conditions have been addressed. The debt crisis has been a major area of concern in these and other prescriptions. We shall highlight only a few of these responses.

At the 1987 Venice Summit of the Group of Seven—the United States of America (USA), the United Kingdom (UK), Japan, West Germany, France, Italy, and Canada—the African crisis was discussed and a decision was reached on the possibility of "applying lower interest rates on their existing debt, and agreement should be reached, especially in the Paris Club, on longer repayment and grace periods to ease the debt burden."[37] Of course, this recommendation was hardly pushed far enough by the Group of Seven, and by the time they met in Houston in 1990 they had completely abandoned Africa and diverted their attention towards Eastern

Europe. This diversion of attention, interest, investments, and assistance away from Africa to other regions reflects the tenuous enthusiasm with which international financial institutions and Western governments have pursued other prescriptions on how to resolve Africa's debt overhang, which include: ad hoc financing, case-by-case rescheduling, interest rate capitalization schemes, zero coupon bonds, debt-equity swaps, comprehensive restructuring, drastic and serious check on waste and corruption, freezing of interest rates, reduction of debt-service ratios, moratoria, the increased use of the so-called "Soft Window" by the World Bank through its International Development Assistance (IDA), the implementation of stabilization and adjustment programs, an intensified export drive policy to increase foreign exchange earnings, selling off outstanding debt at a discount, and the introduction of another Marshall Plan. It has also been suggested that "banks should be entitled to charitable tax deductions for claims on low income countries that they donate to public or private aid agencies. These agencies could then sell such claims to the debtor government for local currency or continue to collect the local currency equivalent of the debt service due, using the proceeds in the debtor country to fund development projects."[38]

As part of the 1987 initiative of the Group of Seven, which was reinforced in 1988 at its Toronto Summit, certain categories of debt have been reduced or written off. At the end of 1990, about $7.6 billion had been cancelled by the Group of Seven members. Some developed nations have cancelled Official Development Assistance (ODA) loans amounting to $2 billion between 1987 and 1988 and $5 billion between 1988 and 1990. For instance, "Canada cancelled 35% of outstanding and disbursed debt on concessional terms during 1988–90, France, 20%, and Germany 19%. Overall 11% of concessional debt was cancelled, with many creditors far below the average."[39] Countries like Tanzania, Benin, Cameroon, and Morocco have benefitted from various packages aimed at reducing the pains of debt servicing and debt repayment. But this is just a tiny, almost inconsequential amount, considering the magnitude of the region's debt. For instance, while the United States cancelled debts for Poland and Egypt, it has resisted doing so for even poorer and much needier African nations. This shows that there is no standard yardstick and that many cancellation programs are politically determined or motivated.

While the Trinidad terms that were formulated in 1990 had proposed a two-third reduction of the total debt stock of a qualifying nation, the Toronto terms offer repayment of outstanding debts over a 25-year period with a 14-year grace period. The United States has stuck to the latter, thus receiving subsidies from nations who adhere to the former. There have also been a spate of activities around the issue of "debt for development swap" options which allows Western financial institutions to make tax-deductible write-offs of debts owed them as donations for specific development projects in Africa and other developing nations. Such "donations" were to be directed at policies and programs in health, education, social services, rural development, and so on. A typical instance of such swap option was the "donation" of $1 million by American Express Bank Limited in Nigerian obligations to the International Foundation for Education and Self-Help (IFESH) "to fight hunger, health problems, unemployment and illiteracy in Nigeria."[40] In 1988, the Midland Bank also "donated" to UNICEF the sum of $800,000, with arrangements for the Bank of Sudan to service UNICEF in local currency and for the money to be "solely invested in water, sanitation, reforestation and health education programmes in the Kordofan region of Sudan."[41] Other European and American banks have participated in the "debt for development swap" option. France has created a "conversion fund" to facilitate the conversion of $1 billion in debt from Cote d'Ivoire, Gabon, Congo, and Cameroon into investment, infrastructure and environmental protection.[42] Again, though the direct and immediate benefit goes to the financial institution in that it indirectly gets back its funds through tax deductions, this option hardly addresses the critical issues in Africa's debt problem.

From the continent and the Third World in general, prescriptions on the need to form a debtors' cartel, outright default, repudiation, and the creation of powerful anti-debt movements have been advanced as possible alternatives to prescriptions from the West. The major problems with the West's prescriptions are, first, their implications for the empowerment of the poorer countries, which obviously is not in the interest of some developed countries as it would drastically reduce their subservience and vulnerability to foreign manipulation and second, their lack of harmonization in both the demands from Africa and the responses from the West. While the UN Conference on Trade and Development (UNCTAD) at its eighth meeting in Cartegna, Colombia, called for an 80 percent cancellation of Africa's debt and the balance repayable in local currency and spent on development programs, the Western nations have not taken such calls seriously. Rather, they have proposed an array of options and solutions: the Baker Plan, the Brady Plan, the Toronto Plan, the Enhanced Toronto Terms, The Trinidad Terms, the Group of Seven Plan, the IMF's March 1986 Structural Adjustment Facility (SAF) and its December 1987 Enhanced Structural Adjustment Facility (ESAF), and a whole range of responses, even from private banks, international donors and so on. With these numerous and now confusing responses, African countries hardly know which option is best suited to their conditions. Yet, the West and international financial institutions have resisted the calls for an international conference on the debt crisis.

True, some Western Governments, in particular the Federal Republic of Germany, France, and Sweden, have cancelled debts owed to them by low-income countries. Countries like Canada and the Netherlands have cancelled aid loans to African states, while Belgium is accepting repayment in local currency, as many African states have demanded for years in the face of declining foreign exchange earnings. France has cancelled the official debt of all low-income countries in Africa, while Japan has used grants to refinance aid and export credits. The total cancellation of aid debt owed by low-income African countries to Canada, the Federal Republic of Germany, the Scandinavian countries, and the United Kingdom in 1988 exceeded $3.2 billion, with a possibility of reducing debt service by $125 million. The OECD likewise agreed to reschedule official credits, while the low-income countries benefitted from the 1987 "new grace and maturity ceilings of 10 to 20 years."[43] Denmark, the Netherlands, and Norway have assisted Uganda with debt-servicing obligations to the World Bank and the African Development Bank. Denmark, Sweden, and Switzerland are also assisting Uganda with payments to the IMF.

These policies, while significant for resolving the debt crisis, have not gone far enough. In the first place, they seem to be based on moralistic and humanitarian grounds, reflecting the old paternalistic response of the West to the historically determined underdevelopment, weaknesses, and crises of developing formations. The West waits for the debts to mount, for the poor countries to cry and plead for assistance, then with fanfare and all the possible publicity, certain concessions are announced. This will simply not do.

The second problem has to do with the fact that grace periods, rescheduling, higher maturity periods, and so on, simply address the manifestations rather than the *causes* of the debt crisis. The responses have not looked at the gross inequality in the global system, the lack of access to developed-country markets, falling commodity prices, declining investments, by the developed countries, the net transfer of resources from the continent to the West, especially in debt-servicing obligations, and the deep-rooted internal constraints to production and exchange which were in the first place responsible for the mounting debt crisis. Finally, the responses, so far, seem to overlook the need for a comprehensive solution to the debt crisis by making a linkage between debt, development, and democratization within the region and in the international system. This is because such a critical linkage would expose the weaknesses in Western responses to the African crisis, empower the African region, and affect the unequal flow of global resources which currently works to the benefit of the developed economies. With the existing situation, Africa remains at the mercy of Western governments and institutions and lacks the capacity to develop institutions, technologies, and structures that would make the region effectively competitive in the global market. Yet, as the World Bank noted in its 1989 report, Africa is obviously incapable of competing in an increasingly complex, technologically sophisticated, and highly competitive global market.[44]

In its major position paper on "External Debt Crisis of Africa" produced in 1986, the OAU noted that the solution to the debt crisis has to be *political*. It then advanced several possible short-and longer-term options: suspension or freezing of debt-service payments for a period of ten years; reduction of debt-service burden to a level compatible with export earnings and the gross domestic product; a linkage between external debt repayment and the prices of export commodities; a 15% ceiling on export earnings allotted for servicing external debts; extension of the grace period to "synchronize the economic impact of the projects financed with external loans with the debt repayment burden;" multilateral debt cancellation; and a linkage between "debt rescheduling and the imposition of structural adjustment programs on the debtor countries by the international financial and monetary institutions not conversant with the specific realities of African economies." The OAU also asked for repayment of debts to regional and multilateral financial institutions in local currency "either in part or in full;" the establishment of a new financial institution "with a joint capital contribution by African countries and the creditors to refinance Africa's debts;" the reduction of interest payments on commercial loans and a "further rescheduling of interest payments moratorium with ten-year grace period and a 20-year repayment period;" relief terms to debtor countries without financial charges; and finally, due attention to the differences within and between African states and their debt problems "since their experiences of external debts differ from one country to another. Some export oil, others do not."[45] Since these proposals were advanced by the OAU, they have not been taken too seriously by the global community.[46]

At the special session of the OAU Summit in Addis Ababa in late 1987 the OAU gave publicity to these prescriptions and added a few other possibilities: conversion of commercial credits into transferable securities with maturity of at least twenty-five years and lower interest rates; no conditioning of debt rescheduling on IMF stabilization programs; easing multilateral agencies' conditionality and no cross-conditionality; a new Special Drawing Rights (SDR) allocation of at least SDR15bn to ease developing countries' liquidity shortage and doubling of the World Bank's capital; raising of the eligibility ceiling for IDA resources; and restoration of repayment and grace periods for IDA loans to fifty and ten years, respectively.[47] These are certainly very comprehensive and realistic responses, which make no allusions to issues of default, cartellization, or repudiation which seem to scare lenders in spite of the rather small size of Africa's debt. But one major issue was missing.

The OAU, in typical fashion, was silent on the internal dimensions of the debt crisis: a bloated bureaucracy, widespread corruption, economic mismanagement, misplaced priorities and poorly planned investment programs, unnecessary defense and security expenditures, and the concentration of the elites in unproductive sectors of the economy. The organization was also silent on the use of the state for accumulation, as against legitimation purposes, and the general misuse of decades of foreign aid, foreign exchange earnings, and foreign loans. A country like Nigeria, in spite of the fluctuations in the global oil market, has squandered the hundreds of billions of dollars it collected from the production and sale of oil, especially since 1973. Today, the country is heavily in debt, and social, political, and other forms of contradictions plague the state and society.[48] How does one explain the grinding poverty, hopelessness, and dehumanization that characterizes Zaire today, an otherwise resource-rich nation? What led the Ghanaian economy into ruins from which it is yet to recover, in spite of a very favorable disposition of the Bank and donors towards its reform agenda? How did the United National Independence Party (UNIP) in Zambia, which had promised in 1964 that every Zambian would be able to afford a pint of milk and an egg a day by 1970, drive the economy aground and to the verge of total bankruptcy by 1989? It is obvious that unless these issues are seriously addressed there is no way the debt crisis can be resolved, irrespective of whatever concessions might come from the international level. So far most African leaders have found it more convenient to overlook or neglect these internal conditions, which have contributed immensely to the net illegal transfer of resources abroad and the rapid increase in the foreign debt profile of the continent.

Beyond the Debt Crisis: Africa in the New Globalization

The debt crisis, as we have argued, is only an aspect of the deepening crisis of the continent. It cannot be addressed in isolation from other contradictions and constraints on growth and development. The big question that African leaders must answer is: who will do business with a bankrupt economy that is also under severe pressure? Who will invest in an economy ravaged by inflation, poverty, unemployment, and obvious inability of the state to service its debt, not to speak of repaying the principal on loans contracted decades ago? As the ECA noted in its 1990 report on Africa, the continent "cannot overcome its present economic predicament without an early resolution of the problem of debt overhang."[49] The report also noted that none of the initiatives so far proposed has "captured or encompassed the holistic approach" advanced by the OAU as discussed earlier. Even the IMF agrees that there is a need to "establish principles for settling the question of Africa's external debt" and that "[c]learly, the existing repayment obligations of the African countries are still too onerous."[50] There is no doubt that structural adjustment and other stabilization programs, which have been widely prescribed, have not provided a lasting or far-reaching solution to the debt crisis of African states. In virtually all instances, foreign debt profiles as well as debt-service ratios have more than doubled and the economies have been plagued with political tensions, coups, instability, and social crisis in the context of state decline and delegitimization. For instance, when Nigeria introduced its structural adjustment program in 1986, its foreign debt stock was $18 billion dollars. By the end of 1991, its foreign debt stock has climbed to over $30 billion. Zambia's debt increased from 40 percent of GDP in 1975 to 400 percent of GDP in 1986.[51] The pressures generated by adjustment have likewise compelled several African states to resort to repression, violence, human rights abuses, and the expansion of defense expenditures in a desperate move by the elites to hold on to political power and contain mounting popular opposition to the pains of adjustment. This pattern of reaction has become rather frequent because the painful and unprecedented adjustment programs were imposed without programs designed specifically to protect vulnerable, even privileged, groups directly affected by adjustment.

It is true that donors and the West, in a post-cold war global environment, are no longer interested in Africa.[52] The complaints about "aid fatigue" and "compassion fatigue" as well as the redirection of interest, investment and aid to other regions, especially Eastern Europe, attest to this.[53] The inability to show practically any achievement for decades of development assistance, however limited such assistance was, has frustrated some donors. Political instability, economic mismanagement, uncertainty, corruption, and declining purchasing power of the majority have scared off investors or forced them to shift their operations to other regions within the Third World and to the new-found markets of Eastern Europe. One fact is, however, clear. There is a fundamental political dimension to the African crisis. The suffocation of civil society, widespread repression, and erosion of democratic rights and basic freedoms have contributed to declining productivity, the mass exodus of productive segments of society to foreign lands, and increasing reliance on unorthodox, often extra-legal mechanisms of accumulation. In countries like Togo, Nigeria, Burundi, The Sudan, Somalia, and Liberia, political crisis, war, and insecurity have effectively grounded productive activities as rural producers have withdrawn to production for subsistence or are busy smuggling their products to neighboring markets.

In the *African Charter for Popular Participation in Development and Transformation* published in 1990, the ECA argued that the African crisis was in several ways more political than economic (see Chapter One). The crisis has to do with the lack of empowerment of popular organizations, absence of accountability of leaders to the people, the suffocation of civil society, the noninvolvement of women, youths, and the rural majority in the decision-making processes and the general opposition of most African governments to the democratization of society.[54] Similarly, Adebayo Adedeji has argued that the African crisis cannot be resolved until Africa undergoes a "fundamental structural transformation and diversification" and that only the "democratization of development will inevitably accelerate the restructuring process and the expansion of domestic market."[55] This, ultimately, is the only way to check lack of financial discipline, unbridled corruption, waste, mismanagement, and the piling up of huge internal and external debts at the expense of the poor majority.

Without doubt, African governments not initiating and pursuing policies that open up society, empower the people, and create a conducive environment for domestic investment, production, and accumulation should receive no foreign aid or any sort of debt relief. The same leaders who piled up the billions of dollars in foreign debt by looting their treasuries, displacing peasants and farmers from the land, chasing professionals and scholars abroad, and engaging in prestige projects cannot be expected to pursue policies which would resolve the debt crisis. Hence, there is an urgent need for serious and far-reaching political responses at levels which strengthen civil society and encourage people to invest, be creative and productive, attract back those who fled from the country as well as foreign investors, and generate conditions for growth and development.

There is certainly an urgent need for an international conference to discuss the African crisis in general and the debt crisis in particular. Such a conference should provide a forum for addressing all existing prescriptions with a view to identifying the best options to the crisis within the rather confusing options currently suffocating the international system. Resolving the debt crisis is equally in the interest of the developed economies. An Africa without debt would divert its resources to productive activities with the right political leadership and environment. Such an Africa would be less dependent on foreign food and other aid, be a better trading partner, throw up fewer civil wars, give rise to fewer refugees, and experience fewer conditions requiring frequent international intervention. The OAU is correct in arguing that unless "the fundamental factors underlying Africa's economic and social crisis are attacked at the root through durable and long-term structural transformation, *Africa will perforce remain the sick child of the international community.*"[56] With the end of the cold war, another "debt war" between the developed and developing countries must not be allowed to dominate international economic relations. Only a preparedness for dialogue and mutual concessions can resolve the deepening crisis of the continent. As Karamo N. M. Sonko has rightly noted, "even if all of the debt is cancelled today, many problems which led to the current crisis will continue to exist. Therefore, major policy changes in both creditor and debtor nations are required in order to generate long-term economic prosperity in Africa."[57] Recovery in Africa will mean less dependence on the developed nations, fewer upheavals, fewer coups and counter-coups, and a major reduction, at the very least, in conditions that hinder productivity and militate against the ability to manage existing debt profiles. With the recent developments in the Middle East and Eastern Europe, Africa has been further removed from the focus of international attention. Most donor nations are in deep economic crisis and their politicians are looking more inward. Ultimately, the debt crisis is an African crisis. Going about and begging for debt forgiveness will not resolve the problem even if it provides temporary relief.[58] Given that the twenty-first century will be extremely trying for Africa, the need for urgent comprehensive internal restructuring in order to create a viable environment for productivity and recovery cannot be overstated if Africa is to overcome its current marginalization in global power and economic relations.

Endnotes

1. Organization of African Unity, *African Priority Programme for Economic Recovery 1986–1990 (APPER)*, (Addis Ababa: OAU Secretariat, 1990).

2. Javier Perez de Cueller quoted in United Nations, Office of the Secretary General, *African Debt: The Case for Debt Relief* (New York: Africa Recovery, UN Information Unit, 1991).

3. Boutros Boutros-Ghali, Statement to the Panel of High-Level Personalities on African Development, Geneva, 28 December 1992.

4. See Thandika Mkandiwaire, "The Road to Crisis, Adjustment and Deindustrialization: The African Case," *African Development* 13, 1 (1988).

5. Adbou Diouf, Address to the UN General Assembly in his capacity as Chairman of the Organization of African Unity, 30 September 1992.

6. General Ibrahim B. Babangida, Address at the 46th Session of the UN General Assembly, New York, October 4, 1991, p.6.

7. See Nii K. Bentsi-Enchill, "Bank Reports on Poor Adjustment Results," *Africa Recovery* Vol. 6 (4) (December 1992–February 1993); Economic Commission for Africa, *Economic Report on Africa 1992* (Addis Ababa: E/ECA/CM.18/2, ECA Secretariat, 1992); and "Rising Debt Threatens Reforms," *Africa Recovery* Vol. 5 (4) (December 1991).

8. North-South Roundtable, *The Challenge of Africa in the 1990s* (New York: North-South Roundtable, 1991), p. 19.

9. Michael Holman and Edward Balls, "Foreign Debt: Still Caught in the Vice," *Financial Times* (September 1, 1993), p. VII.

10. "UNICEF Call: Strike Off Chains of Africa's Debt," *Africa Recovery* Vol. 5 (4) (December 1991), p. 48.

11. "African Countries Lead Misery Index," *Africa News* (May 25–June 7, 1992), p.3.

12. Layashi Yaker, Keynote Address at the International Conference on "Africa in Transition: Challenges and Opportunities," held at the American Graduate School of International Management, Glendale, Arizona, February 18–20, 1993.

13. See the works of Claude Ake, Walter Rodney, Frantz Fanon, Aime Cesaire, Albert Memi, and Ade Ajayi on the nature and implications of colonialism on Africa.

14. Quoted in His Majesty King Mosheshe II,"Alternative Strategies for Development: A Clarion Call!", *Development Dialogue* (1) (1987), p.79.

15. Economic Commission for Africa, *ECA and Africa's Development, 1983–2008: A Preliminary Perspective Study* (Addis Ababa: ECA,1983), p.93.

16. See World Bank, *Sub-Saharan Africa: From Crisis to Sustainable Growth- A Long-Term Perspective Study* (Washington, DC. World Bank, 1989).

17. The South Commission, *The Challenge to the South: The Report of the South Commission* (London: Oxford University Press, 1990), p.227.

18. Ibrahim Babangida, Statement at the 46th Session of the UN General Assembly, New York, October 4, 1991.

19. World Bank, *Sub-Saharan Africa...*, op. cit., p.18.

20. The South Commission, *The Challenge to the South:*, op. cit., p.227.

21. Tony Killick and Matthew Martin, "African Debt: The Search for Solutions," *UN Africa Recovery Programme Briefing Paper* No. 1, June 1989, p.4.

22. See Julius O. Ihonvbere, "Banking on Poverty and Crisis: The Impact of World Bank and IMF Policies on Sub-Saharan Africa." Paper presented at the conference on "Is a Democratic World Order Possible?" organized by the Campaign for Peace and Democracy, New York, New York, April 17, 1993.

23. See Julius O. Ihonvbere, "The Crisis of Structural Adjustment Programs in Africa: Issues and Explanations," *Philosophy and Social Action* Vol. 18 (3) (1992).

24. United Nations, *African Debt...*, op. cit.,p.1.

25. See "IMF in Africa," *Africa Recovery* (4) (December 1987), pp.5–6.

26. United Nations, *African Debt...* op. cit., p.1.

27. Ibid, p.1.

28. Ibid.

29. Ibid, p.2.

30. See Organization of African Unity, "External Debt Crisis of Africa: Summary of Information, Statistical Data, and Proposed Actions," Addis Ababa, 20–21 November 1986.

31. Joshua Greene, "The Debt Problem of Sub-Saharan Africa," *Finance and Development* (June 1989), p.9.

32. Therese Sevigny, "From Crisis to Consensus: The United Nations and the Challenge of Development." New York: Africa Recovery Unit of the Communications and Project Management Division of the UN Department of Public Information, November 1990.

33. Killick and Martin, "African Debt...," op. cit.,p.4.

34. Roy Laishley, "Creditors Consider Improved Debt Relief: Larger Part of Africa's Burden Remain," *Africa Recovery* Vol. 6 (3) (October 1993), p. 3.

35. Ibid, However, with recent positive developments in the Ugandan economy and the new overtures by the West and donors towards Uganda, these anticipated problems might be contained in the 1990s. Uganda, today, is seen as one of the best performing economies with a focused leadership in Africa

36. See "Rising Debt Threaten Reforms," *Africa Recovery* Vol. 5 (4) (December 1991) and Roy Laishley, "Renewed Calls for Less Debt, More Aid," *Africa Recovery* Vol. 6 (4) (December 1992–February 1993).

37. "African Debt Continues to Mount," *Africa Recovery* Vol.2 (1) (March 1988), p.23.

38. Ibid, p.24.

39. The Global Coalition for Africa, *African Social and Economic Trends* op. cit., p.16.

40. Stephany Griffit-Jones and David Williams, "Donations of LDC Debt by Banks to Charities," in S. Griffit-Jones (ed.), *Third World Debt: Managing the Consequences* (London: IFR Publishing Limited, 1989), p.100.

41. Ibid,

42. The Global Coalition for Africa, *African Social and Economic Trends*, op. cit., p.16; and "French Debt Deal for Four African Countries," *Africa Recovery* Vol. 6 (3) (November 1992).

43. Killick and Martin, "African Debt...," op. cit., p.5. See also contributions to G.O. Olusanya and A. O. Olukoshi (eds.), *The African Debt Crisis* (Lagos: NIIA, 1989).

44. World Bank, *Sub-Saharan Africa: From Crisis to Sustainable Growth* op. cit., p.3.

45. OAU, "External Debt Crisis of Africa...," op. cit. See also ECA, *African Alternative Framework to Structural Adjustment Programmes for Socio-Economic Recovery and Transformation* (Addis Ababa: ECA, 1989).

46. See Boutros Boutros-Ghali, *New Concepts for Development Action in Africa* op. cit.; and Kidane Mengisteab and Bernard I. Logan, "Africa's Debt Crisis: Are Structural Adjustment Programs Relevant?" *Africa Development* Vol. XVI (I) (1991).

47. "OAU Summit Adopts Debt Strategy," *Africa Recovery* (4) (December 1987), p.2. See also "African Debt Continues to Mount," op. cit.; "Africa Needs New Strategies for Debt and Investment," *Africa Recovery* Vol. 5 (4) (December 1991); and "UN Secretary-General Urges Fresh Approaches for African Development," *Africa Recovery* Vol. 6 (4) (December 1992–February 1993).

48. See Julius O. Ihonvbere," Economic Crisis, Structural Adjustment and Social Crisis in Nigeria," *World Development* Vol. 21 (1) (1993) and Dele Omotunde and Dare Babarinsa, "This Government has Run Out of Ideas-Interview With Sam Aluko," *TELL* (Lagos, Nigeria) (March 29, 1993).

49. ECA, *Economic Report on Africa 1990*, op. cit., p.33.

50. Michael Camdesus, Managing Director of the IMF speaking at the 1991 review of UNPAAERD in *Africa Recovery* Vol. 5 (4) (December 1991), p. 27.

51. Therese Sevigny, *From Crisis to Consensus: The United Nations and the Challenge of Development* (New York: UN Communications and Project Management Division, 1990), p.6.

52. See Julius O. Ihonvbere, "Surviving at the Margins: Africa and the New Global Order," *Current World Leaders* Vol. 35 (6) (December 1992).

53. See Carol Lancaster, *United States and Africa: Into the Twenty-First Century*, (Washington, DC: Overseas Development Council, 1993).

54. See Economic Commission for Africa, *African Charter for Popular Participation in Development and Transformation* (Addis Ababa: ECA, 1990).

55. Adebayo Adedeji, "Transforming Africa's Economies," *Africa Report* (May–June, 1986), p.5 and 7.

56. OAU, "Africa's Submission to the Special Session of the United National General Assembly on Africa's Economic and Social Crisis," 13 May, 1986.

57. Karamo N. M. Sonko, "Debt in the Eye of a Storm: The African Crisis in a Global Context," *Africa Today* Vol. 37 (4) (1990), p.26.

58. The North-South Roundtable is clear on the fact that the scores of "official initiatives" have so far "had only minor effects upon the transfer of resources to Africa;" that most of the relief measures have come "both too little and, of course, too late;" and that the gains made by low-income African countries would usually be "deducted from bilateral ODA commitments …leaving them literally no better off than before." See *The Challenge of Africa in the 1990s*, p.20.

Chapter Three

Banking on Poverty and Crisis: The World Bank and the Politics of Adjustment in Africa

> IMF prescriptions are designed by and for developed capitalist economies and are inappropriate for developing economies of any kind; the severe suffering imposed on a developing society through IMF conditionality is endured without any real prospect of a favourable economic outcome and without an adequate foundation of social-welfare provisions to mitigate the hardships experienced by the people.[1]

> When did the IMF become an International Ministry of Finance? When did nations agree to surrender to it their power of decision making?...The problems of my country and other Third World countries are grave enough without the political interference of IMF officials. If they cannot help at the very least they should stop meddling.[2]

> ...the World Bank was not created with the problems of the Third World in mind and has always been dominated by the Western powers.[3]

African nations are today practically under the hegemonic control of the World Bank, the International Monetary Fund (IMF), donors, and other international financial institutions. In most African countries, national budgets and development plans are made known to and are discussed with officials of the World Bank and the IMF before they are made known to nationals. Educational policies, social programs, foreign trade and all international economic transactions are determined, conditioned, and in many instances, dictated by officials of the Fund and Bank once a nation adopts stabilization and structural adjustment programs. Most Central Banks, as well, are under the control of both institutions. The powerful influence exerted by these institutions on African states in the current era has generated a new debate on the recolonization of Africa. African states are having to deal not only with profit and hegemony-seeking transnational corporations but also with these powerful financial organizations backed by the Western powers.

If nothing can be said about their role in the consolidation and reproduction of Africa's marginalization in the global division of labor and its chronic underdevelopment, we can state with certainty that Africa's pitiable conditions today attest to the failure of IMF and World Bank programs, prescriptions, and interference in African affairs. Their so-called experts, planning missions, and development models have failed woefully in addressing the specifics of Africa's underdevelopment and have, in fact, deepened contradictions, conflicts, and crises in African social formations. How else can we explain the deepening crisis of the region in spite of over a decade of commitment to IMF and World Bank prescriptions? Of course, both institutions have been guarded in their pronouncements about the achievements of African economies. At the very best they speak of "some growth" and are very careful to avoid the word "development." While both institutions were originally not designed to respond to the problems and realities of underdeveloped societies, the truth is that since attaining political independence and joining the IMF and World Bank, African states have not succeeded in getting the institutions to reconceptualize their methods, restructure their programs, and redesign their approaches to African problems.

What happened was that as the global economy became more bifurcated and as African states experienced more deterioration, the powers of the IMF and World Bank, on behalf of their Western sponsors, increased over all aspects of life in the region. This increasing power strengthened the control of IMF and Bank officials and further reduced possibilities for a more realistic and sympathetic understanding of the historical experiences of African states. What was been more frustrating, at least until very recently, was the very poor appreciation of the internal dynamics of power and social relations within Africa. This was evidenced in the superficial treatment of the state, its institutions, and custodians; the neglect of social constituencies and communities; the failure to provide genuine support for popular institutions, and the neglect of the *political* dimensions of the African predicament.

For the Fund and the Bank, everything was conceived and executed in the context of the cold war. As Cranford Pratt has noted, development assistance to developing formations by the Bank "was seen by many in the West as an important check on the spread of communism. It is in effect a dovish expression of the anti-communist concern to contain the Soviet Union."[4] This ideological purpose was not only evident in its policies and insensitivity to criticism, but also informed its mode of analysis, its models, its prescriptions, and its global politics. As the former president of Tanzania, Mwalimu Julius Nyerere has noted, very few people "honestly believe that the IMF is politically or ideologically neutral. It has an ideology of economic and social development which it is trying to impose on poor countries irrespective of their own clearly stated policies."[5]

Of course, the World Bank is not in a different position. Though in 1989 the Bank's so-called "long-term perspective study" tried to give the impression of increasing sensitivity to African realities and to belatedly acknowledge the *political* dimensions of the African crisis, it remained committed to its conservative international Keynesian perspectives and prescriptions to African states. The truth is that both institutions work together, and the World Bank has consistently linked its structural adjustment policies to the conservative stabilization policies of the IMF. As Pratt notes,

> The Bank has become increasingly arrogant and ideological in its approach to development issues in the Third World...Increasingly the Bank operates on the assumption that it already knows the policies it wishes to insist upon before it enters negotiations with individual Third World countries...When an IMF mission comes to a country to negotiate a stand-by credit, its negotiators actually arrive with a prepared text for the letter they wish the finance minister of that country to send to the IMF...Bank officials have no doubt about the policy changes they wish to require of a country...Bank officials not only suffer from a messianic complex but also...every few years they change their gods. The present god they worship is export promotion...[6]

African states are thus caught in a very difficult situation. They are poor. They lack the resource base. Their economies are dominated by foreign capital. They lack a resilient technological base. They lack control over the prices of their exports as well as the prices of their imports. Their currencies are either overvalued or not convertible. They are not only politically unstable, they are marginal in the international division of labor and power. Under these circumstances, how can they deal with powerful organizations like the Bank and the Fund? The World Bank for instance, "is the Mount Everest of development lending institutions; aside from the huge amounts of money it lends...it has arrogated to itself a position as the institution coordinating many other sources of aid and loan money, including a number of bilateral aid programs."[7] It chairs the consultative groups of aid consortia, co-finances commercial banks and tries to influence the direction of their lending, it has cooperative relationships with several specialized agencies of the UN and clearly influences policies in these organizations, and it has a huge reservoir of technical experts that are badly required in developing formations.[8] How can poor African states stay away from the influence of such a powerful organization?

In the rest of this chapter we seek to discuss the responses of the Fund and Bank to the African crisis, and examine critically the possibilities for recovery based on their monetarist prescriptions.

The African Predicament: The Basis of Stabilization and Adjustment

Africa is in a very desperate situation today. A combination of internal and external factors and forces have combined over the years to generate unprecedented and debilitating crises. As Adebayo Adedeji has noted:

> According to the UNDP Human Development Report 1992, countries of the world are classified into three groups—countries with high human development, countries with medium human development, and countries with low human development. Of the 47 countries belonging to the first category, there is not a single African country. Of the 48 countries in the second category, there are six African countries—South Africa, Libya, Tunisia, Gabon, Botswana, and Algeria. All the remaining African countries covered (42 in all) are classified among the 65 low human development group, with Sierra Leone and Guinea taking the two bottom positions and Nigeria occupying the 128th position out of a total of 160.[9]

Adedeji goes on to note that "for sub-Saharan Africa, only an estimated 26 per cent of the rural dwellers have access to safe water compared to 74 per cent of those who live in urban areas. Sub-Saharan Africa's under five and maternal mortality rates are the highest in the world and its life expectancy not unexpectedly, the lowest. More than half of the population has no access to public health services and tropical diseases afflict a high proportion of the population."[10] These are very somber statistics which are equally shocking because of the rich resource and human endowment of the African continent.[11]

Unfortunately, in spite of the region's wealth, its annual economic growth rate of 1.5 percent is the lowest in the world. With a population of over 500 million people, its combined GNP of about $150 billion is equivalent to that of Belgium with a population of a mere 10 million. Yet, the World Bank estimated that by A.D. 2010, Africa's population would have increased to 1 billion. Food production levels are 20 percent lower than they were in 1970. According to the World Bank, "More and more Africans are going hungry. Severe food shortages were exceptional in 1960; now they are widespread."[12] Africa produces half of the world's refugees, there is only one doctor for every 28,000 Africans, and its population growth rate of 3.2 percent is the highest in the world. AIDS is devastating many of the countries, and according to President Museveni of Uganda, the disease is expected to cut Uganda's population by 20 percent by A.D. 2000. It is estimated that by A.D. 2000 some 70 million Africans will be HIV positive. There are eleven active wars going on in Africa, and in countries like Somalia and Liberia, the state simply disintegrated. In the vast majority of African states, one can hardly speak of a government. Governments are either at war with their own citizens or have been so delegitimized that they exit just in name.[13] The continent is increasingly seen as the "development challenge" of the next century.[14] With thousands of Africans dying daily from war and hunger, and with another 40 million starving, the region has become a dumping ground for toxic wastes from the West. Seventy of every 1000 Africans are destitute, unemployment has increased fourfold since 1980, commodity prices continue to decline just as do foreign aid and foreign investment.[15]

The conditions highlighted above have not gone unnoticed, even if they have not attracted the interest of donors, lenders, and the Western powers. The World Bank in its 1989 report acknowledged these deteriorating conditions. It also acknowledged that for sub-Saharan Africa, "the disintegration of paved highways, the collapse of the judicial and banking systems," and the fact that most governments are "wracked by corruption and are increasingly unable to command the confidence of the population at large"[16] have mediated the recovery process. It is in the context of the African predicament, as discussed above, that we can appreciate Edward Jacox's view that:

> The second oil shock of 1979, followed by steep global recession, reconfigured the development landscape...Sub-Saharan Africa was in an especially vulnerable position because its basic economic structures and capacities were weaker than anywhere else.

> The region had no industrial base to speak of, its human resource and management skills were extremely thin, its infrastructure was sparse and often run-down, its technological options were limited, and it was rapidly losing its competitiveness to other developing regions. Wrong-headed policies fed into and exacerbated these basic problems. Grossly overvalued exchange rates, excessive taxation of exports, widespread price controls and subsidies, state interference in internal and external trade, and generally poor management of the revenues from the commodity price booms of the 1970s—all these left Africa in the early 1980s with a major development crisis on its hands.[17]

It was upon this frightening, desperate, and very dangerous political, economic, and social terrain that the IMF and the World Bank were to deposit their orthodox stabilization and structural adjustment packages in the 1980s. But did their responses work? Can we truly say that the orthodox responses laid the foundations for a more productive, more stable, and more democratic Africa? Can we truly say that the Africa of today is better in any respect than the Africa of a decade ago? Let us now examine why adjustment is not working in Africa.

The Limitations of Africa's Adjustment Programs

It is true that African states need adjustment. Their economies are in deep crisis (see Chapter One) and they have no options except a comprehensive adjustment and transformation of their respective political economies. Adjustment, as packaged by the multilaterals, have brought in some "rewards" or "benefits" (see below). Yet, orthodox adjustment programs, as packaged by the Bank, have a limited chance of success if they fail to take proper cognizance of existing socioeconomic and political power balances, coalitions, and contradictions. The fact remains that ultimately it is the internal character of power, politics, and social relations that determine and influence the ability of the government to implement the often harsh prescriptions of the IMF and the World Bank. African governments are agreed that some adjustment is inevitable in the face of current deepening crisis and further marginalization in the global system. In a global system in which the market is the main driving force, even the most recalcitrant African leaders recognize the importance of market reforms. The ECA, too, is not opposed to the idea of structural adjustment, though it contends that it must be "adjustment with transformation." The disagreement between the IMF and the World Bank on the one hand, and African governments, the OAU, and ECA on the other, is on the content, context, and manageability of the adjustment program.

Eboe Hutchful has provided an outline of issue areas to be considered in the implementation of adjustment programs in view of the "significant implications for the reproductive space and dynamics of political regimes."[18] Though Hutchful concentrates on Ghana, in this section we shall draw examples from other experiences with structural adjustment. The first point to note is the depth of the preadjustment crisis, as well as the "rate and severity of the decline" before adjustment. In the case of Ghana the economy was already in ruins and hardship had become part of the people's reality. The harshness of the IMF and World Bank prescriptions therefore made very little difference to the people. In Nigeria, the reverse was the case. The oil boom had given the impression that the problem was how to spend the money, not how to generate it. By 1986 when the adjustment package was introduced, most Nigerians were of the view that the setbacks were going to be temporary; after all, the country was still in the oil-producing business. What this means is that the rate at which adjustment is introduced and the severity of the policies must pay due attention to the existing preparedness of the people to withstand the pains of restructuring. Hence, in Ghana, opposition was not as violent and persistent as it was in Nigeria and Zambia, where it has been the source of coups, violent political upheavals, and a rapid delegitimization of the state.

Second, the degree of adjustment required is important to the possible success or failure of the package itself. The lending institutions have tended to impose very harsh conditionalities on African countries, conditionalities that pay very little regard to the structural differences, regime types, and opportunities for regime and elite manoeuvre, internally and externally. As Hutchful has rightly noted, "almost all African programs belong in the high conditionality end of the scale," and this situation implies that regimes have less room to set their "own reform agenda and construct the appropriate coalitions"[19] required for successful implementation of the program. This situation has been another major source of opposition to structural adjustment in Africa. The funding institutions assume that all that is required are so-called "stabilization" and "adjustment." The real questions are, the adjustment of what? And, of course, the stabilization of what? How do you "stabilize" and "adjust" a badly organized, badly managed, badly coordinated, corruption-ridden, dependent, foreign-dominated, unproductive, and marginalized economy? In addition, the package is seen as foreign-formulated, foreign-inspired, and foreign-imposed in a grand strategy to recolonize the continent under the supervision of the IMF and the World Bank. The specifics of stabilization and adjustment, which involve the privatization of national institutions and symbols and the unprecedented influence of foreign institutions and "experts," have only fuelled resentment to foreign-dictated recovery programs. Because of the stringency of the conditionalities, African regimes have had very limited room for 'domesticating' their packages, and local innovations easily become incorporated into set patterns handed down by the lending bodies. This has encouraged very weak commitment to the program and generated popular opposition to it from opposition politicians, nationalistic sections of the military, and popular groups. In Ghana, Nigeria, and Zambia, in spite of local efforts to give adjustment a domestic face, it was often seen as foreign-inspired and foreign-directed.

Third is the external environment, which affects the ability to draw international support, resources, and technical assistance to mediate the harshness of adjustment in conditions of poverty and underdevelopment. With the changes in Eastern Europe and the apparent redirection of international interest and support away from Africa, this becomes an even more pressing issue. The record of waste, mismanagement, misplaced priorities, and widespread corruption in African states has contributed immensely to eroding possible support from the international environment.[20] To initiate a stabilization and adjustment program is one thing. Generating the required resources to lubricate the harsh edges of the program and to meet various financial obligations is another. The Fund and the Bank have not worked hard enough to adjust the gross inequalities in the global economy, in which African states are not just marginal but are victims of unbridled exploitation and manipulation. Interest rates are still very high; terms of trade have not improved; commodity prices are still stagnant or on the decline; skills, technology and new investments are not flowing into Africa. These facts show clearly that the environment for mounting such far-reaching restructurings is hardly favorable to poor and underdeveloped nations. Complaints about "aid fatigue" and "compassion fatigue" only serve to rationalize growing disinterest in the region. For a nation like Zambia, the paucity of foreign assistance, in spite of promises following the stunning victory of the Movement for Multiparty Democracy (MMD), is a typical example. Zambia has not received an appreciable amount of foreign assistance to keep development projects afloat. The new democratic government has been unable to fulfil its promises and has faced over a hundred strike actions from its major constituency, labor.

The fourth issue area is the "nature of national constituencies and sociopolitical actors, their composition, interests, tolerance thresholds, their 'discourse of resistance,' and their ability to resist adjustment"[21] which are of utmost importance to the success of adjustment. Unfortunately, the lending agencies have over the years tended to treat these matters, critical as they are, rather lightly. Specifically, this point is about the sites and dynamics of politics and power: the ways in which political constituencies and communities are structured and mobilized, and the nature of interaction between and within political constituencies. This point also has to do with the track-record of the dominant elites, the character of their politics, their ability to reproduce themselves through the careful manipulation of power and ideological discourses, their dominant world-view, their relations to nonbourgeois forces, the character of their relations to foreign interests, and the role of the state in the overall patterns of production and accumulation. In Africa, the dominant elites are mostly responsible for the deepening crisis today through their records of waste, mismanagement, social and economic irresponsibility, corruption, nepotism, and commitment to the reproduction of unequal exchange relations with foreign capital. Also, their tenuous relation to production has contributed significantly to the expansion of the bureaucracy, parastatals, and commerce and the stagnation of productive activities.

The Nigerian example is of particular relevance. The bourgeoisie has never been known, save for a tiny fraction, to be interested in production. The state has always been a means to capital accumulation. The hegemony of the dominant classes has always been tenuous, and it has since political independence relied on the manipulation of religion, ethnicity, and region to retain political dominance and win access to the state. The bourgeoisie has always been concentrated in the real estate, service, and import-export sectors of the economy as against involvement in agriculture and other productive activities. Finally, its factionalization and fractionalization, inability to build hegemony, its corruption, and incapacity to effectively manage society and improve on the living conditions of the majority have alienated the people from the state and its agents and agencies. When such a dominant elite comes up with harsh monetarist policies, it cannot mobilize support. Rather, it will ignite opposition, riots, and counterorganization to its programs. Hence, in Nigeria, Zambia, the Sudan, and Cote d'Ivoire, adjustment programs have met with strong opposition from the people; they see these programs as another attempt by the dominant elites to make life difficult for the already poor and disadvantaged. It is instructive to note that the funding agencies and Western governments are very familiar with the decadent and corrupt character of African elites and governments. Assuming that stabilization and adjustment packages were designed to promote self-reliance, efficiency, and effectiveness in the deployment of resources, elimination of waste, and the promotion of accountability, why on earth did they expect the very same regimes that ran down their respective economies and generated deep-rooted contradictions, which now militate against political stability and productivity, to take such policies seriously or to be capable of implementing them?

A fifth point has to do with what Hutchful calls "regime dynamics": the composition and character of ruling coalitions; mechanisms for securing "vertical and horizontal solidarities;" the nature of political discourses; and the "relationship between technocrats and politicians, and between political and technocratic rationality and decision-making centres in individual regimes, in particular the autonomy and insulation from political pressures enjoyed by the technocratic staff."[22]   Again, lending agencies hardly go beyond the surface in their negotiations with African power elites for adjustment support. Where the bourgeoisie has historically depended on the state for largesse or accumulation, adjustment is unlikely to be palatable to it. Policies that emphasize financial rationality, accountability, and discipline are usually resisted by elites who are used to accumulation through inflated contracts, stealing from public coffers, using public positions for reproducing complex patron-client relations, and relying on connections with public officers to get rich. This has been the case in Nigeria, Zambia, and Zaire. If stabilization makes it more difficult for the elites to accumulate through access to the state, the whole process of corruption can become more desperate and brazen. This only erodes the effectiveness of the adjustment package and reduces the credibility of the political elites, who impose harsh policies on the people and turn around to loot public resources without restraint in order to maintain their preadjustment life styles and living standards.[23] This reduces the credibility of the state, its agents and agencies, as well as the credibility and viability of the adjustment package. Since adjustment was introduced in Nigeria in 1986, corruption, violence, scams, and armed robbery have risen to unprecedented proportions.[24]

Sixth, while adjustment packages usually demand devaluation, desubsidization, deregulation, privatization, massive retrenchment of workers, and the general withdrawal of the state from economic activities, such recommendations not only run contrary to the expectations of African peoples but often address the wrong issues. The nationalist struggles involved the urban-based elites and the masses of the people. Political independence witnessed the capture of political power without economic power. The colonial state had ensured the domination of all sectors of the economy by profit and hegemony-seeking transnational corporations. Thus, the state was the only instrument of power available to the new elites with which to protect the weak, create opportunities, and restructure the economy. The inability of the elites to effectively expand into the economic and more productive spheres of their respective economies is partly due to the high levels of foreign domination and the obstacles placed on the path of indigenous entrepreneurs by foreign investors. This reality is often not appreciated by the Fund and the Bank. Hence, they call for trade liberalization, privatization, deregulation and so forth, which means actually increasing the levels of foreign participation and domination of the local economies. Under such conditions, already weak and disadvantaged local investors and businesses cannot compete or survive. The reality is that if the African elite had been sufficiently strong and productive, the current crisis might not have occurred. Ironically, as is evident in the trade war between the United States and Japan, the protection of local industries and the local market for local exploitation is a critical portion of the accumulation process. Yet, the opposite is prescribed without regard to the African specificity.

The seventh point is that the excessive focus on the state and the prescription for rolling it back is often misplaced, unrealistic, and ahistorical. The focus is often on state intervention, not on the character and nature of the intervention. Even in the advanced capitalist societies, the state is still very prominent in promoting private accumulation and in protecting the poor and disadvantaged through health subsidies, unemployment insurance, cheap housing, subsidized public transportation, subsidized school lunch for kids, and even free primary education, with hundreds of thousands of fellowships and scholarships for higher education. In Europe and North America, farmers receive huge tax breaks and subsidies from the state. The American government pays sugar farmers above the market price. At the end of 1991, the then American President George Bush undertook a tour of Japan and Australia to win trade concessions for American producers. This is precisely what African peoples expect of their governments. The blanket rolling back of the state and the unmitigated exposure of millions of vulnerable poor peasants, women, rural people, youth and children to the harsh forces of the market has led to more crises and instability, which are then used by investors as excuses for holding back or redirecting investments to other regions. However, adjustment has meant higher food prices, stagnating incomes, devalued wages and salaries, scarcity of essential goods, inflation, retrenchment of workers, imposition of user-fees on social services, higher costs of education, and higher house rents for workers. These policies have tended to generate opposition to the state and adjustment while leading to riots. The state has often responded to these challenges with repression, in the effort by its custodians to hold on to power. Without doubt, the "neoclassical basis of structural adjustment," as outlined above, "contradicts...the tenets of nationalism, statism and welfarism and their embedded notions of entitlements which are central to many African regimes."[25] National development programs and public statements by African leaders since political independence in the 1960s have focused on the need for mobilization and the responsibility of the state to cater to the needs of the majority in society. There is no way in which a regime that has lost its legitimacy and credibility before the vast majority of the people can promote mass mobilization and implement far-reaching policies. Under adjustment, African regimes are now compelled to go against all the promises they had made to the people over the years. It becomes very difficult to push through a completely different set of prescriptions which go directly against the tenets of nationalism and welfarism, which are still strongly enshrined in African culture and value systems.

The eighth point relates to the internal factionalization and fractionalization within the ranks of dominant classes as well as the depth of contradictions between the elites and nonbourgeois forces. Such divisions and contradictions pose major challenges to the success of adjustment. They have also been responsible for coups, countercoups, and other underground coalitions and challenges to regimes that try to implement difficult programs of reform. Bureaucrats tend to support adjustment because they have to implement them anyway. Not all factions of the officer corps in the armed forces support adjustment; hence, as mentioned earlier, it has become one major excuse for coups and countercoups. In Nigeria, both the Vatsa coup attempt of 1986 and the Orka/Mukoro coup attempt of 1990 were opposed to structural adjustment; at least, that was what they claimed in their broadcasts and trial statements. While a fraction of the bourgeoisie, in league with foreign capital, tends to support adjustment, local investors are often in opposition because floating interest rates and devaluation make it difficult to borrow, lower wages, and depress the buying power of workers, while trade liberalization removes all the protection they previously enjoyed against imports. Politicians are often divided into three groups: those who support adjustment whole heartedly, those who oppose adjustment from a populist angle so as to win the support of nonbourgeois forces in their political objectives, and those who oppose adjustment purely from a nationalistic position. Such divisions make it difficult for the government to effectively mediate or contain popular pressures and maintain a steady course on the implementation of adjustment programs. Of course, the fluidities of national solidarities that accompany intensifying intra- and interclass divisions equally impede the ability of the regime to confront societal crisis in a holistic fashion while responding to the urgent demands of social interests within the limits of available resources.

The ninth issue has to do with the "moral and political credibility of the leadership (the perception that the leadership is not personally corrupt and can be relied upon to decide wisely in the national interest)," as well as with its ability to play constituency against constituency, juggle accountability to international interests and national constituencies, "create a 'discourse of reform' and effectively exploit political symbolism" and with its skill in sharing the costs of adjustment between interest groups. These leadership attributes are very critical and can make a major difference to the implementation of adjustment. Lending institutions waste their time when they expect leaders who are generally perceived by their people to be untrustworthy, corrupt, inept, and unjust to implement even harsher policies than those that already alienate the people from them. Typical examples are Zaire and Nigeria. In the case of Ghana, Jerry Rawlings had a good rapport with the left, students, and academics (at least at the beginning), he had the legacy of Kwame Nkrumah and the socialist and Pan Africanist rhetoric and philosophy of the early days of political independence to rely on, and given the very vibrant intellectual culture of the country, it was easy to get the people to debate and experiment, even at the grassroots level, with ideological positions previously debated in the university campuses. The reverse was the case in Nigeria. Ibrahim Babangida declared a 'war' against trade unions, students, and the left. He branded them as "extremists" and barred them from the political process. He proscribed trade unions, rehabilitated disgraced and discredited politicians and military men, and had no patience with ideological discussions. Babangida also lacked any national symbols, he accentuated the retreat into ethnic, regional, and religious basis of acquiring and using political power, shielded corrupt public officials from punishment and was himself accused of corrupt practices. When the military terminated the already disorganized march to a third republic in November 1993, the suffocation of civil society, corruption, and the politics of diversion continued. The point, therefore, is that such leaders are not trusted and are widely perceived as incapable of improving the living conditions of the people. Poor leadership qualities easily erode the relevance and credibility of public policies, no matter how well intended. In Nigeria, the numerous debates sponsored on housing, foreign policy, political restructuring and so on, were perceived as diversions. The political manipulations and repressive actions of the military convinced many Nigerians that the government could not be trusted or relied upon to lead the country out of its economic predicament.[26] More importantly, the military and civilian (including interim) regimes since 1986 have been unable to share the costs of adjustment equally; a few rich have become super-rich as contractors, military officers, and top bureaucrats and their friends collaborate to enrich themselves, while the majority are subjected to retrenchment and other harsh consequences of the adjustment program. Regimes since 1986 have therefore found it very difficult to mobilize and retain the support of critical social actors. Under such conditions adjustment can make little progress and often remains bogged down in financial manipulations, while the *structures* of the political economy experience no adjustment.[27]

The point remains that the more repressive and undemocratic a regime is, the less its chances of effectively implementing adjustment programs. It might be able to show, in the short term, impressive "gains" on some economic indicators. However, repression and human rights violation encourage opposition elements to develop concrete political programs to oppose the regime and negate its economic "achievements." One way of advancing the interest and visibility of the opposition is to discredit, and where possible sabotage the policies of the government, and the adjustment programs are easy targets in this area. In Zambia, the MMD's campaign against Kenneth Kaunda received a major boost from the economic failures of the incumbent regime. A more open and democratic regime can convince the people to make sacrifices, convince the people that there is hope in the future, and convince external supporters that it is not only in command but that it has the support of the people in the process of change no matter how painful. Coalitions, conflicts, and contradictions are easily managed or mediated, and organized interest groups in particular, the labour unions and students as well as peasants and local investors, give support and openly defend market positions in the collective effort to find solutions to the deepening crisis. This is possible only where the regime is fairly institutionalized, enjoys some credibility, is not steeped in corruption, and is capable of accommodating alternative positions and interpretations of the path to progress and reform.

Finally, tenth, is the near total exclusion of Africans in the design of adjustment programs. Of course, the lending institutions do not consult with local popular groups and intellectuals in the design of adjustment packages. Their Western "experts" are competent enough to understand what is possible and what is not. Though some Africans are now being consulted in the process of evaluating the programs in the face of widespread failure and general rejection of orthodox structural adjustment as a solution to the African predicament, they are still in a minority and it is doubtful their views are taken very seriously. Certainly, the World Bank has several groups of African "experts" which include ex-presidents and ex-ministers. But these are not the people who will feel the impact of adjustment and whose feelings and expectations need to be paramount. It is instructive to note that though the World Bank employs some "80,000 expatriate consultants" to "work on Africa alone," "less than 0.1 percent are Africans."[28] The net result of this intellectual apartheid is that Bank policies, analyses, prescriptions, and projections are flawed right from the beginning, reflecting, in most cases, the views and interests of a tiny minority concentrated in the exile community, government, and the urban centers. Of course, Africans bear the brunt of such miscalculations by Bank "experts" and "consultants." Structural adjustment is just one of such policy prescriptions, designed without consultation and appreciation of the historical experiences and specificities of Africa, and imposed through direct and indirect manipulation and pressure on poverty-stricken, debt-ridden, and desperate African regimes. The midterm review of UNPAAERD presented to the UN General Assembly by the secretary-general on the impact and "achievements" of structural adjustment in Africa was summarized thus:

> The implementation of structural adjustment programmes has given rise to general concerns. The limited objectives and short-term perspectives of those programmes are sometimes viewed, by African countries and others, as being at variance with the objectives of more balanced long-term development. Their human and social costs have often been seen as out of proportion with their real or intended benefits. The most vulnerable population groups, in particular women, youth, the disabled and the aged, have been severely and adversely affected, directly, and indirectly, by such measures as the withdrawal of subsidies on staple food items, the imposition of limits on wage increases at or below inflation rate, the retrenchment of civil servants and private sector personnel frequently belonging to the lowest salary categories, and the cutting of expenditures on social services, including health and education, and on basic infrastructure. Access to food has become more difficult for large segments of the population, with the result that malnutrition has increased, particularly among children, infants and pregnant women...Moreover, some of the main ingredients of the programmes, such as re-alignments of exchange rates and rises in producer prices, are not generating the full expected benefits because of the structural rigidities that characterize the current stage of development of most African countries.[29]

Finally, the United Nations Research Institute for Social Development (UNRISD), in a 1995 review of adjustment, reached the conclusion that

> ...the experience of recent decades in indebted countries has shown that dogmatic economic prescriptions are of limited value—and can be dangerous...For most developing countries debt remains an enormous stumbling block to successful adjustment and to renewed economic growth...Stabilization and adjustment have,...implied hardship...Even adjustment programs that are typically held up as "success stories" have been social failures. Some governments may have dealt more effectively than others with the threat of economic instability-but they still remained mired in intractable social crises. Most people in highly indebted African states...suffered a sharp drop in living standards. Between 1980 and 1990, their per capita incomes declined markedly, and for the poorest people the drop was even more precipitous. Many people in the formal sector lost their jobs and had to seek much more precarious and ill-paid work in the informal sector.[30]

IMF and World Bank Responses to the African Crisis

It is quite true that "in virtually every case, African countries have gone into adjustment only when they were absolutely desperate."[31] Perhaps the reluctance to go to the IMF and the World Bank was borne out of the realization that not only were these organizations not set up for developing social formations but also that, historically, their responses have overlooked the specificities of poor nations and have tended to worsen their already bad situations. Further, the two organizations are well noted for their "willingness to impose harsh conditionalities on already poor countries and to disregard the state of human rights within countries as a criterion for loans."[32] Moreover, and rather unfortunately for African leaders and bureaucrats, their conditions of desperation put these countries in a very weak position to bargain with the donors, lenders, and Western governments who control the IMF and World Bank. They are therefore unable to negotiate better terms, resist pressures, make the imposed packages more responsive to local realities, and dictate the timetable for implementation. Ironically, the poor and desperate conditions of African states have also increased the insensitivity and leverage which the lenders exercise over supposedly independent states.[33] As Cranford Pratt, who has been involved in such negotiations on behalf of Tanzania, has noted,

> The World Bank is staffed by able men and women. They are confident in themselves to the point of arrogance. They have, as a result, sought to expand the responsibilities and power of the Bank...

> There is a further important aspect to the shift that has been occurring in the attitude and operations of the World Bank these last several years. The Bank has become increasingly arrogant and ideological in its approach to development issues in the Third World.[34]

Thus, though African states met in Lagos in 1980 and adopted *The Lagos Plan of Action and Final Act of Lagos*[35] as instruments for the socioeconomic and political transformation of Africa, the World Bank quickly moved to contain the document by releasing the so-called "Berg Report" in 1981, contradicting practically every prescription in the OAU document (see Chapter One).[36] While the LPA emphasized self-reliance and programs to check Africa's dependence and vulnerability in the global system, the "Berg Report" advocated liberalization and outlined the basic instruments of stabilization and structural adjustment. Given that most African states "could not import enough goods and could also not produce enough essential goods domestically...there were queues everywhere and domestic prices rose, almost everyday. Life was expensive and national currencies were nearly valueless...Finding themselves in a tight and desperate situation, African countries sought financial assistance from the World Bank and the IMF family *mainly because they could not get any assistance elsewhere.*"[37] In fact, donors and credit clubs like the London and Paris Clubs, lenders, and Western governments openly refused to guarantee imports for African states, even for essential commodities like food and drugs, and pressured African governments to reach stabilization and structural adjustment agreements with the IMF and the World Bank. With spiralling inflation, urban tensions, food riots, threats of military coups, and decaying institutions and infrastructure, African governments discovered that they had practically no room for manoeuvre in the capitalist-dominated international division of labor. As the ECA's *African Alternative Framework* put it:

> So, in essence, the World Bank and the IMF became primary lenders to most of the African countries and quite naturally they made such assistance available on their own terms. Their objectives were less to help African countries than to 'discipline' them, and above all, reorient their economic policies to the market economy model.
>
> In this policy reorientation which is often described as policy reforms, the World Bank and the IMF took as their model for proper economic functioning in Africa the classical free-market system, in which prices are set by supply and demand and profitable enterprises provide the engine of economic growth...[38]

The Bank and the Fund actually contended that domestic food prices were too low and ought not be subsidized by the government; import duties should be lowered, even if it would result in the death of local infant industries; national currencies were grossly overvalued; budget deficits were wrong and ought not be tolerated on any account; the public services were too large and ought to be reduced in many cases by as much as 60 percent; and user-fees ought to be imposed on social services while all subsidies on energy, education, transportation, and so on should be eliminated. The classical package imposed on poor, debt-ridden, desperate, and crisis-ridden African states therefore included: devaluation, deregulation, desubsidization, privatization/commercialization of public enterprises, regular debt-servicing, irrespective of the country's financial conditions, imposition of new levies, taxes and tolls, massive cuts in government spending, the retrenchment of hundreds of thousands of able-bodied workers, elimination of import controls, and the tight control of money supply. The Bank and the Fund made it very clear to African governments that "to qualify for loans—any type of loans—borrowing countries would have to adopt structural adjustment programs (SAPs)"[39] through the implementation of the "shock measures" highlighted above. As indicated earlier, IMF officials often came with prepared texts of letters of invitation and commitment to harsh stabilization policies as well as to SAPs as prescribed by the Bank for ministers of finance to sign before any negotiations took place. They had no illusions that their prescriptions for "stabilization" and adjustment

> ...would solve the fiscal and trade imbalances and improve the capacity of the governments to service their debt obligations. The 'fat' of government spending and intervention in the economy would be cut away, leaving the 'muscle' of a reinvigorated private sector to push development forward. Government development projects and social service initiatives would be suspended until adjustment was carried out. Africa would import less and export more...[40]

It is interesting to note the attitude of the Bank and the Fund in their prescriptions for Africa's economic recovery. In several instances they demonstrate crass ignorance or a rather superficial conceptualization and analysis of the structural roots, dimensions, and implications of the African crisis. The fact that their policies have not in any way affected Africa's marginal location and role in the global division of labor attests to how ineffective they have been. Moreover, the fact that more African states have joined the ranks of least-developed countries and are all in deeper crisis in spite of stabilization and adjustment makes doubtful the "benefits" of the programs. We have already examined above why adjustment programs have failed, in particular the critical issues often trivialized or overlooked by the Bank and Fund. The Fund and Bank assume that their prescriptions would work in all African states without acknowledging the *political* context of the African crisis. In short, the Fund and the Bank fail to appreciate the terrain of politics and political economy in Africa, ignore the region's historical experience, reify the state, embrace an unproductive bourgeois class because it is conducive to the entry and domination of the local economy by foreign capital, and overlook the implications of Africa's technological backwardness and marginalization in the international division of labor. Only very peripheral attention is paid to declining commodity prices, declining foreign aid, declining terms of trade, massive repatriation of capital by transnationals and other financial interests, sectoral disarticulation of the economies as reproduced by foreign investors, rising interests rates, and the inhibitions of a grossly unequal, undemocratic, and very exploitative international division of labor. The generally ahistorical and, in fact, politically opportunistic nature of IMF and World Bank strategies in Africa have led both organizations to assume, in their wildest imaginations, that corrupt leaders like Eyadema, Babangida, Abacha, Moi, Mobutu, and Bongo, to name a few, could be relied upon to implement serious and painful adjustment programs.

It was only in 1989, following the gross failure of stabilization and adjustment policies all over Africa, that the World Bank moved some distance from the IMF in its analysis and prescriptions for the African crisis: it acknowledged the *political* dimensions of the crisis, emphasized the need to protect vulnerable groups, bureaucratic decentralization, a check on corruption and waste at all levels, the empowerment of the people and their organizations, democratization of the society, rural development, and capacity-building as very necessary aspects of adjustment and recovery.[41] It must be mentioned however, that while this shift represented a victory for popular forces and scholars who had criticized the orthodox packages imposed on African states, it has not in any way moved the Bank away from its commitment to monetarism and supply-side economics.[42]

Prescriptions for Recovery or for Disintegration? The Adjustment Debate

There is now almost unanimous agreement among intellectuals and policy makers in and outside the African continent that adjustment programs, are not working, or at least, not as promised.[43] At a more general level, attention has recently become focused on the negative consequences of structural adjustment programs which do not pay particular attention to existing socioeconomic and political inequalities in underdeveloped social formations. To be sure, economic and other fiscal prescriptions have been complicated by natural disasters and political stalemates in most adjusting countries. Why did the World Bank fail to anticipate such developments? After all, Africa was already in deep crisis prior to the imposition of the reform packages. As Pope John Paul II has declared, the implementation of adjustment programs, in particular, the commitment of substantial proportions of foreign exchange earnings to debt-servicing, "cannot be met at the price of asphyxiation of a country's economy, and no government can formally demand of its people privations incompatible with human dignity."[44] M. de Larosiere, of the IMF, similarly argued that public support is essential for the success of adjustment programs and that if there are "no pay-offs in terms of growth...while human conditions are deteriorating," it would be impossible to continue the adjustment program. He concluded that "human capital is after all the most important factor of production."[45] Michel M. Camdessus, Managng Director of the IMF also confessed that it is "the poorest segment of the population that have carried the heaviest burden of economic adjustment."[46] Of course, this realization did not in any way encourage a fundamental change in the prescriptions of the IMF restructuring processes in underdeveloped countries. *Africa Recovery*, published in the office of the secretary-general of the United Nations, has noted that "adjustment programs do not necessarily work in low-income countries where unemployment and malnutrition are already high and which do not have a resilient industrial base."[47] The United Nations Development Programme (UNDP)'s *Human Development Report 1990* is clear on the fact that "structural adjustment programmes...have increased the burden of poverty of recipient nations and their people."[48] In the last five years, the UNDP has restated this position. In its two-volume study of the impacts of structural adjustment programs in the third world, *Adjustment With a Human Face*, UNICEF drew attention to the need to include "poverty alleviation" programs in adjustment packages if they are not to cause more problems than envisaged by policy makers.[49]

Specifically in the case of Africa, attacks against structural adjustment have arisen not from opposition to the need for change but from a recognition of the negative political, economic, and social contradictions and conflicts that the program has tended to accentuate or generate. Carol Lancaster argued, in a study of adjustment in sub-Saharan Africa, that by 1983 "it had become clear that few of the nearly 20 agreements between the IMF and the African governments had been successful."[50] She also took the position that the IMF adjustment model "has almost never worked in sub-Saharan Africa."[51] In a more recent study, noting that over 33 African states had adopted stabilization programs as a requirement for more aid or debt rescheduling by 1992, she concludes that the "anticipation" of restraining domestic demand, attracting investment, controlling or managing balance of payments, and resuming growth have "proved false."[52] In 1988, the United Nations Programme of Action for African Economic Recovery and Development (UNPAAERD) in its continent-wide review of adjustment programs conceded that there were a few gains in "a handful of countries...in certain macroeconomic indicators" such as reduced inflation rates and higher export volumes. It, however, concluded that "for the majority of African states, there has not been even a hint of recovery."[53] Incidentally, during the 1991 review of UNPAAERD, it was clear that the rosy picture of growth and recovery painted all so often by the Bank and the Fund was out of touch with reality. Though the new emphasis was on democratization and human rights, there was near unanimous agreement that the adjustment policies, which formed the core of UNPAAERD, had not led to recovery in Africa. As Chu Okongwu, then Nigeria's Minister of Budget and Planning, speaking on behalf of the OAU, noted,

During the life span of [UNPAAERD], African economies did not witness any significant change for the better...from all economic indicators, the continent of Africa appeared to have been by-passed by [the] positive developments in the world system.

African countries were required to make...adjustments and achieve economic growth in the face of severely compressed incomes and rising debt over-hang. This is an impossible dilemma...The hardships caused by the decline in incomes were so severe that structural adjustment came to be associated with privation in several countries.[54]

At the same forum, the then Zambian minister of state, J.C. Chizu, criticized structural adjustment programs because "African debt has continued to soar, and resources to Africa have declined." In addition, Mr. Chizu noted that "it is now widely recognized that the 1980s generation of structural adjustment programmes have been deficient because they were short-term in character..."[55] Claude Ake has noted that adjustment programs are being pursued by African states in a "desperate attempt to contain the crisis [of the continent] and save the state." However, he has argued that policies of "massive retrenchment of public employees, the withdrawal of government subsidies, and the dismantling of welfare schemes, the privatization of public corporations, the deindigenization of the economy...are replete with contradictions and address the symptoms and not the causes of the problems." It is Ake's contention that stabilization and adjustment programs under the supervision of the IMF and World Bank will inevitably deepen the crisis of the continent because they address neither the specificities and implications of the historical experiences of African countries nor the content and character of contemporary politics and political balances and struggles:

...the withdrawal of welfare measures, minimal in the first place, in a context where the most elementary needs are lacking only intensifies the contradictions between the rulers and the subordinate classes. And so does the mass retrenchment of workers. Privatization can only deepen the class contradictions for it is bound to mean the cheap sale of public stock to the few who are already well-off; the attempt to make public corporations efficient and profitable cannot work because the political class must continue to use them as a means of accumulation; deindigenization of the economy entails the strengthening of those exploitative ties and the dependence which underlies underdevelopment. In any case, destatization can only go so far because the objective conditions which produce statism remain as strong as they have always been.[56]

Ake's position was supported by the United Nations Economic Commission for Africa (ECA) when it argued in its *Economic Report on Africa 1990* that "policy prescriptions widely adopted during the decade (1980–1990), based on conventional adjustment programmes, have failed to address the fundamental structural issues in Africa's development; hence their failure to arrest the downward trend, less reverse it and bring about a sustainable process of development and transformation."[57] In fact, the ECA sponsored the meeting of nongovernmental and grassroot organizations that issued the *African Charter for Popular Participation in Development and Transformation*, which has been adopted by the Organization of African Unity (OAU). This document is very specific on the rejection of IMF and World Bank adjustment packages when it declares: "We also wish...to put on record our disapproval of all economic programmes, such as orthodox Structural Adjustment Programmes, which undermine the human condition and disregard the potential and role of popular participation in self-sustaining development."[58] Adebayo Adedeji, as the Executive Secretary of the ECA, in a keynote address at the thirty-third annual meeting of the African Studies Association (ASA) in 1990 was quite direct in his opposition to this approach when he stated that orthodox adjustment programs demonstrate vividly the "tension between economism and ethics of development." He further argued that "on-going SAPs are single-mindedly pre-occupied with stabilizing internal and external financial balances primarily through price and other financial adjustments in order to achieve economic performance criteria anchored to GDP, exports, balance of payments equilibrium, debt servicing, etc. In the process, enormous social costs have been imposed on the vulnerable segments of the population; the human resources for transformation are crippled; domestic structural inequalities increase and the marginalization of Africa proceeds apace."[59] In like manner, Kofi Awoonor, Ghanaian ambassador to the UN, who also served as chairman of the Group of 77 in 1990, noted, the structural adjustment program is not working because it assumes that the African economy is only "slightly out of adjustment," whereas the reality is that "our economies need total upheaval." He also pointed at the "glaring contradiction" in conditionality, which in Ghana had done great harm to local production and industrial development, and at liberalization, which had destroyed Ghana's textile industry by the dumping of cheap mass-produced textiles.[60] As well, in his study of the African crisis, Richard Sandbrook took the position that the "structural adjustment programs have had mixed, but generally disappointing, results."[61] Finally, in a surprising though not unexpected move, the World Bank shifted some distance away from the IMF when in its 1989 report on

Africa: *Sub-Saharan Africa: From Crisis to Sustainable Growth* it admitted its own past failures in Africa and embraced the call for protecting vulnerable groups, empowerment of the people, democratization, and adjustment with a human face.[62]

To be sure, adjustment has its own supporters, largely to be found in the private sector, in Western governments, and in most African governments. The latter support it largely because they have very little choice. Western governments and international banks support it because adjustments open African markets and ensure the steady servicing of debt obligations. Yet, it is obvious that structural adjustment programs forced on African states by mounting problems and deepening socioeconomic and political contradictions have not achieved the goals set by the IMF and the World Bank: increased production, investment and growth achieved through the efficient use of resources. The policy shift by the World Bank is certainly a reaction to this realization and a response to criticisms from the ECA and others who have shown concern for the deepening crisis in the continent in spite of commitment to adjustment and stabilization as prescribed by the Bank and Fund. Unfortunately, this "shift" has not resulted in a serious, consistent, and democratic policy output and action by the Bank. It has been slow in admitting its own mistakes, and it continues to blame mostly internal policies for the deepening crisis of Africa, when in reality its own earlier adjustment policies contributed in very large measure to deepening the crisis of African economies.

The Real Impact of Adjustment on Africa

Why have these adjustment programs, in spite of vitriolic propaganda in certain quarters, failed in Africa?[63] Why have adjustment programs led to violent political upheavals in most of Africa? Why has adjustment failed to bridge political interests and narrow the differences between political communities and constituencies? Finally, why has adjustment failed to restructure or redefine Africa's marginal location and role in the global division of labor?

Going by the general impact of IMF and World Bank prescriptions on African states, it is very difficult to see recovery.[64] In IMF and World Bank documents, though, there are often glowing reports about the achievements of the structural adjustment programs. True, some countries have experienced some growth, especially in the export sector. Such growth has only enabled them to better service their foreign debts. Hence, the growth rates are usually not reflected in the overall conditions of living. Of course, the policies of adjustment and stabilization have also made some gains, even if they have been quite modest and are hardly sustainable. Many Africans have come to realize that they can no longer rely on the government for everything; communities and individuals are realizing that the government cannot subsidize every activity and every public service; and a new culture of "saving for the rainy day" is gaining ground more than ever. Further, there is a new "return to source" culture in Africa as more people now patronize locally made goods. Governments are being forced to be more prudent and to take fiscal matters more seriously. They are more conscious of the fact that their financial records can no longer be kept secret from donors and lenders. The drive for foreign exchange has increased, and increasing attention is being paid to sectors of the economy that earn foreign exchange. African governments are more appreciative of the dynamics of global politics as they realize their weaknesses and marginalization in the global order on the one hand and, on the other, the unprecedented revolutions in science and technology taking place in other parts of the world. The economic difficulties and uncertainties imposed by adjustment are forcing Africans to plan their families and to abandon extravagant ways of living, which drain scarce resources. Finally, the private sector is expanding in certain areas such as manufacturing, investors are becoming more creative, there is a boom in the informal economy, and new businesses dealing with a range of services are emerging all over the major cities.

While the above and more are certainly taking place, and the Bank has succeeded in identifying Ghana as the only real successful case of adjustment in Africa, that claim has been challenged, even by Ghanaians. Also, documents from the OAU and ECA, as well as several pro-developing countries organizations like the Group of 77, disagree that orthodox adjustment is laying the foundations for growth, not to mention development. The fact that at the beginning of the middle of the 1990s, African states had not experienced any significant recovery capable of empowering them to exploit the new globalization is adequate testimony to the failure of over a decade of externally designed prescriptions for growth: foreign debts are up, inflation is out of control, exports have not increased, political and social tensions have increased, unemployment has increased, there are more riots and violent demonstrations in most African countries, foreign investors have not been attracted in spite of very generous incentives, foreign aid continues to decline, and there is a very visible marginalization of Africa in the emerging 'new' global order.[65] Of course, many African states have joined in the manipulation of statistics to give the impression that their reform programs are yielding results. The best measure of success, however, beyond clear improvements in trade indicators, foreign reserves, and the strength of the local currency, is in the quality of life of the people and the extent to which adjustment has empowered the people and their communities.

The ECA has noted that "there is documented evidence that in many cases sustained economic growth has not materialized, the rate of investment rather than improve has tended to decrease, budget and balance of payments deficits have tended to widen after some temporary relief and debt service obligations have become unbearable."[66] Adebayo Adedeji, in his Foreword to the *African Alternative Framework* argued that

> The overall assessment of orthodox adjustment programmes has led to the conclusion that, although these programmes aim at restoring growth, generally through the achievement of fiscal and external balances and free play of market forces, these objectives cannot be achieved without addressing the fundamental structural bottlenecks of African economies...An adjustment programme that marginalizes people is doomed to failure.[67]

The *African Alternative Framework*, in its evaluation of IMF and World Bank adjustment programs, reached the conclusion in 1989 that it had "become abundantly clear by now that, both on theoretical and empirical grounds, the conventional SAPs are inadequate in addressing the real causes of economic, financial and social problems facing African countries which are of a structural nature."[68] Finally, the ECA contends that "No programme of adjustment or of development makes sense if it makes people indefinitely more miserable."[69]

For instance, prescriptions for cuts in government expenditures, the retrenchment of hundreds of thousands of workers, and even a freeze on employment ignore the historical and structural reasons why the government in most African states became the main employer, main contractor, and leading actor in the economy. Simply removing subsidies and laying off workers in a society, without any welfare or social security programs, hardly addresses the structural issues of production, exchange, and accumulation patterns and relations; the domination of the economy by profit and hegemony-seeking transnational corporations; and the very tenuous relation of domestic elites to productive activities. Such policies have only increased the rate of crime, urban violence, suicides, marital violence, child abuse, frustration, and cases of mental illness.[70] In any case, as the ECA has rightly noted, prescriptions for desubsidization have been directed at the so-called "soft sectors": of the economy-health, education, housing, sanitation, counselling, transportation and so on. They have not addressed the need for reduction of redundant embassies, reduction in security votes and military expenditures, and cutbacks in other unproductive areas which governments maintain to keep their visibility in international politics. Consequently, "cuts in government expenditure end up harming the welfare of the people."[71]

Desubsidization policies in societies characterized by gross inequalities in power and opportunities have hardly affected the elites and the custodians of state power. Africans have, since the 1960s, come to rely on the state and public parastatals to survive grinding poverty and the ruthlessly exploitative activities of foreign corporations. True, many of the corporations were subsidized. But subsidy of government and other businesses is not typical in Africa. The U.S. government and other Western nations subsidize thousands of public and private interests and individuals. Subsidization is not responsible for the inefficiency and poor performances of the companies. To suddenly, in the name of "shock treatment," remove the subsidies without safety nets is a direct invitation to deepening social crisis, violence, alienation, corruption, and inefficiency.

Policies of devaluation are very important in finding the real value of national currencies. But implementing such policies across the board and as "shock treatments" has only generated more crisis than recovery in Africa.[72] While devaluation is supposed to make imports more expensive and African exports cheaper, it has in fact culminated in the closure of industries from inability to import spare parts, the destruction of the industrial bases of African states, and capital flight as real wages are depressed and people are unable to buy from the market. In addition, floating interest rates have affected the ability of local investors to borrow, and African central banks have simply lost control of the devaluation process and most currencies have become worthless as the US dollar has become the legal tender in many countries. Given that African states are heavily import-dependent, "generalized currency devaluation also makes imported spare parts, fuel, and other inputs more expensive, thereby raising the cost of doing business."[73] In any case, since developed-country markets are not necessarily open to African exports, and Western governments have devised complex ways of protecting domestic investors, devaluation has not increased foreign exchange earnings. What is more, currency devaluation has not attracted investors, as poverty, declining purchasing power, unemployment, and urban tensions have made the economic environment very risky. The secretary-general of the UN noted recently that "long-term financial flows into sub-Saharan Africa declined from $10 billion to $4.7 billion between 1982 and 1990. Eighty-four per cent of this reduction can be accounted for by the decline in private flows. One of the positive parts of the Africa story is that many African countries have taken courageous steps to reform their financial and monetary systems. They have created a framework which should attract private investment. *Yet that investment is not materializing.*"[74] High interest rates and currency devaluation have increased trade in money, foreign-exchange speculation, smuggling, speculative investment, the proliferation of so-called merchant banks, and economic stagnation.

The privatization of public enterprises is in itself a misplaced prescription. It fails to address why the corporations are not making profit and why they are overstaffed. It ignores the social functions of these parastatals, and in the effort to constrain the strengthening of the African state, the World Bank and IMF confuse the symptoms of peripheral capitalism with the structural causes of Africa's predicaments. In fact, the Fund and the Bank pretend that state interventionism is peculiar to developing nations, particularly Africa. They argue that African governments are inefficient and corrupt, overlooking the fact that corruption in the whole of Africa is nothing when put side by side with the degree of waste, mismanagement, and corruption in the United States, to take just one non-African example.[75]

As discussed earlier, the American state is heavily interventionist. In any case, virtually all the major inefficient parastatals in Africa are joint ventures with foreign partners who have consistently reaped billions of dollars in profits over the years through very complex mechanisms. From car assembly plants and beer breweries, through iron and steel to textiles and hotel chains, Africans and their governments have always relied on the "expert" advice of foreigners. When the going was good for these parastatals, and governments in Africa had a lot of foreign exchange to throw around, the "experts" from the IMF and World Bank were silent. The sudden attack on the Africa state is a wrong step in the wrong direction.

It is completely wrong for the Fund and Bank to pretend that the state has not always been a major force and actor in the process of capital accumulation and the strengthening of the market. Wholesale privatization and commercialization of all government-owned enterprises in Africa would hardly address the problem. It would be tantamount to a recolonization of the African economic landscape. The state came to dominate the economy in the context of the postcolonial weaknesses and marginalization of indigenous producers and the domination of the economies by foreign capital. After all, in the American and other Western, as well as in the Japanese economies, there are sectors where the state limits the degree of foreign participation, such as in the airline and news media sectors. Where are the indigenous business interests that would take over these privatized corporations? If they were that good, why have they not effectively competed with and/or displaced the state since political independence? The majority of African countries lack the local private capital base to take up the management of the parastatals. The net result of privatization and commercialization would be that foreign business interests with foreign exchange and the capacity to easily source for capital locally would take over the African market at a time of increasing protectionism in Europe and North America. The solution is to address the weaknesses of local investors, curtail the role and participation of foreign investors, support and protect small businesses (just as is done in the West), and strengthen the efficiency and effectiveness of the African state.

Finally, prescriptions for trade liberalization in open, weak, unproductive, and vulnerable economies in the contemporary world are rather suspect prescriptions. Which Western nation has fully liberalized its trade and opened its market to the entire world without restrictions? If this were the situation, then why all the negotiations through GATT and UNCTAD? The protectionist policies of Western nations and Japan directly negate the prescription that African states should remove all trade restrictions and open up their economies to all sorts of imports and foreign investors. The United States in mid-1995 was seriously considering sanctions against Japan for not opening up its economy to American products. In the same year, the United States it responded firmly to unequal trade in shoes with China, and both countries constantly get involved in trade arguments over import quotas and other restrictions. Moreover, as we have seen since SAPs were put in place, trade liberalization has permitted the dumping of second-hand and inferior goods, local products have been chased off the store shelves, local industries have been undermined, and a massive process of taste transfer is taking place. With the massive devaluation of the local currencies, people are unable to buy the imported substitutes in many cases.

At a fundamental level, IMF and World Bank prescriptions have only deepened the crisis of the region and consolidated its marginalization in the global division of labor.[76] This is not just because they are orthodox in a general sense, but specifically because the policies were imposed on a sea of contradictions and conflicts that were bound to undermine effective implementation. As we have seen in country after country, schools are closing down, and malnutrition and disease are widespread. The majority of states have been badly delegitimized. Destitution has become widespread and parents are losing control of their children and families. The rural areas are being abandoned. In countries like Nigeria and Zaire, adjustment doubled the rate of corruption, with the U.S. dollar and pound sterling becoming "little gods." Agricultural production has not increased, and as local industries pack up, foreign corporations have not been around to replace them. The limited autonomy of the state from foreign control has been eroded as economic and social, even political policies are dictated by foreign interests.[77] The ECA was very clear on the failure of SAPs when it noted that

> As the 1980s drew to a close, it became clear that economic turnaround had not occurred in almost all of the countries that had tried SAPs...Even the countries that followed adjustment programmes with the most rigor were barely holding their ground. Most were suffering further set-backs including high inflation, lower spending on health, education, housing, sanitation and water. Also, laying off people from their jobs or the declining real wages caused suffering to reach unbearable proportions.[78]

In most African countries, the introduction of the World Bank package culminated in violent riots and massive destruction of public property. The Sudan, Zambia, and Nigeria have experienced several riots directly related to desubsidization, privatization, and retrenchment. One of the reasons for the 1990 coup attempt in Nigeria was to rid the country of the structural adjustment program.[79] Siyaad Barre's regime in Somalia was not helped by the introduction of the IMF stabilization package in 1985 when the Fund "imposed a devaluation, the floating exchange rate, an end to trade restrictions, and constriction of the money supply. But no new money was forthcoming from the Fund, because of back debt owed."[80] How did the Fund expect a poverty-stricken, least-developed country like Somalia to survive the imposition of such draconian "shock measures"? Today, we can see the effect in Somalia's unprecedented disaster.[81] At the end of 1995, in spite of over a decade of experimentation with stabilization and adjustment packages, Africa remains poor, weak, indebted, marginalized, and very unstable.[82] As Adedeji has argued, "[i]nstead of putting in place a transformation process that will change our entire political economy and thereby arrest the process of relentless peripheralization in our continent we pursued narrow purely economistic and mechanical programmes of adjustment; we have continued to chase growth rather than economic justice, development and transformation; we have installed despotism, authoritarianism and kleptocracy in place of democracy, accountability and political and economic empowerment."[83]

Many Africa countries, in the effort to understand and implement the World Bank's package, have begun to make a fetish of the dollar and pound sterling and to engage more in financial/monetary adjustment than in *structural* adjustment. Writing on the Nigerian case, Sam Aluko, one of the country's leading economists, evaluated the experience with structural adjustment thus:

> Our economy is poorer today in production level than in 1986, even our agriculture. I have not seen anything gained from SAP...Our debt has become more difficult to pay. The rate of interest has risen so we cannot borrow money to do business. Any economy that does not encourage long-term investment and production, that economy can never make it. SAP has destroyed the incentive to invest and produce. There are no new investment arena except for those who are stealing money. What is happening now is that people are trading in money. Production has collapsed. The cost of machinery has increased several folds since 1986. In 1986, you (could) buy a car for N10,000, now it is N300,000 and yet earnings have not increased...Nigerians have gone to other countries to do slave labour, insecurity has increased, armed robbery has increased. There are more industrial strikes today than we had before. The middle class has been wiped out. You can travel the length and breadth of this country and you will not find a single road mender because the ministry has no money to mend roads.[84]

Not much need be said about the failure of the IMF and World Bank prescriptions in Africa, and the pains and feeling of hopelessness they have imposed on Africans.

Conclusion: Beyond World Bank and IMF Prescriptions

The point of discussion in this chapter is not about the need for or the relevance of adjustment in African economies. Certainly, African states without exception require very serious and sustained adjustment. The bureaucracy needs to be cut and the state needs to move away from its present involvement in several wasteful and irrelevant ventures. As well, we do not put all the blame for Africa's woes and predicaments on colonialism and external sources or on structural adjustment.

Our position is that the World Bank and the IMF have been unable (unwilling?) to adjust to the realities and specificities of African social formations. The delegates to the Kampala Forum in 1990 were quite clear in their conviction that "Africa can not emerge out of her current economic problems on the basis of orthodox structural adjustment programmes."[85] So far, the Bank and the Fund have failed to come up with a holistic agenda for reconstruction and development that will alter Africa's marginal place in the global economy.[86] Both organizations have failed to take the side of the majority to design a political agenda based on the experiences, aspirations, and struggles of the African people that will alter and recompose the political landscape in such a manner as to make the implementation of a realistic adjustment program possible. In fact, the policies of the IMF and the Bank have tended to weaken African states, weaken African producers, and expose African economies to foreign domination and exploitation, and they have emphasized cash crop production at the expense of food crop production in the name of export-led development, thus encouraging a dependent food policy. In addition, policies and prescriptions by the Fund and the Bank have tended to impoverish the vast majority, particularly disadvantaged and vulnerable groups—women, children, and the unemployed; and have increased social and political tensions. The policies have promoted clan as well as ethnic, religious, and regional conflicts, and through policies of debt-servicing, promoted the massive drain of resources from the region. Finally, the impoverishment of the middle classes has encouraged unprecedented emigration of skilled workers and professionals abroad, reduced the efficiency of institutions, weakened the educational sector, and encouraged atavistic, violent, uncompromising, repressive, and corrupt political and social attitudes. The degree of human rights abuses, repression and massacres witnessed in the African continent in the 1980s, the era of adjustment, is unprecedented in the history of the continent.[87]

In the context of these failures and the social crises generated by adjustment and other externally induced recovery prescriptions, what are the options for Africa?[88] The options for Africa are clearly articulated in the documents of the OAU and ECA discussed in Chapter One. Moreover, whatever one might say about the problems and pains of adjustment, they have contributed to the massive crystallization of political positions, the invigoration of dormant constituencies, and political action. Thus we have seen, all over Africa, in the past decade a dynamic process of recomposing and reconstituting the political landscape particularly among the masses.

Unable to take the pain of adjustment any longer, Africans are asking new questions, forming new popular organizations, reviving banned organizations, forging new alliances, and organizing themselves beyond the traditional constraints of region, religion, ethnicity, gender, and class.[89] Hundreds of popular and grassroot organizations have emerged all over Africa in the last decade or so. Human rights organizations have sprouted all over African countries. We see a new determination by students, workers, women, and professionals to be involved in the political processes and to have a say in determining not just public policies but also the futures of their respective countries. In a way, the prescriptions of the Fund and Bank have had an unanticipated effect of delegitimizing African leaders and governments, exposing them to popular attack, and encouraging the masses to struggle for participation and democratization.[90]

The impact of this new momentum has been the opening up of political spaces, a reconstruction of the patterns of political alignments and realignments, and the emergence of alternative political organizations and political parties.[91] While this process is still tenuous and unsteady, it has become obvious that the future of Africa in the emerging complex and unequal global order is in the empowerment of the people, the strengthening of civil society, and popular participation in decision-making at all levels. It is only through the strengthening of civil society and the involvement of the people in decision-making that effective policies and programs for recovery, growth, and development can be initiated and implemented. As the *African Charter for Popular Participation* has rightly noted, "nations cannot be built without the popular support and full participation of the people, nor can the economic crisis be resolved and the human conditions improved without the full and effective contribution, creativity and popular enthusiasm of the vast majority of the people."[92] If the people are involved or consulted before decisions are taken, and an atmosphere of democracy and accountability prevails, they are unlikely to oppose such policies and they would be in a better position to withstand or absorb the pains and shocks of adjustment. Moreover, conditions of democracy, democratization, empowerment, and accountability of the leadership would promote creativity, patriotism, productivity, and stability, and would redirect expenditures from "military defense" to "social defense." Foreign-inspired economic and political models would be openly debated, adjusted, and made to reflect the specificities of each society and the objective needs of the people.

In addition to the need for democratization and empowerment, African states must take regional integration more seriously and move away from current political posturing and rhetoric on regionalism (see Chapter Five). The adoption in June 1991 of the African Economic Treaty, designed to culminate in the establishment of an African parliament and common market in A.D. 2025 is a positive step, though the timetable is rather long and hardly demonstrates a full appreciation of the desperate nature of African economies. African states, however, need to develop the required political will, check waste and corruption, promote rural mobilization and development, and strengthen local institutions.[93]

Endnotes

1. Michael Manley, "Message to the South-North Conference on the International Monetary System and the New International Order," *Development Dialogue* (2) (1980), p. 5.

2. Julius K. Nyerere, "No to IMF Meddling," *Development Dialogue* (2) (1980), p. 7.

3. R. Cranford Pratt, "The Global Impact of the World Bank," in Jill Torrie (ed.), *Banking on Poverty: The Global Impact of the IMF and World Bank* (Toronto: Between the Lines, 1983), p. 56.

4. R. Cranford Pratt, "The Global Impact of the World Bank," op. cit., p. 57.

5. Julius K. Nyerere, "No to IMF Meddling," op. cit., p.8.

6. R. Cranford Pratt, "The Global Impact of the World Bank," op. cit. p. 65.

7. Cheryl Payer, "Researching the World Bank," in Jill Torrie (ed), *Banking on Poverty*...op. cit, p.79.

8. Ibid

9. Adebayo Adedeji, "The Nigerian Economy at the Dawn of the Third Republic," *The Guardian* (Lagos) (March 25, 1993), p.19.

10. Ibid

11. See Fantu Cheru, *The Silent Revolution in Africa* (Harare and London: Anvil and Zed Press, 1989); Bonnie Campbell and John Loxley (eds.), *Structural Adjustment in Africa* (London: Macmillan, 1986); and John Ravenhill (ed.), *Africa in Economic Crisis* (London: Macmillan).

12. World Bank, *Sub-Saharan Africa: From Crisis to Sustainable Growth- A Long-Term Perspective Study* (Washington, DC: World Bank, 1989), p.7.

13. See I. William Zartman, (ed.), *Collapsed States: The Disintegration and Restoration of Legitimate Authority*, (Boulder, CO: Lynne Rienner, 1995).

14. See United Nations, *African Debt Crisis: A Continuing Impediment to Development* (New York: The United Nations, 1993).

15. See Michael Chege, "Remembering Africa," *Foreign Affairs* Vol. 71 (1) (1991–1992).

16. World Bank, *Sub-Saharan Africa: From Crisis to Sustainable Growth* op. cit., p.3. The Bank also notes the problems of "declining level and inefficiency of investment, compounded by accelerating population growth," excessively high investment and operating costs, fall in real wages by "about a quarter on the average across Africa since 1980," "deteriorating quality of government, epitomized by bureaucratic obstruction, pervasive rent seeking, weak judicial systems, and arbitrary decision-making," and of the fact that "Africa is simply not competitive in an increasingly competitive world," (p.3). For the very first time, the World Bank, quite unlike the IMF, acknowledges the *political* dimensions of the African crisis, when among other positions, it states that Africa needs "better governance" and a type of government that would decentralize responsibilities, check corruption, ensure the autonomy of the judiciary, and "create a leaner, better disciplined, better trained, and more motivated public service, with competitive salaries..." (p.5), and when, among several conclusions, the Bank notes that "To attract investors, a stable economic and political environment is essential."(p.9).

17. Edward Jaycox, *The Challenges of African Development* (Washington, D.C.: World Bank, 1992), p. 15. Jaycox also noted that "While the trade of other developing regions was growing, Sub-Saharan Africa's international market share dropped from 3 per cent in 1960 to just over 1 per cent in 1988. This choked off Africa's central source of growth and limited its means for paying its way. Africa borrowed more to fill the gap. Its external debt rose from $6 billion in 1970 to $130 billion in 1987." (p.16).

18. Eboe Hutchful,"Structural Adjustment and Political Regimes in Africa". Mimeo,University of Toronto,1990,p.1.

19. *Ibid*,p.2.

20. See Trevor Parfitt and Stephen P. Riley, *The African Debt Crisis* (London: Routeledge, 1989) for excellent discussions of the cases of Nigeria and Zaire. See also Richard Joseph, "Class, State, and Prebendal Politics in Nigeria," *Journal of Commonwealth and Comparative Politics* Vol. 21 (3) (1984), pp.21-38, and Edwin Madunagu, *Nigeria: The Economy and the People-The Political Economy of State Robbery and its Popular-Democratic Negation* (London: New Beacon, 1983) for detailed discussions of the Nigerian case.

21. Ibid.

22. Ibid.

23. See Julius O. Ihonvbere, "Economic Crisis, Corruption and the Crisis of State Power in Nigeria, 1985–90." Unpublished manuscript, The University of Texas at Austin, December 1993.

24. For a rather misinformed and unfair characterization of all Nigerians as corrupt, see the views of retired General Colin Powell in Henry Louis Gates, Jr., "Powell and the Black Elite," *The New Yorker* (September 25, 1995).

25. Eboe Hutchful, "Structural Adjustment and Political Regimes.." op. cit.

26. See Julius O. Ihonvbere,"Structural Adjustment, the April 1990 Coup and Democratization in Nigeria". Paper presented at the 33rd Annual Meeting of the African Studies Association, Baltimore, Maryland, November 1–4, 1990.

27. See Mokwugo Okoye,"A Time of Sadness," *The African Guardian* (September 24, 1990); Ademola Ogunlowo, "From Boom to Burst: A Review of the Economy," *Sunday Concord* (Lagos) (September 30,

1990) and "Five Years of Strangulation," *Newbreed* (Lagos) (1 October, 1990).

28. George B.N. Ayittey, "Why Structural Adjustment Failed in Africa," *TransAfrica Forum* Vol. 8 (2) (Summer 1991), p.50.

29. General Assembly Document No. A/43/500 of 10 August 1988.

30. United Nations Research Institute for Social Development, *States of Disarray: The Social Effects of Globalization*, (Geneva: UNRISD, 1995), pp. 39, 40, and 42.

31. Edward Jaycox, *The Challenges of African Development* op. cit., p. 4.

32. Mel Watkins, Foreword to Jill Torrie (ed.), *Banking on Poverty* op. cit., p.10. Watkins also notes that in the era of Reagan and Thatcher their "approach was increasingly neoconservative and monetarist: that is, following stringent fiscal and monetarist policies-notwithstanding recession and unemployment."

33. See Cheryl Payer, *The Debt Trap: The IMF and the Third World* (New York: Monthly Review Press, 1974) and her *The World Bank: A Critical Analysis* (New York: Monthly Review Press, 1982).

34. R. Cranford Pratt, "The Global Impact of the World Bank," op. cit., pp. 63 and 64.

35. See Organization of African Unity, *The Lagos Plan of Action for the Economic Development of Africa 1980–2000* (Geneva: Institute for Labour Studies, 1981). For a critique of this document see Julius O. Ihonvbere (ed), *Political Economy of Crisis and Underdevelopment in Africa: Selected Works of Claude Ake* (Lagos, Nigeria: JAD Publishers, 1990) and Timothy M. Shaw, "Debates About the Future: The Brandt, World Bank and Lagos Plan Blueprints," *Third World Quarterly* Vol. 5 (2) (April 1983).

36. See World Bank, *Accelerated Development in Sub-Saharan Africa: An Agenda for Action* (Washington, DC: World Bank, 1981).

37. William Minter (ed.), *Africa's Problems, African Initiatives* (Washington DC: Africa Policy Information Center, 1992), p.13 (emphasis added). This document reproduced portions of important African initiatives such as the "African Alternative Framework," "The African Charter for Popular Participation," and "The Kampala Document."

38. Ibid.

39. Ibid.

40. Ibid, p. 14.

41. See World Bank, *Sub-Saharan Africa: From Crisis to Sustainable Growth* op. cit

42. See Linda de Hoyos, "1990s Decade: Breaking Point for the IMF or Africa?" *Executive Intelligence Review* Vol. 20 (1) (January 1993); Bjorn Beckman, "Empowerment of Repression? The World Bank and the Politics of African Adjustment," *Africa Development* Vol. XVI (1) (1991); and Adebayo Adedeji, "Economic Progress: What Africa Needs," *TransAfrica Forum* Vol. 7 (2) (Summer 1990).

43. See World Bank, *Sub-Saharan Africa: From Crisis to Sustainable Growth* (World Bank, 1989); Economic Commission for Africa, *Economic Report on Africa 1990* (Addis Ababa: ECA,1990); Institute for African Alternatives (IFAA), *Alternative Development Strategies for Africa* (London: IFAA, 1989) and Julius O. Ihonvbere (ed.), *Structural Adjustment and Prospects for Recovery in Africa* proceedings of the Workshop on Structural Adjustment and Prospects for Peace and Development in Africa, sponsored by the Social Science Research Council (Toronto, 1990).

44. His Holiness Pope John Paul II, Message to the celebration of World Peace Day, December 27, 1986.

45. M. de Larosiere, Address to ECOSOC, July 4, 1986.

46. M. M. Camdessus, Address to ECOSOC, June 1987. See also Richard Jolly, "From Speeches to Action: Implementing What is Agreed," *IDS Bulletin* Vol.19 (1) (January 1988), and Giovanni Andrea Cornia, Richard Jolly, and Frances Stewart, *Adjustment with a Human Face, Volume 1: Protecting the Vulnerable and Promoting Growth* (Oxford: Clarendon Press, 1987). Volume II, *Country Case Studies* was published in 1988.

47. "Social Costs of Adjustment," *Africa Recovery* (Office of the Secretary-General of the United Nations, Information Unit) (4) (November 1987), p.15.

48. *West Africa* (June 11, 1990), p.968.

49. See Giovanni Andrea Cornia, Richard Jolly, and Frances Stewart (eds.), *Adjustment with a Human Face...Volumes I and II* op. cit.

50. Carol Lancaster, "Economic Restructuring in Sub-Saharan Africa," *Current History* Vol.88, (538), (May 1989), p.213.

51. *Ibid.*

52. Carol Lancaster, *United States and Africa: Into the Twenty-First Century*, (Washington, DC: Overseas Development Council, 1993), p. 15.

53. See E. Harsch, "Recovery or Relapse?" *Africa Report* Vol.33 (6) (1988), p.57.

54. "UNPAAERD speeches debate issues of debt, governance, and aid flows," *Africa Recovery* Vol. 5 (4) (December 1991), p.24.

55. Ibid, p.25.

56. Claude Ake," The Present Crisis in Africa: Economic Crisis or A Crisis of the State?" in Julius O. Ihonvbere (ed.), *The Political Economy of Crisis and Underdevelopment in Africa: Selected Works of Claude Ake* (Lagos: JAD Publishers, 1989), p.48.

57. Economic Commission for Africa, *Economic Report on Africa 1990* (Addis Ababa: ECA, 1990), p.VII.

58. Economic Commission for Africa, *African Charter for Popular Participation in Development* (Addis Ababa: ECA,1990), p.19.

59. Adebayo Adedeji," Development and Ethics..." op. cit.,p.6.

60. "Africa's Way Forward," *Africa Recovery* Vol. 5 (4) (December 1991), p.29.

61. Richard Sandbrook," Taming the African Leviathan," *World Policy Journal* (Fall, 1990), p.675.

62. World Bank, *Sub-Saharan Africa: From Crisis to Sustainable Growth* op. cit., p.1.

63. This sort of propaganda can be found in the World Bank's *Accelerated Development in Sub-Saharan Africa: An Agenda for Action* (Washington DC: World Bank, 1981).

64. To be sure, in World Bank and IMF documents, glowing reports on the successes of adjustment are presented. It is argued by both organizations that the situation would have been worse if adjustment had not been imposed on African states and a distinction is made between the achievements of so-called "strong reformers" and the failures of "non-reformers." Ironically, the ECA, using similar data argues that orthodox structural adjustment programs have undermined "the human condition" and shows a disregard for "the potential and role of popular participation in self-sustaining development," (p.19). For both positions see Edward Jaycox, *The Challenges of African Development* op. cit., and Economic Commission for Africa, *African Charter for Popular Participation in Development and Transformation* (Addis Ababa: ECA Secretariat, 1990).

65. See Boutros Boutros-Ghali, "New Concepts for Development Action in Africa," (New York: United Nations, Department of Public Information, 1993); Akinlo E. Anthony, "African Domestic Structure, Deepening Crisis and the Current Adjustment Program," *Africa*

Development Vol. XVI (1) (1991); Therese Sevigny, "From Crisis to Consensus," (New York: United Nations Communications and Project Management Division, 1990); Karen Lange, "Horn of Misery," *Africa News* (May 11–May 24, 1992); and "African Countries Lead Misery Index," *Africa News* (May 25-June 7, 1992). See also "Conference to Counter Africa's Marginalization," *Africa Recovery* Vol. 6 (2) (August 1992).

66. Economic Commission for Africa, *African Alternative Framework to Structural Adjustment Programmes for Socio-Economic Recovery and Transformation* (Addis Ababa: ECA, 1989), p. i.

67. Ibid, pp. ii and iii.

68. Ibid, p. 25.

69. Economic Commission for Africa, *African Alternative Framework- A Popular Version* (Addis Ababa: ECA 1991), p. 1. For very critical evaluations of structural adjustment programs in Africa, see various issues of *Africa Recovery* published by the UN Department of Public Information.

70. See Julius O. Ihonvbere and Darlington Iwarimie-Jaja, "The Political Economy of Mental Health in Nigeria: A Case Study of Port Harcourt," *Man and Life* Vol. 17 (1-2) (January-June 1991).

71. William Minter, *Africa's Problems, African Initiatives* op. cit., p.14.

72. See Elizabeth Obadina, "Currency Devaluation Saps Nigeria," *Africa Recovery* Vol. 6 (2) (August 1992).

73. Economic Commission for Africa, *African Alternative Framework...* op. cit., p. 25.

74. Boutros Boutros-Ghali, "New Concepts for Development Action in Africa," op. cit., p. 2. (emphasis added).

75. More money is stolen in America every day than most corrupt African governments would ever dream of. From insurance fraud to all

sorts of scams, the American economy is sustained by its dynamic technological base, the integration of its sectors, a strong international trade, a very productive agricultural sector, and a consumer culture that permeates the entire society. The money that disappeared in the savings a loans ('S and L') scandal of the 1990s dwarfs what many African leaders embezzle. The difference is that most of the stolen funds did not leave America. While this is not an attempt to justify corruption in Africa, the point is that corruption is inevitable in any capitalist (much more dependent capitalist) system. The root of the African crisis cannot be simply anchored on corruption.

76. See "Bank Lending Policies Under Fire," *Africa Recovery* Vol. 5 (2) (December 1991); Melvyn Westlake, "Fears Over Development Cash," *Africa Recovery* Vol. 5 (2) (December 1991) and The Global Coalition for Africa, *1992 Annual Report* (Washington, DC: The Global Coalition for Africa, November 1992).

77. See Julius O. Ihonvbere, "Political Conditionality and Prospects for Recovery in Sub-Saharan Africa," *International Third World Studies Journal and Review* Vol. 3 (1–2) (January-June 1991) and his "The Economic Crisis in Sub-Saharan Africa: Depth, Dimensions and Prospects for Recovery," *The Journal of International Studies* (27) (July 1991).

78. William Minter (ed), *Africa's Problems, African Initiatives* op. cit., p. 16.

79. See Julius O. Ihonvbere, "A Critical Evaluation of the Failed 1990 Coup in Nigeria," *The Journal of Modern African Studies* Vol. 29 (4) (1991).

80. Linda de Hoyos, "1990s Decade: Breaking Point for the IMF or for Africa?" op. cit., p. 11.

81. See Julius O. Ihonvbere, "Beyond Warlords and Clans: The African Crisis and the Somali Situation," Forthcoming; Africa Watch, *Somalia-Beyond the Warlords: The Needs for a Verdict on Human Rights Abuses* (New York: Africa Watch, 1993); and Ernest Harsch, "Somalia: Restoring Hope," *Africa Recovery Briefing Paper* (7) (15 January 1993).

82. "African Countries Lead Misery Index," *Africa News* (May 25–June 7, 1992), p. 3.

83. Adebayo Adedeji, Statement at the "Brainstorming Meeting on a Conference on Security, Stability, Development and Cooperation in Africa," Addis Ababa, Ethiopia, 17–18, November 1990.

84. Dele Omotunde and Dare Babarinsa, "This Government Has Run Out of Ideas: Interview With Sam Aluko," *TELL* (Lagos, Nigeria) (March 29, 1993), p.32. See also Julius O. Ihonvbere, "Economic Crisis, Structural Adjustment and Social Crisis in Nigeria," *World Development* Vol. 21 (1) (1993) and his "Structural Adjustment and Nigeria's Democratic Transition," *TransAfrica Forum* Vol. 8 (3) (Fall 1991).

85. Olusegun Obasanjo and Felix G. N. Mosha, (eds.), *Africa: Rise to Challenge*, (New York: Africa Leadership Forum, 1993), p. 353.

86. For rich and powerful organizations like the IMF and World Bank it is indeed shocking that all they have presented to Africa are post-hoc responses and policies which pay very little attention to national and regional peculiarities. For instance, it was only in 1989 that the Bank came up with a policy to protect vulnerable groups and to recognize the place of politics in the African crisis. By that time, the damage had been done and African economies were already on the verge of total disaster.

87. See Mike Agwu, "Endless Nightmare," *African Concord* (11 January 1993). See also several country reports from Africa Watch and Amnesty International.

88. Nigeria is a typical case where there was a public debate. The people soundly rejected the IMF loan and its conditionalities. The Ibrahim Babangida regime turned around to accept loans from the World Bank and to implement all the conditionalities of the Fund and Bank while claiming that it was pursuing a so-called homegrown alternative!

89. See Julius O. Ihonvbere, "Is Democracy Possible in Africa? The Elites, The People and Civil Society," *QUEST: Philosophical Discussions* Vol. IV (2) (December 1992).

90. See Julius O. Ihonvbere, "Building and Sustaining Democracy in Africa: Impediments and Possibilities." Mimeo, Department of Government, The University of Texas at Austin, 1993.

91. See Bade Onimode et. al, *Alternative Development Strategies for Africa Volume 1: Coalition for Change* (London: Institute for African Alternatives, 1990).

92. Economic Commission for Africa, *African Charter for Popular Participation* op. cit., p. 17. The African Charter is one of the most progressive documents to have come out of the region in recent times. It clearly outlines the responsibilities and obligations of the international community, African governments, women, the media, youth, the people and their organizations, NGOs and VDOs, and organized labor. More importantly, the document outlines ten major conditions for monitoring popular participation and democratization in Africa. If African states fail to commit themselves to the implementation of the Charter as well as to other declarations and charters, they would not have embarked on the road to recovery. For an evaluation of the Charter, see Julius O. Ihonvbere, "The African Crisis, The Popular Charter and Prospects for Recovery in the 1990s," *Zeitschrift fur Afrikanstudien (ZAST)* (11-12) (1991).

93. There is no reason why African states cannot strengthen the African Development Bank (ADB) and make it an alternative source of funding for development projects. Currently, the ADB is under the heavy influence of non-African members like the United States and Japan. Eventually, it will be unable to respond to African interests. See Roy Laishley, "Donors Curb ADB Expansion," *Africa Recovery* Vol. 6 (2) (August 1992).

Chapter Four

The State, Human Rights, and Democratization in Africa

With one or two exceptions, I think it is correct to say that today, African states are guilty of tyranny and oppression towards the masses of Africa in the same way as the colonial powers were. Indeed, it can be said that the African states concerned are guiltier...[1]

Freedom of speech and expression means nothing to a largely illiterate and ignorant society and similarly, the right to life has no relevance to a man who has no means to livelihood.[2]

African governments have had a terrible human rights record. A combination of historically determined coalitions, contradictions, conflicts, and crises have combined with external issues to create an environment that made the violation of human rights in the most wicked form part of the African political equation since the 1960s. What has been missing in the recent accounts of political and economic developments in Africa is the way in which human rights abuses delegitimized the state, encouraged, albeit inadvertently, the emergence of civil liberties organizations, and prompted challenges to the repressive neocolonial state structures, and how the new democratization agenda in the region relates to the struggles for human rights. In this chapter, we begin with a brief examination of the nature of the state and state power in order to explain why human rights abuses were so commonplace; we then examine the extent of human rights violations and the responses to these abuses. We conclude by locating the discussion in the ongoing struggle for democracy and democratization in Africa. One issue we have tried to avoid is detailed cataloging of human rights abuses, largely because of the magnitude of the abuses and the tendency for such an exercise to divert attention from a discussion of deeper structural issues.

The issue of human rights, especially its violation, has become topical in the past decade or so. In Africa, the traditional neglect has given way to increasing concerns, which have in turn encouraged the emergence of hundreds of human rights and civil liberties organizations, as well as pro-democracy and popular groups with interest in human rights issues. In Nigeria, for instance, while no civil liberties organization existed until the late 1970s, there are today well over a dozen well-structured and active organizations like the Universal Defenders of Democracy (UDD), the Civil Liberties Organization (CLO), the Committee for the Defence of Human Rights (CDHR), and the Constitutional Rights Project (CRP). The activities of these bodies have complemented the works of Amnesty International, Africa Watch, Africa Rights, Human Rights Internet, and other international human rights organizations. Another major departure from the past is the way in which other popular and community-based organizations have come to include and incorporate human rights issues in their regular activities. Trade and students' unions, womens' movements, farmers' associations, lawyers, journalists, academics, and so on, now have human rights issues written into their constitutions, and in many instances they have units that deal exclusively with human rights issues.

Conceptualizing Human Rights in Africa

Though the concept of human rights is of fairly recent origin, the idea of "natural law" has a much earlier origin, dating back centuries. In fact, early European philosophers held the view that human beings had natural rights that preceded formal governments. While the French Revolution was anchored on a struggle for liberty, equality and fraternity; the United States Declaration of Independence fully acknowledges the "inalienable rights" of its citizens. Similarly, the 1948 Universal Declaration of Human Rights, in its preamble, acknowledges the rights of peoples to be "equal and inalienable."

Yet, the debate on the need for an appropriate definition or conceptualization of human rights has been quite intense.[3] At the core of the debate is whether the conception of human rights is culturally relative or universal. On the one hand, there are scholars and writers, especially from the developing world, who contend that conceptions of human rights cannot be universal because they are relative to specific cultures and existed within the philosophical foundations of precapitalist formations prior to recent Western notions of human rights.[4] Then, there are those who contend that human rights are universal rights and notions of "human dignity" must not be confused with "human rights," which are "individual claims or entitlements against the state."[5] Consequently, there cannot be such a thing as "African human rights" or human rights in precolonial African societies, because "there is only one conception of human rights and that is Western."[6] While it is attractive, even enticing, to argue for an African concept of human rights, I would contend that there is no such thing. True, there are specificities and particular historical conditions which must be considered. But justifying human rights abuses on the grounds of cultural relativity simply allows bourgeois forces to rationalize and legitimize the brutal, irresponsible, and exploitative ways they have organized the suffocation of civil society and their peoples. After all, there is no particular "African hunger," "African poverty," "African illiteracy," or "African death." Hunger, poverty, illiteracy, and death know no color, race, or location. In any case, the cultural basis of so-called African rights is not static, and in most communities these have been eroded, mediated, or completely transformed by the onslaught of capitalist penetration and market relations.

In addition, the issue of whether it is necessary, indeed, inevitable, to trade political rights for socio-economic and cultural rights has been a major aspect of the debate. Unfortunately, such debates have tended to divert attention from the real issues: why has the African state, its agents, and agencies come to rely heavily on the abuse of human rights? Why does the state suffocate civil society and asphyxiate popular groups in spite of the negative implications for change, stability, resource generation and management, development, growth, and even its own legitimacy? An appropriate approach to understanding these issues requires that we locate such debates within the specificities of African social formations as well as the dynamics of power, politics, production, and exchange relations.[7] In fact, it is not surprising that researchers in developing and developed formations do not see human rights from a similar perspective. This difference in perspective is understandable once there is some agreement on basic minimums for rights, liberties, and obligations.

On both sides of the global division of labor and power, experiences and expectations differ, the role and nature of the state, and of civil society, differ, and the strategies and tactics of struggles differ. The priorities of people also differ, depending on a range of factors and forces, and these are bound to affect which issues are determined to be primary at any moment in time. For instance, while in the developed nations, where institutions are stable and predictable, rights are guaranteed, there is separation of powers, justice is not only available to the rich, and basic needs are more or less guaranteed, there might be a tendency to focus on civil and political rights. After all, the free-market ideology still leaves human survival at the individual level even if there are several opportunities to cushion the effects of exploitation on the disadvantaged. In developing formations however, where nothing is predictable or guaranteed, and where hunger, disease, homelessness, unemployment, lack of access to health facilities, and gross inequality between the few rich and the majority poor characterize society, the emphasis might be on socioeconomic and cultural rights. In both instances, there does not need to be a trade-off; rather, organizations, communities, and individuals should struggle for political and economic rights while paying due attention to the specificities of their environments.

At the cultural level there are equally differences. In the developed formations, modernization, a complex and powerful consumer culture, excessive regulation, and the impact of the media and technology have atomized the family and reduced human beings to more or less mechanical objects. It was not surprising to see so-called "family values" become a campaign issue in the 1992 presidential elections in the United States, though none of the candidates linked the erosion of traditional family values to the pervasive influence of market relations. Possessive individualism is what reigns supreme. Under such a cultural milieu, the emphasis in the perception and discussion of human rights is influenced by a pervading individualist culture rationalized in complex ways. In developing formations however, in spite of the negative impacts of peripheral capitalism, vulnerability in the global system, and increasing incorporation into Western-style consumer culture, the village, community, and family remain very strong. Collectivism overrides individualism, and in an environment without formal safety nets, the family, community, and mass-based organizations continue to protect the individual, irrespective of location. Here, human rights are perceived as part of group and community rights. Yet, these cultural differences only sensitize us to the specifics and environments in which rights are enjoyed or denied. They do not in any way justify or necessitate the trade-off of one set of rights against another.

It is not really appropriate to argue that human rights are "irrelevant to African societies." In fact, those who argue for an African concept of human rights do so essentially to draw attention to the distinctive character of the African condition, its particular historical experiences, and its special location and role in the capitalist-dominated global division of labor.[8] As Claude Ake has argued,

> [T]he Western notion of human rights stresses rights which are not very interesting in the context of African realities. Even when they are interesting their salience is questionable. There is much concern with the right of peaceful assembly, self-determination, free speech and thought, fair trial etc. The appeal of these rights is sociologically specific. They appeal to people with a full stomach who can now afford to pursue the more esoteric aspects of self-realization. The vast majority of our people are not in this position. They are facing the struggle for existence in its brutal immediacy. This is a totally consuming struggle. They have little or no time for reflection and hardly any use for free speech. There is no freedom for hungry people, or those eternally oppressed by diseases. It is no wonder that the idea of human rights has tended to sound hollow in the African context.[9]

In spite of the position above, Ake insists that Africa "ought to be interested in human rights because it will help us to combat social forces which threaten to send us back to a more violent barbarism. Because it will aid our struggle for the social transformation which we need to survive and to flourish."[10] What this position advocates is to link the struggle for human rights, to the struggle for the transformation of society. It is insufficient to simply struggle for human rights because the factors and forces which abuse or abridge the rights of people are located in the totality of power structures in society. If the nature of the politics and political economy are responsible for human rights abuses, it follows that it is not adequate to isolate human rights and to confront the problem without confronting the laws, institutions, groups, individuals, and the state which perpetuate the abuse of natural and other constitutionally guaranteed rights.[11] This is not to deny that wanton abuse of rights take place on a daily basis. Perhaps. But even more important is the point that such abuses have taken place because of the character of the state, its custodians, and its institutions, as well as because of the weak nature of a civil society that is completely incapable of checking the excesses of political leaders. In the context of deepening socioeconomic crisis, oppressed constituencies have sometimes been forced to resort to armed struggle as the only viable option.

A holistic and historical approach to the problem will demonstrate the inextricable linkage between underdevelopment and human rights violations. We argue, therefore, that the underdeveloped and dependent conditions of the African continent generate contradictions, pressures, and crises that enhance insecurity, conflicts, and the violation of human rights by the state and its custodians. It is the underdeveloped and vulnerable character of the political economy that breeds the conditions of violence, instability, insecurity, corruption, and nonaccountability that in turn culminate in human rights violations. An underdeveloped economy, presided over by an underdeveloped state and elite, is a direct prescription for human rights abuses. It is no wonder that the more poverty-stricken, underdeveloped, and marginal a nation is in the global system, the more insecure its elites, the more unstable its production and accumulation patterns, and consequently the higher the propensity for human rights abuses. Of course, there are a few exceptions here and there, but there is a direct relationship between underdevelopment and the containment or suffocation of individual and collective rights. This is not to excuse the state and its institutions or to contend that because the social formation is underdeveloped, human rights abuses must necessarily take place. On the contrary, we wish to point out that the pressures, contradictions, and implications of underdeveloped state and social structures, weak political traditions, and the preponderance of survivalist strategies among nonbourgeois forces, which become more important in the context of a weak unstable, repressive, and desperate state, make human rights violation almost inevitable in the African context.

The importance of this approach is to direct our attention to *structural* aspects of the problem. Merely writing a constitution guaranteeing rights will not do; neither will cataloging what civil rights are. In fact, African governments, have, since the 1960s, demonstrated outstanding skills in constitution-making and in creating institutions dedicated ostensibly to the guarantee of rights and liberties. The problem is to address the nature and behavior of the state and its custodians within the total context of the political economy.

Researchers have tended to overlook these issues when they undertake the more fanciful project of cataloguing the gruesome record of African leaders in the area of human rights.[12] Of course, such accounts do perform the function of sensitizing the public to the state of human rights abuses and, in many instances, have encouraged the formation of human rights organizations. To be sure, our conceptualization of human rights encompasses rights such as freedom of speech, the right to vote and be voted for, and freedom of movement. We contend, however, that a proper analysis and understanding of human rights in any society can only be made by looking at the socioeconomic or material foundations of society.[13] Hence, political institutions and processes, the existence of more than one political party, periodic elections, and constitutionally guaranteed rights hardly tell the real story because they all depend on the patterns of power, production, and exchange, the relations among and within social classes, and the location of social formations in the international division of labor. If the processes of growth and development fail to mobilize the people, empower them and their organizations and communities, strengthen democratic and other civic associations, and meet the basic needs of the vast majority, then it can be argued that such a process of development is actually consolidating the narrow and exploitative interest of the minority at the expense of the majority. This implies that civil, political, cultural, and socioeconomic rights cannot be discussed in isolation because they reinforce each other and inform the overall composition and character of political systems.[14]

It is undesirable to generalize on the issue of human rights. At the same time, it is inappropriate to transpose standards of evaluation and determination of human rights from one society to the other. The historical experiences of particular social formations and the consequences of these experiences must be taken into consideration at all levels. Well-worded declarations, charters, covenants, and laws do not necessarily guarantee human rights, as the African situation has clearly shown. Though African states adopted the *African Charter on Human and Peoples' Rights* in 1981, in which they agreed to pay "particular attention to the right to development and that civil and political rights cannot be dissociated from economic, social and cultural rights in their conception as well as universality and that the satisfaction of economic, social and cultural rights is a guarantee for the enjoyment of civil and political rights,"[15] not one African state has lived up to the provisions of the Charter. In fact, not one African state has shown any respect for the Charter, and as Ake has noted, "[n]obody can accuse Africa of taking human rights seriously. This remains true whether one is thinking of human rights philosophically, ideologically or politically."[16]

Human rights are not "things" or "benefits" that benevolent leaderships grant to the people. It is true that by virtue of being human beings on earth, people have natural rights which are inalienable. But despotic governments, desperate in the struggle to hold on to power and ward off challenges from popular constituencies, do not subscribe to the notion of natural or inalienable rights. Historically, rights have been won through constant and consistent struggles between those who have reasons to deny these rights to the majority and those who, by their contribution to the growth and development of society, feel they should enjoy such rights, as the experiences of the United States, European nations, and most recently, South Africa clearly demonstrate. In other words, the level of rights enjoyed in society reflects the intensity, content, and context of class contradictions and struggles. Further, rights, once won, do not remain static. They change with the times and with the changing character of politics and society. This means that only a strengthened and vibrant civil society can guarantee the sustenance and reproduction of a political environment conducive to human rights protection.[17]

It is quite easy for organizations, individuals, and governments in the Western world to insist, as they have done in the past decade or so, on the primacy of civil and political rights.[18] In fact, such insistence is sometimes made at the expense of socio-economic and cultural rights. As well, Western governments, particularly the United States, have not hesitated to sacrifice human rights principles on the alter of economic and political or strategic interests. How else can we explain the romance the West had with apartheid in South Africa for decades even after the United Nations declared the system a "crime against humanity"? The same considerations currently inform America's relations with China, where human rights issues are treated as distinctly separate from economic issues because of the lucrative nature of the Chinese market. But, for nations that were never colonized, dominated, and underdeveloped, such insistence on the primacy of civil and political rights makes sense only because the state and its custodians use the "abundance" of civil and political rights to hide gross social and economic inequalities. Political and civil rights "naturally" emanate from a well-integrated and productive material base that reproduces itself through the interaction of internal forces using viable and stable political institutions to guarantee a positive atmosphere for capital accumulation and the domestication of the opposition. Once civil society was constituted, the market strengthened, and institutions of politics put in place and routinized, it was easy for a bare minimum of rights to be established on which society was to build. However, for countries that have known no peace, stability, or progress since their contact with the forces of Western imperialism, civil and political rights have little meaning, for they are constantly mediated by pressures, expectations, contradictions, and conflicts emanating from the condition of mass poverty, backwardness, dependence, underdevelopment, and peripheralization in a very unequal and exploitative international division of labor and power.[19]

This is one area where Western nations and some analysts have overlooked the specifics of Africa in the prescriptions on human rights issues. To expect debt-ridden, poverty-stricken, nonindustrialized, dependent, and foreign-dominated economies, presided over by corrupt, repressive, unproductive, and largely subservient elites who see the capture, retention, and manipulation of state power as coterminous with their survival, to guarantee and protect human rights means that the real issues are not being addressed. Moreover, it must be realized that as a precipitate of the colonial divide-and-rule politics, ethnic, regional, religious and other primordial matters had become severely politicized and that this has eroded possibilities for tolerance, political accommodation, consensus, and rational politics. As the cases of Liberia, Somalia, the Sudan, Rwanda, and Burundi clearly demonstrate, clan, religious, regional, and ethnic suspicions remain very critical matters that prompt violence, massacres, and war.

African History and the Legacy of Repression

An attempt to catalogue human rights abuses in any five African states would be an enormous undertaking. The record, in terms of dimension, brutality, and impact is extremely bad. It is as if *political* independence was an excuse to terrorize the people, squander resources, mortgage their respective economies, and brutalize those who had supported the struggle against colonial domination. As John Hatch has noted,

> Events during the 1960s largely destroyed the euphoria aroused by independence, replacing expectancy with cynicism or resignation. A score of regimes, created in the high point of anti-colonial nationalism, were unconstitutionally overthrown. The use of violence, actual or threatened, supplanted political processes over large areas of the continent. The goal of pan-African unity, for many nationalists a central objective of the anti-colonial campaigns, receded beyond the horizon, a forgotten Utopia. Instead of national prosperity, anticipated from the collective national efforts released by independence, stagnation in the countryside, massive unemployment in the towns and ostentatious luxury for a tiny minority became the general experience.[20]

Furthermore, because of the failings above and the disarticulations in the system, the new governments could not maintain law and order or meet the basic needs of their peoples. Consequently, the leaders "opted for political repression. In the course of this they militarized not only politics—it became a violent struggle with the norms of welfare—but also social life."[21] In addition, "detention without trial, public executions, inter-communal massacres, commonly succeeded colonial rule. Freedom to organize trade unions, political parties or co-operatives was curtailed. The right to publish newspapers, to hold public meetings, was widely curtailed. Theft and rapine violence spread through town streets and country paths. Corruption became rampant, graft common-place. Africa seemed to be fast imitating not only the societies of New York, Chicago, Dallas, Hamburg, Marseilles or London..."[22]

Compared to the contemporary situation, the African condition that Hatch described in the 1960s can be described as a golden age. Africa Watch has summarized the violation of human rights within the academy in Africa thus:

> ...summary executions of academics and students; torture; arbitrary arrest and prolonged detention without charge or trial; imprisonment under conditions that are cruel and degrading; restrictions on freedom of expression, assembly, association and movement; dismissal of faculty staff; expulsion of students; university closures; banning of student organizations and staff unions; the prohibition of "political activity" on campus; discrimination against students on the basis of race, ethnic or regional origin; censorship of teaching and reading materials and manipulation of curricula. Lesser forms of coercion are also used as a means of intimidation, such as denial of promotions and tenure to outspoken academics; restrictions on travel abroad for research or meetings; refusal to grant scholarships to politically active students; and the requirement that students who

have been implicated in political disturbances sign pledges of "good behavior" in order to resume their studies.[23]

The tactics of human rights abuses in academic institutions outlined above apply to all African countries without exception. It is merely a matter of degree. While it might be low in Botswana (probably because of the large number of expatriates at the University of Botswana, but also because of its fairly democratic government), it is much worse in Nigeria and Kenya, where the governments seem to be waging an unending battle against the academy. At the Universities of Benin, Maiduguri, Port Harcourt, Ife, and at the Ahmadu Bello University in Nigeria, hundreds of students have been handed over to the police, rusticated, or suspended, at times, without fair trial and over manufactured charges. Also, in collusion with the Federal government, especially under the military, several faculty have been fired for being active in the faculty union and for opposing government erosion of academic freedom.[24] Describing the human rights situation in Zaire in 1990, the Lawyers Committee for Human Rights has noted that:

> For nearly 25 years the people of Zaire have lived under a repressive system which has institutionalized...abuses. Since President Mobutu took power in a military coup in 1965, thousands of Zairians have been killed, or subjected to torture, cruel treatment, or prolonged arbitrary detentions. Throughout this period, and until today, Zaire's security forces have routinely engaged in harassment, arrest, detention and physical abuse as a means of controlling the population and quashing any perceived threat to the President's authority. This has led to a total breakdown in the rule of law in Zaire.[25]

The fragility of state structures, the occurrence of coups and countercoups, the vulnerability to external manipulations, and the corrupt and unproductive deposition of the dominant forces have continued to deepen contradictions, insecurity, uncertainty, and conflicts.[26] The industrial, agricultural, and service sectors of the various economies are either stagnating or declining. Import substitution industrialization strategy, religiously embraced in the early period of technology transfer, failed to promote an appreciable level of sectoral integration. Periodic improvements in production levels, trade balances, foreign reserves, GDP, and so on, were not reflected in the living conditions of the majority of Africa; poverty, illiteracy, disease, hunger, and marginalization from political and decision-making processes came to characterize life on the continent.[27] The terrible economic and social conditions in contemporary times are so devastatingly obvious that we can appreciate Michael Holman's conclusion that "Today, more people in Africa are poorer, and more children are dying. Other signs of stress are rampant, beginning with the distressing list of countries that have effectively ceased to function as modern nation states: Zaire, Somalia, Liberia, Sudan, Angola...Former "success" stories and "role models" of the 1960s have since become cautionary tales...The technological gap between Africa and the world has widened, and the continents's management is weak..."[28] The squandering of available limited resources on prestige projects, importation of modern and sophisticated military gadgets, and misplaced national priorities prevent African governments from responding concretely to the contradictions and pressures generated by the continent's backwardness. In the attempt to divert attention and contain popular pressures and opposition, the rights of citizens are wantonly violated.[29]

The point we wish to emphasize here is that wanton human rights abuses in Africa cannot be extricated from the desperate economic conditions of the region. As elites find it difficult to run governments, as parastatals crumble due to heavy debt burdens, as foreign exchange earnings go to debt-servicing, and as workers, women, students, and peasants engage in open opposition to the state, the governments devise legal and extralegal ways to hold on to power and contain the opposition. In fact, the state becomes the target of all opposition elements, and the custodians of state power see such challenges as direct challenges to them as persons and to their capacities to serve as leaders. In the absence of a democratic political culture or propitious environment for effective mediation of conflicts and contradictions, the state, which monopolizes the means of coercion, easily abuses the rights of nonbourgeois forces.

To be sure, the crisis of the continent cannot be understood only from the internal perspective. The harshness of the international environment, rising debt-service ratios and interest rates, frequent increases in the cost of imports, direct military violation of the territorial integrity of African states, until recently, Western support for apartheid in South Africa, and declining foreign assistance have contributed significantly to the plight of the continent. The end of the cold war and the diversion of interest, investment, and foreign aid to Eastern Europe only laid bare the devastation which the so-called confrontation between the East and the West caused in Africa.[30] Africa was simply a pawn in the East-West game. While the superpowers never went to war against each other, a poor and underdeveloped region like Africa received high dosages of military aid. It is not an accident that the most repressive and most corrupt regimes in Africa were the darlings of the West during the era of the cold war. In Zaire, Kenya, Liberia, the Sudan, and Somalia, leaders threw all ideas about human rights overboard and dealt devastating blows to students, trade unions, academics, social activists, and civil society. They massacred protesting peasants and women, closed universities, executed alleged coup plotters, and plunged their wretched nations into civil wars. Scarce resources went into setting up notorious security agencies and in building presidential fortresses. In all these and more, activities which directly and/or indirectly violated all known rules of rational and civilized behavior, the governments of the West continued to give material and diplomatic support to the leaders. Today, though the cold war has ended and Russia is receiving support from all Western nations, Africa has been left high and dry, and the impact of years of intimidation and harassment of popular forces remain there for all to see.

To these we can add the tolerance of the political excesses of African leaders until very recently, the absence of an international body capable of censoring repressive leaders and imposing sanctions for wanton disregard of international covenants, and the impact of the international arms economy which ensured that nations that could not boast of two functioning factories had their streets littered with the latest and sophisticated bombs, guns, grenades, and other weapons of mass destruction. Vulnerable communities and individuals, especially women and children, have been the victims of the arms economy, as the experiences of Somalia and Rwanda clearly show.

The marginal location and role of Africa in the international division of labor militates against the region's ability to generate sufficient resources to promote development and thus contain negative political pressures. Further, the domination of African economies by powerful transnational interests erodes their autonomous ability to be creative. It facilitates massive profit repatriation, technology distortion, corruption of the political elites, taste transfer, cultural bastardization, and general vulnerability of the weak African economy to foreign pressures. As the current "new" world order shows, Africa is almost an irrelevant actor in the global movement of resources and capital.[31] Its rich resources are merely to be exploited and its market bypassed for those of other regions of the world. Lacking stability internally, and lacking a viable constituency abroad, Africa remains in the backwaters of the policy-making concerns of the developed world. As the Lagos Plan of Action, adopted by African leaders in 1980, laments: "The effect of unfulfilled promises of global development strategies has been more sharply felt in Africa" and taken together, the promises and politics of international aid have only made conditions within the continent much worse.[32]

The adoption of monetarist policies, particularly those recommended by the World Bank and the International Monetary Fund (IMF), sharpened these tendencies and contradictions within the state structures on the continent.[33] Policies of desubsidization, deregulation, privatization, commercialization, and devaluation, among other monetarist programs imposed on already fragile and poverty-stricken African states, contributed immensely to the abuse of people's rights and liberties in Africa. As these policies failed to improve the specific and overall conditions of African economies, regimes became the more desperate. Inflation, unemployment, tensions, prostitution, crime, and military coups and countercoups became commonplace. Violent riots organized by trade unions, students, and other vulnerable groups who were left unprotected by structural adjustment made governments insecure and violent in their response to popular challenges. Of course, the IMF and the World Bank had failed to take into consideration the character of domestic constituencies, the ability of nonbourgeois forces to resist adjustment, and the very fragile legitimacy of corrupt and repressive leaders in the region. Hundreds of Africans were killed by the police, army and special security squads during protests against adjustment in Zambia, Zaire, and Nigeria. Human rights activists and intellectuals were harassed and jailed for opposing structural adjustment. The record of adjustment in Africa is one of accentuating already tense situations, promoting the massive abuse of socioeconomic and political rights, and widening the gap between an alienated populace and the insecure, desperate leaders.[34] Yet, the current orientation of the African economy is mostly one of attempting to service dependent capitalism, implement harsh monetarist programs, and contain popular responses through the use of violence, draconian decrees, repression, diversionary tactics, and outright violation of personal freedoms and liberties (see Chapter Three).[35] Clive Thomas has addressed this issue in relation to the Third World generally, but it has great implications for Africa:

> One of the many outstanding features of the Third World, one which is of particular concern, is the prevalence of repression, political assassination, disappearances, and other evidence of installed dictatorships… The prevalence of these repressive political forms is the direct counterpart of the absence of internal democratic practices and the virtual outlawing, within these countries, of representative political institutions, multiparty political systems, due process and equality before the law, free and fair elections and so on. Where repression prevails, the possibility of political and social advances for the broad masses…has also lessened.[36]

Under such conditions, as highlighted by Thomas above, it would be (and indeed is) a waste of time to preach human rights or complain about human rights violations without simultaneously addressing the historical socioeconomic and political processes and relationships that culminate in the violation of human rights. In other words, the campaign for human rights must include direct *political* demands in order to recompose and redirect the nature of politics, power, production, and exchange relations. Claude Ake is right when he laments:

> We Africans have never had it so bad. The tragic consequences of our development strategies have finally come home to us. Always oppressed by poverty and deprivation, our lives become harsher still with each passing day as real incomes continue to decline. We watch helplessly while millions of our people are threatened by famine and look pitifully to the rest of the world to feed us. Our social and political institutions are disintegrating under pressure from our flagging morale, our dwindling resources and the intense struggle to control them.[37]

The militarization of Africa's political landscape has encouraged human rights abuses. Coups and countercoups have precipitated civil wars. Failed and successful coups have led to mass executions in Somalia, Ghana, Liberia, Nigeria, virtually everywhere. Samuel Doe of Liberia made a public show of executing top officers of the Tolbert Government, including Tolbert himself. Rawlings of Ghana prides himself in having executed three former Ghanaian heads of state and several top officers. Nigeria has practically eliminated a whole generation of young military officers through public executions for their involvement in failed or leaked coup plots. Mengistu Haile Mariam, the former military dictator in Ethiopia massacred several leading officers of the Dergue to satisfy his hunger for raw power. In the Sudan and Somalia, it was not unusual to manufacture coup plots to facilitate the elimination of real and imagined opposition. The military simply suspend the constitutions and rule by decrees that oust the jurisdiction of the law courts. Human rights received a very low priority under the military, no matter how benevolent it pretended to be.

> In roughly thirty years, Africa has experienced some sixty coups d'etat and countless number of coup attempts. Major civil wars have erupted in more than ten countries and are still raging on a large scale in six countries. Fifteen separate border disputes involving thirty countries developed into a military confrontation and tension still exists on certain borders. Ten countries, some not included in the above categories, have been subjected to external military interventions or direct involvement of external forces in attacks against such countries. The continent remains a fertile ground for mercenaries and an object of external security manipulation.[38]

These conditions have thrown up refugees and criminals. They have created conditions that allow corrupt leaders to repress minorities and vulnerable communities and to violate human rights in the name of "national security." In the numerous crises of the region 1.5 million lives were lost in the first nine years of the 1980s, excluding those who died in Chad, Ethiopia, Liberia, Somalia and the Sudan. Suffering caused by war affected "4.5 million in Mozambique, over 2 million in Angola, 4.9 million in Ethiopia, 1.5 million in Liberia, 4.5 million in the Sudan, over 1 million in Somalia."[39] In terms of destruction of property and cost to African economies, war has cost the region well over $60 billion between 1980 and 1989. In 1988, it was over $10 billion. While about $4 billion was spent on emergencies arising from strife conditions in Africa between 1984 and 1986, the United States spent $2 billion in Somalia alone in the early 1990s. These are funds that could have gone into development and nation-building. The main victims of the strife have been the poor, the powerless, and the vulnerable. These conflict and crisis conditions continue because of foreign manipulation, the lack of effective conflict resolution procedures and institutions, greed and unbridled lust for power, primordial suspicions, the failure of the state and elites to inspire a culture of dialogue, harmony and consensus, and the weaknesses of civil society and political institutions. As Yoweri Museveni has argued, "stability has eluded Africa because we have failed to build viable political institutions. Lancerous tyrannies, therefore, emerged to fill the vacuum; they became the institutions and in some extreme instances the state. Africa became an importer of institutions not rooted in her soil."[40]

Finally, it is important to add that human rights abuses continue in Africa because of very limited public information, education, and mobilization. Not only do most Africans know little about their constitutions and the rights it accords them, the various covenants like the *African Charter of Human and Peoples' Rights* and the *Universal Declaration of Human Rights* are virtually unknown and unavailable in bookstores or libraries. Even the struggle against despotism has remained elitist and urban-based. People simply do not know their rights. Generally, due to fear of reprisals, people prefer to remain silent about abuses. This has become more prevalent as the elites appropriate the state and the means of coercion, intellectuals get domesticated and incorporated, and traditional institutions invoke cultural rationalizations for accepting the status quo. This cultural rationalization has encouraged exploitation and the internalization of state-sponsored acts of violence. Women for instance, are unable to seek legal redress over issues of rape and sexual harassment because it is culturally taboo to discuss such matters publicly.

Even cases of rape are kept hidden away from public knowledge because of cultural "sanctions" against a raped woman. Many schools, even universities and political science departments in particular, do not have courses on human rights, and it is not unusual to see newspapers and magazines that shy away from exposing human rights abuses and educating the public on ways to protect themselves or seek redress. In short, human rights issues are yet to receive the widespread attention and discussions they deserve.

The State, Democratization, and Human Rights

The end of the 1980s witnessed a largely unanticipated deluge of democratization efforts in Africa. Dictators were swept out of power. Military regimes were resisted by popular forces. In Zambia, the one-party government of Kenneth Kaunda, which had ruled the country mostly through a state of emergency for almost twenty-seven years, was crushed in popular elections by the Frederick Chiluba-led Movement for Multiparty Democracy (MMD). In Ghana, Jerry Rawlings, who had earlier boasted that he had little patience with politicians and that a transition to democracy was not on his agenda, was compelled by donors and pro-democracy groups led by the Movement for Freedom and Justice (MFJ) to organize popular elections and terminate military rule. In Kenya, the repressive and corrupt one-party government of Daniel arap Moi was starved of foreign aid by donor countries and was compelled to open up the political system to multiparty elections, which saw the opposition, though divided, winning several seats. Finally, in Nigeria, the tricks and unending transition to democracy organized by General Ibrahim Babangida were not sufficient to withstand the massive antimilitary and anti-Babangida campaigns of the pro-democracy groups under the umbrella of the Campaign for Democracy (CD), which forced the ruthlessly repressive and corrupt general to resign as president and retire from the armed forces. In virtually all African countries the upheaval was such that the issues of politics and society that were articulated by the new political actors challenged existing conditions of inequality, exploitation, marginalization of the poor, corruption, and human rights violations. As well, human rights associations, trade and students' unions, political parties, pro-democracy groups, peasants' movements, women's organization, even the unemployed, created new associations and reinvigorated dormant ones that had been driven underground. They forged new alliances. They began to express new ideas, ask new questions, and introduce new issues into the political landscape. Issues of accountability, empowerment, democracy, participation, social justice, human rights, gender equality, and environmental protection came to dominate political demands and discourses. Human rights issues took added prominence: "We have suffered in Africa. Our leaders have not respected their peoples. They not only seized the state but also stole all the resources and used force to buy obedience. Now, we have decided to fight. For the poor majority, what else can they lose?"[41]

A major external development at this point, largely facilitated by the end of the cold war, was the new insistence by international financial institutions, Western governments, creditors, and donors that political pluralism or multiparty politics would become major conditionalities for foreign aid to African states. Again, respect for human rights received a prominent place in the new political conditionalities imposed on African governments by donors and lenders. Douglas Hurd, the British Foreign Minister probably set the tone for the debate on political conditionality in mid-1990 when he declared that

> Countries which tend towards pluralism, public accountability, *respect for the rule of law, human rights* and market principles should be encouraged. Governments which persist with repressive policies, corrupt management and wasteful, discredited economic systems should not expect us to support their folly with scarce aid resources which could be used better elsewhere.[42]

Within a short time this position received the endorsement of Japan, Canada, the United States, and France. At the 1990 Franco-African Summit, Francois Mitterand of France made it very clear that "regimes that behaved in an authoritarian manner, without accepting the evolution toward democracy" can forget about receiving foreign aid from France or other donor nations.[43] These declarations encouraged a more enthusiastic support for human rights in Africa. It was under this new position that foreign aid to Malawi and the repressive Kamuzu Banda regime was cut from L10 to L5 million in 1992. Belgium, under pressure from France also cut off aid to Zaire because of Mobutu's refusal to respect popular wishes and reach accommodation with local constituencies. Kenya was similarly forced to accept multiparty elections because twelve donor agencies and governments suspended foreign aid for six months in November 1991 until the Moi regime instituted multiparty politics and allowed for popular elections.[44]

Many leaders who had revelled in criminal human rights abuse now found themselves pressured to reach agreement and accommodation with domestic constituencies, open up the political system, and respect human rights. They tried to play to the gallery by arguing that such conditionalities amounted to interference in the internal affairs of independent African states. However, pro-democracy groups argued that it was only through such internationally imposed conditionalities that stubborn and repressive African leaders, who had demonstrated no respect whatsoever for their peoples, could be forced to respect human rights and become politically reasonable. In any case, it was anachronistic to speak of the "independence" of neocolonial states when they were dependent on the outside world for virtually everything, and were dominated by foreign capital. Though many African leaders were very uncomfortable with these political conditionalities, they had little or no choice but to accept them because they had already accepted the economic conditionalities of creditors and donors through the structural adjustment and economic stabilization packages of the World Bank and the IMF. In fact, in its 1989 report on Africa, the World Bank for the very first time accepted the argument already made by African and Africanist scholars that the roots of Africa's economic predicaments were largely political.

The new Bank position emphasized issues of misgovernance, unaccountability, overcentralization, widespread corruption, waste, mismanagement, bureaucratic inefficiency, the over-extended role of the state, repression, gender discrimination, and widespread abuse of human rights as major aspects of the African crisis. Among other prescriptions, the World Bank called for the creation of an enabling environment that would allow for democracy, accountability, popular participation in decision-masking, the rolling back of the state, support for the private sector, building human capacities, protecting the vulnerable during structural adjustment, good governance, and above all, ensuring that "ordinary people...participate more in designing and implementing development programs."[45] The sort of "political renewal" demanded by the Bank directly challenged the suffocation of civil society, the privatization of the state and its resources by a handful of elites or by presidents-for-life and military dictators, and served notice that the current global order would no longer accommodate such political excesses. With debt of over $300 billion dollars, with precipitous fall in foreign aid, investments, and with donors complaining of "aid fatigue," African leaders, including those who had boasted previously that democracy did not exist in their dictionaries, were forced to make concessions to civil society and to pro-democracy activists. This singular act, reduced and, in many instances, eliminated the reliance on repression and human rights abuses as a way of retaining political power and excluding the opposition. For instance, under "normal" circumstances, Matthew Kerekou of Benin would not have sat by and watched power snatched from him by a constitutional conference, which he had convened in deference to popular pressures. As well, Ibrahim Babangida in Nigeria would have preferred to massacre the protesters and jail the pro-democracy leaders indefinitely rather than leave office in a hurry. In similar vein, Kamuzu Banda, the self-proclaimed "president-for-life" of Malawi would simply have thrown all opposition forces into "detention without trial." The attitude of the donors and lenders, which coincided with internal demands from popular constituencies, ensured the right to vote, to organize, and to present leaders for public office. It forced elections in the majority of countries and allowed popular and opposition groups to organize openly, canvass for public support, generate new political discourses, and set up strategies to check human rights abuses.

Without doubt, these developments and challenges to the state encouraged some respect for human rights in Africa. Yet, the democratization agenda appears to have provided only cosmetic solutions to the problem of human rights abuses as well as to the hopes for democracy. The rather narrow definition of democracy, especially in procedural terms, has made it easy for African leaders to make concessions to civil society while retaining the institutions and patterns of domination and abuse. Frederick Chiluba in Zambia was forced to impose a state of emergency on the country in 1993, and as his reform policies fail he seems more and more irritated by the numerous opposition parties that have emerged in the country thus far. Several members of the MMD who have shown an interest in the presidency of the country have been victimized, while workers and students have been treated in ways similar to those of Kenneth Kaunda.

It would also appear that African leaders have effectively "adjusted" to the new conditionalities and have designed mechanisms to satisfy the demand of donors for political openness, human rights, and transparency. They have taken some break in *direct* human rights abuses. Of course, some African leaders have learnt nothing from the past and remain hardened to the winds of change. For instance, in April 1990 Mobutu of Zaire announced an end to one-party rule and called on the opposition to form political parties. A few days later, security agents raided the home of Etienne Tshisekedi wa Mulumba, an opposition leader, who was hosting a meeting of activists. They disrupted the meeting, manhandled the participants, used tear gas and bayonets, flogged some and killed three people. Mobutu's government claimed that the gathering was illegal but could not explain why such brutality had to be unleashed on people who were simply holding a meeting at the home of a prominent citizen.[46]

Similar accounts can be found in virtually all African countries. However, most of the repressive policies are now carried out through the manipulation of ethnic, regional, and religious differences and by setting one interest group against the other, dividing the opposition, and creating diversions. This strategy has been perfected in Cameroon, Ghana, Nigeria, and Zaire. It has divided civil society and culminated in the creation of scores of political parties, a condition that ensured victory for Rawlings in Ghana and Moi in Kenya. In Nigeria, the military simply carried out a coup, remilitarized the political terrain, and abolished all democratic institutions through decrees that oust the jurisdiction of the courts. General Abacha followed the remilitarization of politics with the total closure of political spaces and the jailing of pro-democracy leaders and numerous activists. Thus political liberalization is not really changing the political landscape in a drastic and fundamental manner, especially in the area of human rights.

Fortunately for African dictators and unfortunately for Africans, support for liberalization and human rights from the West has been tenuous. Unlike in Eastern Europe, African efforts have been treated with indifference or have received very feeble responses and support. Hence, sanctions on repressive regimes have been light and the conditionalities have not been followed by effective sanctions. In fact, Western governments seem to assume that once a dictator has organized an election, human rights are bound to be guaranteed. This has not been the case in Benin, Kenya, Ghana, and other nations which have used procedural democracy to satisfy Western dictated conditionalities. The military regime of General Sani Abacha, which brazenly terminated democratic processes, received only weak sanctions from the United States, sanctions that have not affected the regime in any meaningful way. Though members of the government were prohibited from visiting the United States, this ban has not been effectively enforced. Even then, this is a very mundane sort of sanction against a regime that showed very little regard for developments in the global system and for human rights. When the Abacha junta hurriedly executed the Nobel peace prize nominee and human rights activist Ken Saro-Wiwa and eight others in November 1995 in what has been generally regarded as a flawed trial, responses from the West were uncoordinated, weak, and opportunistic. Business with the junta continued as usual while a few diplomatic maneuverings went on to pressure the regime to be "reasonable." Rawlings continues to receive support from the World Bank in spite of his manipulation of the transition program in Ghana to civilianize himself in power and retain control of the state. Ghana is more or less a one-party state today as the opposition boycotted the parliamentary elections though it was pronounced fair by international observers. The second open elections in 1996 only confirmed Rawlings' dominant position in Ghanaian politics.

Perhaps, the strongest indicator as to the tenuousness of the current tentative break from unmediated repression and exploitation is that the new democratic agenda in Africa does not include anywhere the dismantling and recomposition of the exploitative, ruthless, repressive, and nonhegemonic state in Africa (see Chapter Six). It must be understood that this is a fundamental prerequisite for democracy, democratization, and the ability to create an environment conducive to human rights. The colonial state, which had visited untold violence and pain on Africans, was not dismantled or restructured at independence. This state, because of its aloof, repressive, and undemocratic character, had alienated the masses of Africa. They saw it as nothing but a weapon of oppression, and its institutions and agencies were to be resisted and sabotaged at every turn. This popular perception of the colonial state became the more prominent during the anticolonial struggles. At independence, this state structure, along with all is ideological and social apparatuses, was handed over to the new elite, which had been groomed under colonialism. The new elite continued to use the state to exploit, intimidate, and repress the people. The people then came to see the new state, manned by local elites, as no different from the colonial state. This accounts for the withdrawal of peasants from the state, the prevalence of the underground economy, scores of peasant and workers' protests, and the frequent reliance on covert modes of resistance and struggle.[47] The postcolonial state simply appropriated the institutions of the colonial state and reproduced the underdevelopment of Africa. Its failure in every respect is attested to by the fact that after political independence, as the World Bank has noted, "Africans are almost as poor today as they were 30 years ago."[48] African leaders also confessed to the complete failure of the African state to promote development when they noted in the 1980 *Lagos Plan of Action* that Africa had almost nothing to show for decades of political independence, especially in the quality of life of Africans.[49] This state, which has so failed to improve the lot of the people and which has had to rely on repression, manipulation, and human rights abuse to retain control of the political terrain, is not being restructured or dismantled as part of the democratization agenda in Africa.[50] Ake has concluded that the current democratization agenda in Africa is simply replacing "self-appointed military or civilian dictators with elected dictators." The type of democracy emanates from such programmed efforts, often designed to satisfy donors and lenders, is "not in the least emancipatory especially in

African conditions because it offers the people rights they cannot exercise, voting that never amounts to choosing, freedom which is patently spurious, and political equality which disguises highly unequal power relations."[51]

It would appear, therefore, that while the ongoing liberalization agenda certainly opens up political spaces for increased political activity, such spaces are in danger of being closed up again because the state structure in charge of this political renewal is exactly the same structure which had closed it up for decades. The custodians of the state have learnt almost nothing and seem to be very unhappy at being unable to repress and intimidate the people with state power because of the new political pluralism. As politicians and ministers in Cameroon, Zambia, and Nigeria have clearly shown, the so-called activists are largely political opportunists, persons who had been excluded from the state and its resources by previous regimes, persons who have very little idea of the meaning of empowerment and democratization and who have simply joined the bandwagon as an opportunity to move closer to the center of power. Such politicians have grounded the government of Frederick Chiluba and turned Zambia into a haven for graft, drug trafficking, and corruption. In Nigeria, the politicians and leading members of the pro-democracy movement who teamed up with the conservative General Abacha to abolish the transition to democracy have demystified the pro-democracy and human rights movement by betraying the popular will.[52] With such state structures and patterns of pedestrian and opportunistic politics left intact, and with organizations in civil society weak, disorganized, poorly funded, and frustrated by cynical and spasmodic responses to their frequent calls for action from the masses, the return to the earlier conditions of human rights abuses might be just around the corner.

Conclusion: The Future of Human Rights in Africa

Thus far, we have tried to present the harsh realities of Africa's underdevelopment. We have contended that human rights must necessarily be violated in the context of dependence and underdevelopment. The condition of underdevelopment in itself constitutes a violation of people's rights. Therefore, under conditions where production and exchange patterns and relationships are under foreign control, and the dominant forces are nonhegemonic and largely incapable of mediating the edges of class contradictions and conflicts, human rights for the poor majority cannot be guaranteed. The new globalization, which is creating a larger global market, will hardly improve the situation. Capital has always been able to do business even under very repressive regimes. As the poor, vulnerable, weak, rural and illiterate get marginalized and further exploited in the emerging global market, desperate regimes, eager to satisfy the demands of the market, are bound to devise more sophisticated ways of surplus extraction and domination. As Julius Nyerere notes: "What freedom has a subsistence farmer? He scratches a bare living from the soil provided the rains do not fail; his children work at his side without schooling, medical care, or even good feeding. Certainly he has the freedom to vote and to speak but these are meaningless."[53]

It is our opinion that the Western conceptions of human rights, which tend to emphasize political and civil rights, are very important, but unfortunately, are too narrow to inform the African situation. In Africa, social, economic, and cultural rights are at least as important as civil and political rights. The rights to education, housing, food, jobs, and health are critical for the enjoyment of the freedoms of movement, speech, organization and the like. An illiterate person is easily intimidated, misinformed, and misled. A hungry person can hardly take advantage of the freedom of movement or of speech. A sick person is of little use to a political organization. A poor person persistently feels inferior and disillusioned because he or she lacks the capacity to be an asset to the immediate family. These realities suggest that the conceptualization of human rights in Africa must be holistic, with particular attention to social and economic rights. The equitable distribution of available wealth, the creation of opportunities, the availability of opportunities to participate fully decision-making cannot be negotiated in the process of development.[54] Indeed, unless the majority of the people are mobilized and the rights of the producers of wealth guaranteed, the tendency will be toward deepening alienation and conflicts. The maintenance of political stability, of course, is important to the process of liquidating underdevelopment. Yet, the guarantee of sociocultural rights and economic subsistence of the majority must be a basic right:

> Within Africa, however, the right to subsistence is now taken for granted (theoretically) whereas rights to physical security and those civil and political freedoms which are necessary for effective political participation are problematic. Often, the position that subsistence rights must take priority over civil/political rights is taken solely for rhetorical purposes to perpetuate the political monopoly of a self-serving elite. Against such an elite, one needs to consider the meaning of civil and political freedoms for the poor and unfree masses.[55]

The commitment of Africa's ruling classes to the reproduction of the inherited unequal alliance with profit- and hegemony-seeking transnational interests and their inability (failure?) to embark on a credible process of structural transformation and self-reliance have deepened underdevelopment internally and peripheralization in the world system. In the new globalization, such conditions of subservience to foreign dictates, aid, technology, information, and loans hardly put them in positions of power to negotiate favorable terms. Rather, they will remain vulnerable, exposed, and marginal. This will in turn make them more desperate, and human rights will suffer setbacks as they seek to make up for the deficiencies in their economies through the brutal exploitation of nonbourgeois forces.[56]

Responding to these deprivations and deformities in African social formations requires a program for political renewal and the total democratization of the political landscape. Yet, this does not appear to be on the agenda either of the new political parties or the opposition movements. Unfortunately, lenders, donors, and pro-democracy forces in Africa, caught in the euphoria of the pseudopolitical openings and the programmed elections organized thus far, fail to see or appreciate the dangers ahead. Africa's dominant classes continue to use the state to accumulate capital, their politics is still normless, their relation to production is still tenuous, politics is still a business, and the masses are nothing but objects of exploitation and manipulation. Under the guise of strengthening the state and economy, these governing classes have initiated

> a highly developed system of terror and repression. Despite poverty and economic crisis, these states finance a large military apparatus...The generalization of terror and repression in these societies is linked to the use of torture, assassination, and other forms of physical violence against opponents, or would be opponents, of the ruling classes.[57]

International declarations, human rights charters, and other well-documented statements on the rights of citizens mean very little to desperate elites who have learned to rely on corruption, repression, and the denial of human rights to reproduce the status quo and maintain their hold on power. To the extent that there is no acceptable "international morality," and to the extent that the Western powers employ double standards and pay lip service to the human rights of others, African leaders will continue to repress their peoples. As well, to the extent that international finance institutions continue with policies that alienate and punish disadvantaged groups, international declarations can at best sensitize Africans to the salience of human rights and provide a global basis for articulating domestic programs for challenging the state.[58]

What would determine the violation or guarantee of human rights, especially in a crisis-ridden and poverty-stricken continent like Africa, would be the extent to which socioeconomic contradictions were resolved through the collective struggles of the people. Claude Ake, for instance, has argued that in view of the existing socioeconomic crisis in Africa, fascism is perhaps inevitable: "all the more dramatic precisely because of the long drawn-out economic stagnation...One thing that would surely be needed in ever increasing quantities in this situation would be repression. As the economic stagnation persisted, the masses would become more wretched and desperate."[59] Ironically, it is exactly in these "desperate" and "repressive" environments that hopes for the guarantee of human rights can be found as class/social fraction and faction challenge each other for hegemony. As contradictions deepen, nonbourgeois forces will transcend the debates about civil, political or socioeconomic rights. The struggle will be one of survival or elimination. Given the domestic and international balance of forces, the struggle can be expected to be in favor of nonbourgeois forces. As Ake has noted,

> Wretchedness and desperation would lead peasants to subversion, workers to induce industrial action, and the lumpen proletariat to robbery and violence. Punitive expeditions would then be sent out to liquidate whole villages, armed robbers would be dealt with by imposing sanctions of exceptional harshness. Striking workers would be chased by police dogs, locked out, starved out, shot at. Any person or group of persons who looked like being a rallying point against the system would be summarily liquidated. All this is already happening. And things are likely to get worse.[60]

We only need to take a look at Somalia, Rwanda, Togo, Burundi, Liberia, Angola, the Sudan, and Nigeria to see the validity of this position.

The future will resemble the present, perhaps in a more gruesome form, if democracy and human rights are pursued outside the context of a structural dismantling of the African state at one level and the strengthening of civil society at the other. A popular national state that reflects the interests and aspirations of the vast majority must replace the current exploitative, aloof, overblown, inefficient, corrupt, and repressive state in Africa. As Boutros Boutros-Ghali has rightly noted, "Reform of the African state is a prerequisite of reform of the African economy."[61] To buttress the survival of the reformed state structure, civil society must be strengthened. It is precisely the weakness and fragmentation of civil society in Africa that has permitted decades of wanton abuse of human rights. The process of empowerment of the people, their communities, organizations, and civil society entails the "transforming of the economic, social, psychological, political and legal circumstances of the currently powerless." It includes the "emergence of group identities (or community), the development of autonomous and coherent popular organizations, and the defence of, and education about, the legal rights of the popular sectors."[62] This process of empowerment, which is the only way to guarantee human rights and democracy in previously brutalized societies, also involves, "access to educational facilities and to the minimum resources needed to sustain households. [Poor] people who must devote all their energies to the bare survival cannot empower themselves. This process further requires that people and their organizations have access to contending opinions and accurate information on the performance of powerholders."[63] It is only through such and other efforts, clearly articulated in the Economic Commission for Africa's *African Charter for Popular Participation in Development and Transformation*,[64] that African peoples can "become important pillars of the democratic system."[65] It is only such a democratic system that can guarantee human rights in Africa. Any current agenda that overlooks or underplays these prescriptions is merely addressing the symptoms of the African predicament.

Endnotes

1. Obafemi Awolowo, *Problems of Africa*, (London: Macmillan, 1977), cited in Olusola Ojo and Johnson Adesida, "Human Rights in Africa Revisited," unpublished paper, University of Ife, Nigeria, n.d., p.1.

2. Femi Falana, quoted in Babatunde Ojudu, "Nigeria: Morning Yet on Human Rights Day," *African Concord* (June 9, 1987), pp. 6–7.

3. Adebayo Adedeji, "Africa: Permanent Underdog?" *International Perspectives* (March–April 1981), p. 17.

4. For a very good discussion, see Issa Shivji, *The Concept of Human Rights in Africa*, (Darkar: CODESRIA, 1989), pp.9–36; Josiah Cobbah, "African Values and the Human Rights Debate: An African Perspective," *Human Rights Quarterly* Vol. 9, (3) (1987); and Yougindra Khushalani, "Human Rights in Asia and Africa," *Human Rights Law Journal* Vol. 4, (4) (1983).

5. See Issa Shivji, *The Concept of Human Rights in Africa* op. cit., p.11. Shivji was summarizing the work of Rhoda Howard, a proponent of this perspective.

6. Ibid. For a discussion see Rhoda Howard, *Human Rights in Commonwealth Africa* (Trenton, NJ: Rowman and Littlefield, 1986).

7. For reviews of the various positions on human rights, see R.H. Green, "Basic Human Rights/Needs: Some Problems of Categorical Translation and Unification." *The Review* 24–27 (1980–1981), and Jack Donnelly, "Recent Trends in UN Human Rights Activity: Description and Polemic," *International Organization* Vol. 35, (4) (Autumn 1981).

8. Rhoda Howard, for instance, has tried to argue against the idea of an "African context" of human rights. This is largely because her work, located in neoliberal ideological foundations, tries to ignore or downplay the specificities of the African reality as well as the implications of intellectual and cultural imperialism. Conceding that responsibility for Africa's present problems is international is diversionary and patronizing. While it is true that civil and political rights are necessary to guarantee

socioeconomic rights, the fact remains that impoverished and marginalized people can hardly articulate their ideas much less, struggle for their rights. Rather than create this dichotomy therefore, it is probably more helpful to merge the two positions, while acknowledging that there is indeed an *African* context of human rights. See Rhoda Howard, "Group Versus Individual Identity in the African Debate on Human Rights," in Abdullahi Ahmed An-Na'im and Francis M. Deng, (eds.), *Human Rights in Africa: Cross Cultural Perspectives*, (Washington, D.C.: The Brookings Institution, 1990), pp.159–183.

9. Claude Ake, "The African Context of Human Rights," in Julius O. Ihonvbere, ed., *The Political Economy of Crisis and Underdevelopment in Africa: Selected Works of Claude Ake*, (Lagos: JAD Publishers, 1990), pp. 86–87. Ake also notes that the Western notion of human rights has evolved in such a way as to make it "relevant to the African experience, although its relevance still remains ambiguous." Ake contends that the Western notion of human rights is rooted in a political economy and theory underscored by possessive individualism; that "it presupposes a society which is atomized and individualistic, society of endemic conflict and anarchy," which is quite different from African society which "puts less emphasis on the individual and more on the collectivity." This might be essentially accurate. However, most African societies, having been incorporated into the orbit of Western capitalism, can no longer lay claim to being essentially "collective" in the precolonial and precapitalist sense.

10. Ibid, p. 88. Ake also notes that this position is not akin to "just a matter of subjectively and arbitrarily selecting an instrumental role for human rights. It is the prevailing objective conditions in Africa which must determine whether human rights are relevant at all and what their relevance might be in the scheme of things."

11. It is this pattern of atomizing the struggle for change that has made the achievements of the more liberal human rights groups rather tenuous and limited. They have found it convenient to restrict their activities to court battles, publications, press releases, prison visits, probono legal activities, and occasionally, peaceful marches. These are important, and many human rights activists have lost their lives or have been jailed. But they are not sufficient. They do not challenge the basis of oppression and human rights abuses; they hardly challenge the power of the state.

12. Africa Watch, *Academic Freedom and Human Rights Abuses in Africa*, (New York: Africa Watch, April 1991).

13. For details, see Julius O. Ihonvbere, "Towards a Political Economy of Human Rights in Africa (With Special Reference to Nigeria), Mimeo University of Port Harcourt, Port Harcourt, Nigeria, January, 1984.

14. See International Labour Office, *First Things First: Meeting the Basic Needs of the People of Nigeria*, (Addis Ababa: JASPA, 1981).

15. Organization of African Unity, *African Charter on Human and Peoples' Rights*, (Geneva: International Commission of Jurists, 1986).

16. Claude Ake, "The African Context of Human Rights," op. cit,. p.84.

17. See Robert Jackson and Carl G. Roseberg, "Why Africa's Weak States Persist: The Empirical and the Juridical in Statehood," *World Politics* Vol. 35, (1) (1983).

18. It will be recalled that respect for human rights was a major foreign policy issue for U.S. President Jimmy Carter. Ronald Reagan interpreted this issue to reflect an antisocialist position with a focus on so-called terrorist organizations. George Bush continued this trend with a war on terrorists and drug traffickers. Yet, the United States was, for a very long time and until the end of the cold war, the greatest supporter of the most repressive and corrupt governments in Africa. Witness its unrepentant support for apartheid South Africa, its support of rebels in Angola and Mozambique, and its support for the governments of Liberia under Doe, Somalia under Bare, Sudan under Nimeiri, Kenya under Moi, and Zaire under Mobutu.

19. See Claude Ake, *Revolutionary Pressures in Africa* (London: Zed Press, 1978) and his *A Political Economy of Africa* (London: Longman, 1982); Neville Brown, "Underdevelopment As a Threat to World Peace," *International Affairs* Vol. 47, (2) (April 1971).

20. John Hatch, *Africa Emergent: Africa's Problems Since Independence*, (Chicago: Henry Regnery, 1974), p. 5.

21. Claude Ake, "The African Context of Human Rights," op. cit., p.88.

22. Ibid.

23. Africa Watch, *Academic Freedom and Human Rights Abuses in Africa*, op. cit., pp.2–3.

24. For a detailed account see Ibid.

25. Lawyers Committee for Human Rights, *Zaire: Repression as Policy-A Human Rights Report*, (New York: Lawyers Committee for Human Rights, 1990), p. 1.

26. See Richard Sandbrook, *The Politics of Africa's Economic Recovery*, (Cambridge: Cambridge University Press, 1993), and Rhoda Howard, "The Dilemma of Human Rights in Sub-Saharan Africa," *International Journal* Vol. XXV, (4) (Autumn 1980).

27. See Hugh M. Arnold, "Africa and the New International Economic Order," *Third World Quarterly* 11, (2) (April 1980), p. 295.

28. Michael Holman, "Africa is Striving for a Fresh Start," *Financial Times* (September 1, 1993).

29. See Claude Ake, *Revolutionary Pressures in Africa*, op. cit.

30. See Steven A. Holmes, "Africa: From The Cold War to Cold Shoulders," *The New York Times* (March 7, 1993); Salim Lone, "Africa: Drifting off the Map of the World's Concerns," *International Herald Tribune* (24 August, 1990); and Julius O. Ihonvbere, "The Dynamics of Change in Eastern Europe and Their Implications for Africa," *Coexistence- A Journal of East West Relations* Vol. 29, (3) (September 1992).

31. See Keith Griffin and Azizur Khan, *Globalization and the Developing World: An Essay on the International Dimensions of Development in the Post-Cold War Era*, (Geneva: UNRISD, 1992).

32. Organization of African Unity, *The Lagos Plan of Action for the Economic Development of Africa, 1980–2000*, (Geneva: Institute for Labor Studies. 1981), p. 1.

33. See World Bank, *Accelerated Development in Sub-Saharan Africa: An Agenda for Action*, (Washington, D.C.: 1981). This document, popularly called "The Berg Report," claims to build on the Lagos Plan of Action. It recommends the dismantling of controls on foreign investment, the collection of user-fees for social services, export promotion (cash crops) to earn foreign exchange, devaluation, and more incentives to private investors.

34. See Adedeji, "Africa: Permanent Underdog?" op. cit., p. 17.

35. The limits of dependent capitalism and dependent development as a strategy of development are clearly discussed in Peter Evans, *Dependent Development: The Alliance of Multinational, State and Local Capital in Brazil* (Princeton, N.J.: Princeton University Press, 1979).

36. Clive Thomas, *The Rise of the Authoritarian State in Peripheral Societies*, (New York: Monthly Review Press, 1984), p. xii

37. Claude Ake, "The African Context of Human Rights," op. cit., p. 88.

38. Olusegun Obasanjo and Felix Mosha, (eds.), *Africa: Rise to Challenge*, (New York: Africa Leadership Forum, 1991), p. 217.

39. Ibid, p. 220.

40. Yoweri Museveni, Statement to the Kampala Forum, Kampala, Uganda,19 May, 1991. Reproduced in Obasanjo and Mosha, (eds.), *Africa: Rise to Challenge*, op. cit., p.266.

41. Interview with Hon. Samuel Miyanda, MMD Member of Parliament for Matero, Lusaka, Zambia, June 1993.

42. Douglas Hurd, cited in "Democracy in Africa: Lighter Continent," *The Economist* (February 22, 1992).

43. Ibid

44. See Russel Geekie, "Kenya: Split Decision," *Africa Report* (March–April, 1993).

45. World Bank, *Sub-Saharan Africa: From Crisis to Sustainable Growth-A Long-Term Perspective Study* (Washington, DC: World Bank, 1989), p.1.

46. For a catalogue of human rights abuses in Zaire, see Lawyers Committee for Human Rights, *Zaire: Repression as Policy-A Human Rights Report*, op. cit.

47. Unfortunately, since the Bank released the 1989 report it has not seriously mobilized resources to support grassroot organizations which are ultimately the only credible forces capable of challenging the current custodians of state power and creating an "enabling environment" for stability, growth, and development.

48. World Bank, *Sub-Saharan Africa*, op. cit., p.1.

49. Organization of African Unity, *Lagos Plan of Action*, op. cit., p.1.

50. Claude Ake, "Is Africa Democratizing?" *The Guardian* (Lagos) (December 12, 1993).

51. Ibid

52. See Julius O. Ihonvbere, "Threats to Democratic Consolidation in Africa: The Zambian Experience," Mimeo, Department of Government, the University of Texas at Austin, April, 1994; Peter da Costa, "Nigeria: The Politics of 'Settlement'," *Africa Report* (November–December, 1993); and "Nigeria: Hope Betrayed," Interview with retired Brigadier-General David Mark, *Newswatch* (April 11, 1994). For publishing this interview, the editors of the magazine were detained by the Nigerian State Security Services (SSS).

53. Julius Nyerere, "Stability and Change in Africa," Address to the University of Toronto, Canada, 1969.

54. Rhoda Howard, "The Full-Belly Thesis: Should Economic Rights Take Priority Over Civil and Political Rights? A Discussion from Sub-Saharan Africa," University of Toronto, Development Studies Program, Working Paper No. A1, April 1983.

55. Ibid., p. 3.

56. Adebayo Adedeji, "Perspectives on Development and Economic Growth in Africa Up to the Year 2000," in OAU, *What Kind of Africa By Year 2000?*, (Addis Ababa: 1979), p. 61.

57. Thomas, *The Rise of the Authoritarian State*, op. cit., p. 89.

58. Renate Pratt, "Human Rights and International Lending: The Advocacy Experience of the Task Force on the Churches and Corporate Responsibility," University of Toronto, Development Studies Program, Working Paper, No. 15. February 1985.

59. Ake, *Revolutionary Pressure*, op. cit., p. 105.

60. Ibid.

61. Boutros Boutros-Ghali, "New Concepts for Development Action in Africa." New York: United Nations Africa Recovery Unit of the Department of Public Information, March 1993.

62. Richard Sandbrook, "Introduction," to R. Sandbrook and Mohamed Halfani, eds., *Empowering People: Building Community, Civil Associations and Legality in Africa* (Toronto: Center for Urban and Community Studies, University of Toronto, 1993), p.2.

63. Ibid, p.3.

64. See Economic Commission for Africa, *African Charter for Popular Participation in Development and Transformation*, (Addis Ababa: ECA, 1990).

65. South Commission, *The Challenge to the South*, (Oxford: Oxford University Press, 1990), p. 81.

Chapter Five

Regionalism and Recovery in Africa: Towards an African Common Market?

The political balkanization of the continent into arbitrary nation–states elicits from Africa the understandable impulse to restructure the fragmented region into a more coherent and stronger economic and political entity. The African sense of oneness and solidarity also sparks off natural sentiments for increased socio–economic co–operation.[1]

No African country, no matter how big it is, can really go it alone in the world we are entering in the 1990s. The economic integration of Africa is part of the solution to the crisis of Africa.[2]

Africa today is in very deep crisis. As the Organization of African Unity (OAU) and the Economic Commission for Africa (ECA) have come to agree, it is a crisis of "unprecedented and unacceptable proportions manifested not only in abysmal declines in economic indicators and trends but more tragically and glaringly in the suffering, hardship and impoverishment of the vast majority of African people."[3] This position is shared by the developed nations, the UN, and the major financial institutions of the world. The World Bank, for instance, takes the position that "the difficulties facing Africa are formidable. The margin for maneuver is indeed slim..."[4] In its *World Development Report 1995*, the World Bank noted that in the area of international trade, sub–Saharan Africa was "Trailing the other regions" of the developing world and did not expand its exports, while its terms of trade have continued to fall.[5] Yet, Africa has not been short of responses to its numerous and seemingly unending crisis: import substitution, nationalization, indigenization, African socialism, Nyayoism, humanism, regionalism, and more recently, structural adjustment and total integration into the emerging global economy. Moreover, these responses have been incorporated into several major declarations and charters, such as *Cultural Charter for Africa* (1976), *African Charter of Human and Peoples' Rights* (1981), *The Lagos Plan of Action and the Final Act of Lagos* (1981), *Africa's Priority Programme for Economic Recovery 1986–1990* (1986), *African Alternative Framework to Structural Adjustment Programmes for Economic Recovery and Transformation (AAF–SAP)* (1989), and *The African Charter for Popular Participation in Development and Transformation* (1990).

These documents, which have come from the OAU and the ECA, have been adopted by virtually all African governments but never implemented in any serious and consistent manner. If anything, pressures from ideological differences, nationalistic interests, the inability to generate sufficient political will, corruption, regime turnover, and political instability have militated against the ability to implement the various charters and cooperation agreements. As well, pressures from debt, debt-servicing, drought and refugee problems, and increasing vulnerability to external pressures, manipulation, penetration, domination, and exploitation have worked against national and regional attempts at growth and development. Thus, in spite of foreign aid, the so–called UN development decades, ideological experimentations, and so on, Africa has simply moved from crisis to crisis since the 1960s. Furthermore, as the APPER has suggested, these internal contradictions constitute only a portion of the African reality.[6] It draws attention to the failure of African leaders and governments to implement "most of the measures recommended in the LPA" which would have "minimized" the "ravaging effects of the current world recession and drought on African economies."[7]

Today, the African condition has elicited all sorts of responses as it continues to slide along the path of decay and dislocation. All the programs of the past three decades have failed woefully in improving the conditions of living. As Olusegun Obasanjo, Nigeria's former head of state, pointed out during the OAU Summit in Abuja, Nigeria, "Africa has more civil wars than any other continent, the largest number of refugees and the highest incidence of famine occasioned by a diversion of energy and resources into protracted wars."[8] Salim A. Salim, the secretary–general of the OAU, noted specifically, the region has eleven active conflicts which have thrown up over five million refugees and twelve million displaced persons. The secretary–general was definitive on the point that "unless conditions of normalcy, conditions of peace, stability and security are established, Africa's meager resources will continue to be diverted to situations of conflicts instead of being used for economic development."[9] General Ibrahim Babangida, as chairman of ECOWAS and the OAU and president of Nigeria, in a rather sober address to the forty-sixth Session of the UN General Assembly in October 1992, reached the conclusion that "the overall performance of the African economy since 1986 has been dismal." He attributed the region's unprecedented and deepening crisis "mainly to the debt burden, the collapse of commodity prices, the low levels of resource flows from the developed countries, as well as natural calamities."[10] Earlier in a major foreign policy address, Babangida had noted that "the international system continues to present difficulties for Africa," that "the economies of many of the countries...have deteriorated further with the heavy debt burden pulling them further into stagnation" and that "the picture that is evolving is one of rapid disengagement from Africa."[11]

To be sure, Babangida belonged to the group of African leaders who frequently invoked external reasons to justify and rationalize the widespread *internal* roots of the African predicament: gross mismanagement, criminal corruption, misplaced priorities, repression and large–scale human rights abuses, the general suffocation of civil society; the reproduction of inherited conditions of poverty, dependence, inequalities, foreign domination and subservience to foreign manipulation; and the use of the state by the elites for accumulation rather than legitimation purposes. It is precisely this tendency to seek mostly external scapegoats and to be silent on the role of internal relations of power, politics, production, and exchange that has made it virtually impossible to generate the required political will to mobilize the masses, make the required concessions and sacrifices for integration, and confront in a fundamental way the limitations and contradictions which continue to polarize the continent and make it impossible to implement usually well–worded declarations and charters. There is, however, a growing consensus that only a more serious approach to regionalism can pull the region out of its current crisis and marginalization in the emerging global order. This growing consensus does not ignore or downplay the role of external factors in the African crisis. On the contrary, it contends that the marginalization of Africa "in world affairs is primarily a result of its proliferating internal conflicts and the diminishing capacity to manage its own affairs."[12] These weaknesses are, of course, precipitates of the failure to radically transform the nature of the African economic and political landscape since the 1960s.

With the ongoing changes in the global system–the redirection of interest and investment to Eastern Europe, the drastic decline in foreign aid, the dismemberment of the Soviet Union as a nation, the collapse of communist and socialist regimes the world over, the unification of Germany, the release of Nelson Mandela and the formal dismantling of apartheid, the emergence of the United States as the sole superpower in the world, the enlargement of the European Union, the creation of the North American Free Trade Area (NAFTA) as well as major economic developments in the Pacific Rim—Africa cannot continue to hide under the usual traditional excuses of "foreign domination," "foreign exploitation," declining terms of trade, declining foreign support and so on. Essentially, these are not new complaints.

There is equally an increasing realization among Africans and their leaders that unless serious socioeconomic and political reforms and transformations take place, the region's current marginal location and role in the global division of labor and power will be consolidated, investors are unlikely to return, foreign aid will remain low, and capital flight will likely increase. As the ECA notes in the AAF–SAP, "the emerging trends in the patterns of world production and trade" make it important for Africa "to break the apron–strings of structural and relational dependence on producing a limited number of increasingly cheap primary commodities for export."[13]

The growing disinterest in Africa, clearly evidenced in Western responses to the crisis in Somalia, Ethiopia, Liberia, and the Sudan, as compared to responses to the crisis in Kuwait, Yugoslavia, and the republics of the former Soviet Union, is given expression in the view of one Victor Chesnault that "Economically speaking, if the entire black Africa, with the exception of South Africa, were to disappear in a flood, the global cataclysm will be approximately nonexistent."[14] Such judgements, while largely ill–informed, demonstrate clearly the growing disinterest and disrespect for Africa in the emerging global order.[15] As Eboe Hutchful rightly notes, the current conditions of declining support, further marginalization and deepening crisis means that "Africa, already at the bottom of the international totem pole, is being pushed yet further down."[16] The secretary–general of the OAU has also lamented on the "fundamental difference in the approach of the West Europeans, Americans and the Japanese to the East European reconstruction" as compared to Africa. He notes that while Europe and America "quickly moved to set up" the necessary institutions "to channel funds to the countries of Eastern Europe," they have repeatedly refused to countenance requests for a 'Marshall Plan' for Africa."[17] These positions support the claims that global interest in Africa is, at the very best, stagnant.

It is in response to the debilitating conditions of the region, its further marginalization in the international division of labor and power, the closure of credit lines and opportunities for external support, and the increasing protectionism in the changing global economy and the emergence of regional trading blocs in Europe and North America among other pressures, that compelled African heads of state and government to meet in Abuja, Nigeria, following several other meetings, to adopt The African Economic Community Treaty on 3 June 1991.

This new move has elicited conflicting responses from within and outside the region. On the one hand are those who hail the initiative as clear demonstration of Africa's resolve to reverse its marginalization and confront existing conditions of dependence, domination, and impoverishment. The new initiative is seen as a collective response to decades of domination and subservience to foreign interests and as a critical move to promote the interests of Africa in the evolving global order. On the other hand, there are those who contend that the Abuja initiative is but one more example of diversion, political posturing, waste of scarce resources, and an opportunity for political leaders to sign documents which, as usual, they have no intention of implementing. This latter position points at the existence of scores of integration and cooperation schemes in the region, mostly duplicating one another, in competition with each other for foreign aid and technical assistance, and in most cases, moribund, inefficient, and irrelevant to the objective conditions of the continent. It is further argued that experimentation with such mostly functionalist, at best hybrid, regionalist schemes since the 1960s, has not improved political and social relations among African states, reversed the unidirectional nature of trade with former colonizers, improved the level of trade among African states, or led to development in any form.[18] Finally, it is contended that in view of the pressing problems of Africa and the rapidity with which the world is changing and trade blocs are being formed, for African leaders to decide in 1994 to set up an economic community in thirty–four years is clear evidence of opportunism and a lack of commitment to radical change.[19] That the ECA, in spite of the Lagos Plan of Action, which had aimed at creating a common market in Africa by A.D. 2000, declared the 1980s as "Africa's lost decade" shows the failure of existing integration schemes.[20] The questions then are: can neocolonial, dependent, and underdeveloped economies successfully integrate without reversing existing conditions? What are the specific and broad obstacles *within* African economies which militate against successful and productive integration? Given Africa's historical experience and the contradictions of underdevelopment and marginalization in the global system, can a common market be built as anticipated by the OAU? What external constraints, arising from the balance of forces in the global system make it unrealistic for Africa to think of a common market by A.D. 2025? Given the general failure of African states to make good on previous declarations and given the weaknesses of generally less ambitious efforts in the past, is there any reason to expect any achievements from the current initiative? Finally, given the generally sorry state of the African economy today, plagued with debt, debt–servicing, widespread corruption, political cynicism, and withdrawal, as well as general economic, social, and political decay and instability, can a common market be built and expected to survive in

Africa? These are very critical questions. Our focus in this chapter will be on the recent initiative. Our evaluation of the initiative will provide some answers to the questions above.

The State of Regionalism in Africa

We have considered the origins, depth, and implications of the African crisis elsewhere (see Chapter One).[21] Suffice, it to note that on all indicators of development, the African region has experienced precipitous declines in the last decade or so. As Omar Ali Juma, Honourable Chief Minister of Zanzibar noted at the conference on "Alternative Development Strategies" organized by the Institute for African Alternatives (IFAA) in 1989,

> Thirty years of independence had not benefited the peoples of Africa...Leaders had become pawns of extra–continental powers, economies remained mere appendages of the metropole and cultural values and beliefs had been discarded.

> Although Africa had 7.5% of the world's population, it accounted for only 1.2% of global GNP, 1.6% of the world's export earnings, and only 1.1% of the total world public expenditure on health...,Thirty years of independence had also brought dictatorships and tyrannical regimes in some countries. Basic human rights recognized by all civilized mankind were denied to millions.[22]

The Africa Leadership Forum has provided a new dimension for studying and analyzing the Africa crisis by linking it to national and regional security. In its main document it outlines this perspective in this way:

> ...security reaches beyond traditional maintenance of military strength to ward off 'aggression' against the state or the expansion of internal security to ensure domestic order. The security of a nation traverses through the complex web of political, economic and social structures and link the whole range of inter–state relations...Africa's socio–economic conditions, as a barometer of security, reveals a serious security situation for the continent as a whole. In the first place, the economy of the continent has been retrogressing for twelve years in succession. Per capita consumption has continued to rapidly decline; basic social services and infrastructures such as health, education, housing and transport have increasingly deteriorated; the overall food self–sufficiency ratio for the continent is a low 80 per cent; an estimated 13 million people in the formal wage sector are unemployed and another 95 million are underemployed. The population explosion in the region and particularly in the urban sectors is unprecedented in human history. These conditions present a serious and a frightening picture for the future of Africa's security.[23]

The Africa Leadership Form was convinced that only collective self–reliance and cooperation at all levels could move Africa out of the predicaments it had outlined.

Unfortunately, regional cooperation or integration as a response to the African crisis has not helped much. As Boutros Boutros–Ghali noted at the first meeting of the high level advisory panel on African development in Geneva in 1993, "African countries will have to join forces if they are to compete effectively in world markets. The existing subregional groupings have failed as an instrument of development...nor have they been able to avert conflicts."[24] As mentioned earlier, most of the functionalist schemes exist in name, remaining just an affair of ministers, some top bureaucrats and political leaders.

Over the decades, African leaders have been unable to use integration as a scheme to fight dependence, underdevelopment, foreign domination, and inequalities in the region's relations with the outside world. In fact, writing on the situation in West Africa, Oliver S. Knowles has observed that there "has been a distinct lack of enthusiasm for implementing the provisions of the treaty."[25] Furthermore—and this is even more serious—African leaders have been unable to sell regional integration schemes to their peoples. The schools hardly study them, the press hardly cover them, and the masses of the people hardly understand what they are intended to achieve. In fact, integration, as evidenced in the case of ECOWAS, has tended to deepen contradictions and conflicts within and between nations rather than serve as a tool for mobilization for self–reliance and growth. Even the World Bank admits that in sub–Saharan Africa, "Progress towards market integration has been disappointing, with the share of intraregional trade in total trade still at the level it was 20 or more years ago. This is due partly to the uneven distribution of benefits and costs."[26]

Though the World Bank, the ECA, and the OAU have now come to endorse regionalism as the real viable continental response to its deepening crisis, the reality of the crisis highlighted earlier shows that we need to be cautious as to the sort of reforms and restructurings required to make integration feasible. In the Communaute Economique de l'Afrique de l'Ouest (CEAO), the Communaute Economique des pays des Grands Lacs (CEPGAL), the Economic Community of West African States (ECOWAS), the Preferential Trade Area for Eastern and Southern Africa (PTA), the Southern African Development Community (SADC) (formerly Southern African Development Coordination Conference (SADCC)), the Union of the Arab Maghreb (UAM), and the Union Douaniere et Economique de l'Africa Centrale (UDEAC) as well as in other smaller groupings in Africa, the story has been the same: dependence on foreign aid, poor political support, nonadherence to their respective charters and protocols, poor financial contributions, over–bureaucratization, inefficiency and corruption, and the absence of a radical program to use integration to reverse conditions of subservience, domination, dependence, and exploitation. The World Bank adds other reasons why integrations has failed in Africa: "...top heavy structures, politicized appointments, the reluctance to give power to regional executives, and the failure of nearly all member countries to give priority to regional issues have reduced the effectiveness of...regional institutions. Many governments—even the better endowed—have failed to meet the financial obligations of membership..."[27] As Victor Omuabor has argued in the case of ECOWAS, the community means "very little really, beyond its widely orchestrated abbreviation, ECOWAS...to the average Nigerian, Ghanaian, Togolese or Senegalese."[28] In addition, Omuabor argues that

> Sixteen years since its inception, citizens of member–countries of the body are yet to enjoy such privileges as free movement within ECOWAS states. At the borders of ECOWAS countries, citizens are still subjected to tedious immigration formalities. The existence of ECOWAS has not necessarily boosted trade within the West African sub–region. Tariffs are still slammed by member countries on most imports from fellow member countries. Many ECOWAS states still owe their primary loyalty to their colonial masters and hold sub–regional interest as secondary. Indeed, member states have never spoken with one voice on any issue affecting the sub–region.[29]

It is on record that the ECOWAS is a deeply divided organization, particularly since the Liberian crisis.[30] In the view of the World Bank, ECOWAS "has made little progress toward economic integration," largely because

> tariff and non–tariff barriers have not been reduced, trade among its partners is at the level of the early 1970s–about 3 percent of the group's international trade. The pattern of trade has not changed. Cote d'Ivoire and Nigeria still dominate the export of manufactures. On labour mobility there has been a setback rather than progress; in 1981 and 1983 Nigeria expelled more than 1 million Ghanaian guest workers. There is no movement of capital within the region because capital markets remained underdeveloped. Furthermore, ECOWAS' rule of product origin has become a source of serious disagreement.[31]

In 1993, ECOWAS revised its 16–year–old treaty "aiming at accelerated economic integration and a common currency by the year 2000."[32] This was merely a restatement of a situation already acknowledged at the December 1992 summit that "little ground had been gained in ensuring the free movement of goods and people."[33] In July 1992, Abass Bundu, the ECOWAS executive secretary, had complained that integration in the subregion had been mediated by "non–implementation at national and community acts and decisions."[34] At the July 1993 summit of the organization, Bundu had cause to lament again that "the pace of integration had been painfully slow with only insubstantial progress made towards the goal of a free trade area. There had been little action…on the one–year minimum agenda, adopted at…the Dakar summit, to lift some non–tariff barriers on intra–Community trade, simplify customs and transit formalities, and eliminate some checkpoints on international roads."[35] Bundu also stressed that smuggling has remained a major obstacle to successful integration in the subregion.

The existence of the CEAO, which voluntarily dissolved itself only recently, continued to divide the subregion between anglophone and francophone interests as both competed for the loyalty and dues of member states and competed for foreign assistance. As well, though the ECOWAS has set up its regional bank, ECOBANK, and encouraged the creation of a West African Chambers of Commerce, the Federation of West African Manufacturers Association, a regional insurance scheme, and since January 1990, has succeeded in getting unprocessed goods and handicrafts traded duty–free in the subregion, it has yet to address the critical issues of low intraregional trade, political conflicts, foreign domination, the duplication of foreign investments, competitive as against complementary exports, and general disunity. Ibrahim Babangida, as Chairman of ECOWAS, was addressing himself to this issue at the 14th Summit of the Community in Abuja, Nigeria in July 1991 when he noted that "only a coherent and revitalized economic grouping can help carry the sixteen member–states through the last decade of this century or beyond. This can be achieved if member states rededicate themselves to the ideals of the founding fathers of ECOWAS as a vehicle for the political and economic integration of West Africa."[36] Yet, ECOWAS is regarded as one of the few strong and potentially more viable integration schemes in Africa.

Though the SADC has tried to reconstitute itself into a more integrated subregion rather than the "loose association" it had been, the ten–member organization is still quite weak.[37] The hopes of building a "comprehensive and binding" integration continues to be mediated by contradictions arising from conflicts, debt, debt–servicing, drought, and declining foreign support as well as poor intraregional trade.[38] The new organization, which enjoins its members to put regional interests above national interests, is based on free–trade arrangements. The SADC has refused to merge with the Preferential Trade Area (PTA) because it wishes to maintain the "distinct objectives and mandates" of both organizations.[39] Yet, eight of SADC's ten members are members of the Preferential Trade Area for Eastern and Southern Africa! The PTA is made up of fifteen countries, with the primary objective of promoting trade in the area, reducing or eliminating tariffs, especially nontariff barriers, and giving preferential treatment to goods which are for import and export, with local firms providing at least 40 percent of the components used in production, and with at least 51 percent of the enterprise owned locally. It, like the other organizations, has had problems with determining the rules of origin, reducing tariffs, and effectively applying the 51 percent ownership requirement. The less–developed members of the PTA have also expressed reservations about possible gains by the larger members like Zimbabwe.

Finally, in spite of the proliferation of integration and cooperation schemes in the continent, trade, which is the main purpose of integration, among African states has remained very low if not stagnant or on the decline in some cases:

> One of the clearest reflections of Africa's economic weakness is the small size of most domestic markets and the low volume of trade among them. The division of Africa into some 50 states, almost half of them with less than 5 million people, means that the continent's economy is fragmented. This has intensified Africa's dependence on external markets and suppliers, with foreign trade equivalent to more than half of the continent's total gross domestic product (Latin America's foreign trade is just a quarter of its GDP).[40]

About 85 percent of Africa's total exports "are marketed in the industrialized countries of the North (compared to 75 percent for Latin America and 68 percent for South and East Asia). A very small fraction of officially recorded African exports, ranging between 3 and 6 percent, goes to other African countries."[41] This is indeed a very poor showing, for all the rhetoric about continental unity, all the declarations and charters, and all the cooperation schemes that dot the continent. In 1988 intra–community trade in ECOWAS was a mere 4.9 percent. In the CEAO, it was 10.5 percent; for UDEAC, it was 3.6 percent; and in CEPGAL, it was only 0.7 percent. In the UDEAC for example, "trade within the group has declined, while trade with nonmembers has increased...the main African trading partner of Congo (a UDEAC member) is Zaire (a nonmember). Almost half of the UDEAC's African trade is with ECOWAS, compared with less than 45 percent within the group."[42] Ironically, it is estimated that about $5 billion worth of goods imported by African states from the outside could easily be supplied by other nations producing or importing similar products.

Beyond these hard facts and contradictions, and beyond inherited structural distortions and disarticulations are the numerous informal and nontariff barriers to integration in Africa. Corruption, crime, the noncompliance of border agents with official rules and regulations, and the total disregard for community–ratified protocols, especially on the movement of production factors, have mediated the success of cooperation and integration schemes across Africa. The bridge linking Liberia and Sierra Leone in the Mano River Union is hardly used because of restrictions and the conduct of border officials on both sides. The flow of refugees all over the region has made travel a very dangerous undertaking. Nigerian immigration, security, and customs officials cannot be relied upon to respect valid travel papers because of corruption. There is hardly any communication between state capitals and the border offices, and if we add to these "cumbersome and antiquated customs procedures, poor operational coordination between modes of transportation—especially at the interface between ports and railways—and weak harmonization of regulations on transit carriers," we can understand why trade is low, uncertain, and hazardous.[43] In what ways will the proposed African Economic Community reverse this debilitating trend?

The African Economic Community Treaty: An Evaluation

The signing of the treaty establishing the African Economic Community (AEC) at the Twenty–seventh Summit of the OAU in Abuja, Nigeria, on 3 June, 1991, has been described as marking "a major milestone in the continent's quest for regional economic integration."[44] Attended by thirty–five heads of state and government, it was the largest such attendance since the founding of the OAU in 1963. This unprecedented attendance, reflected in some way, the renewed commitment of African leaders to finding a viable solution to the region's deepening crisis in the face of further marginalization in "world affairs, both geo–politically and economically."[45] As the ECA has argued, integration is the only viable option for recovery in Africa, given the rapidly changing nature of the global economy. Hence, "Africa urgently needs to integrate its economies. The go–it–alone approach that has characterized Africa's development efforts since independence has proved a total failure."[46]

The Treaty, which contains 106 articles, outlined a timetable "for the phased removal of barriers to intra–African trade, the strengthening of the existing regional economic groupings, and other steps towards African economic cooperation" which are expected to lead ultimately to the formation of an "Africa–wide monetary union and economic community by the year 2025."[47] Article 3 of the AEC treaty affirmed the adherence of the contracting parties to

    a) equality and interdependence of member states;
    b) solidarity and collective self–reliance;
    c) interstate cooperation, harmonization of policies and integration programmes;
    d) promotion of harmonious development of economic activities among member states;
    e) observance of the legal system of the Community;
    f) peaceful settlement of disputes among member states, active cooperation between neighboring countries and promotion of a peaceful environment as a pre–requisite for economic development;
    g) recognition, promotion and protection of human and peoples' rights in accordance with the provisions of the African Charter on Human and Peoples' Rights; and
    h) accountability, economic justice, and popular participation in development.

In Article 4, the treaty spells out the four objectives of the AEC to be:

    a) the promotion of economic, social, and cultural development and the integration of African economies in order to increase self–reliance and promote indigenous and self–sustained development;
    b) the establishment on a continental scale, a framework for the development, mobilization, and utilization of the human and material resources of Africa;
    c) the promotion of co–operation in all fields of human endeavor in order to raise the standard of living of African peoples, and maintain and enhance economic stability, foster close and peaceful relations among member states, and contribute to the progress, development, and the economic integration of the continent; and
    d) the co–ordination and harmonization of policies among existing and future economic communities.

To achieve these objectives, the AEC treaty hopes to, through stages, strengthen "existing regional economic communities" and establish "other communities where they do not exist;" conclude agreements on harmonization and coordination of "policies among existing and future sub–regional and regional economic communities;" promote and strengthen "joint investment programmes in the production and trade of major products and inputs;" and liberalize trade through the "abolition, among member states, of Customs Duties levied on imports and exports and the abolition...of non–tariff barriers in order to establish free trade." The treaty also hopes to harmonize "national policies in order to promote community activities, particularly...in agriculture, industry, transport and communications, energy, natural resources, trade, money and finance, human resources, education, culture, science and technology;" adopt a common trade policy toward third states; establish and maintain "a common external tariff;" establish a common market; gradually remove "obstacles to the free movement of persons, goods, services and capital and the right of residence and establishment;" and establish a Community Solidarity, Development and Compensation Fund. Finally, it is the hope of African leaders that the envisaged community will grant special treatment to least–developed members and adopt special measures to favor land–locked, semi–land–locked and island countries; harmonize and rationalize "the activities of existing African multi–national institutions;" encourage the flow of information, trade, contacts among trading organizations, export promotion; and harmonize and coordinate environmental protection policies. The treaty calls on members to "refrain from any unilateral action" and stipulates that members who fail to "honour its general undertakings under the Treaty or fail to abide by the decisions or regulations of the Community may be subject to sanctions." It then lists six stages of implementation which are expected to "unfold over a period of 34 years," as outlined below.[48]

Stage 1
Strengthening regional economic communities and establishing new ones. 5 years
Stage 2
Stabilizing tariffs, customs duties and other barriers to intracommunity trade; strengthening sectoral integration; coordinating and harmonizing activities of the regional organizations. 8 years

Stage 3
Setting up free trade areas within each regional community. 10 years.

Stage 4
Establishing an Africa–wide customs union, with common external tariff, by harmonizing regional tariff and nontariff systems. 2 years.

Stage 5
Establishing an African Common Market through the adoption of common policies in agriculture, industry, transport; the harmonization of monetary, financial and fiscal policies; and the application of the principle of the free movement of people and right of residence. 4 years

Stage 6
Finalizing the African Economic Community through the consolidation of the common market structure; the establishment of an African Monetary Union, African Central Bank and single African currency; and creation of a pan–African Parliament, elected by continental universal suffrage. Implementation of the final stage for the setting up of the structure of African multinational enterprises. 5 years.[49]

It is clear that African leaders have come to terms with the reality of backwardness and marginalization in the international division of labor. They have also come to better appreciate the implications of noncompetitiveness of the African economy, as well as the political dimensions of Africa's backwardness. As Adebayo Adedeji notes, "there is a realization on the part of each government that this is something that must not be allowed to fail. If it fails, the crisis in Africa will deepen."[50] The real question, therefore, is whether African governments and leaders are prepared for the very challenging tasks and costs of setting up an economic community.

This is not the first time that African leaders are setting up a regionwide organization. Africa has more regional organizations than any other subregion in the world. At the end of 1990, there were some 200 regional organizations dedicated to the cause of integration and cooperation in Africa. Yet, the region has reaped the least benefits from integration and/or cooperation in the last three decades. Right from the establishment of the OAU in 1963, African leaders showed that they were incapable of setting up a strong, viable, financially stable, militant and progressive organization capable of challenging the internal and external forces and interests which militate against Africa's stability and development. The OAU has become more of a spectator in the struggle against the orthodox stabilization and adjustment programs of the IMF and the World Bank. The ECA has come to play the leading role in this struggle against orthodox structural adjustment and in organizing workshops, conferences and research on the depth, dimensions, and implications of Africa's crisis.

When in 1980 the OAU adopted the Lagos Plan of Action, it could not follow up on the Protocols and moved to abandon the nationalistic, even if defensively radical Plan by adopting the more conservative African Priority Programme for Economic Recovery (APPER) in 1986, which incorporated ideas from the World Bank's "Berg Report." Such demonstration of lack of commitment and the frequent rush to draft new treaties and declarations have led to poor policy coordination, waste, confusion, and dissipation of energy on irrelevant programs. It is interesting to note that African ministers, meeting in Addis Ababa under the auspices of the ECA in May 1991 argued that "Africa does not lack strategies and policy frameworks, and therefore should resist the temptation to draft new ones. What Africa needs to do is implement the existing plans and translate them into operational programmes."[51]

The AEC treaty itself shows very clearly the unseriousness of African leaders. For a region which houses the largest number of cooperation and integration schemes in the world, which has had experience with integration at all levels, it is ridiculous that it has mapped out thirty–four years to achieve an economic community. This is in spite of the rapid changes taking place all over the world, the emergence of trade blocs even in the developed regions of the world, and the rather desperate conditions of African economies. While we recognize the need to be gradual, the reality of the African condition dictates an urgent and serious response to its deepening crisis and impoverishment. The world is not going to wait for Africa to take its time in a rapidly changing and increasingly complex global system. Africa is not Europe, and the OAU has no business aping the European Community is addressing its peculiar conditions of backwardness, dependence, domination, vulnerability, poverty, and underdevelopment. Given that none of the current leaders will likely be in office by A.D. 2025, the current decision to finalize arrangements for a regional community in thirty–four years appears to be an attempt to buy time and give the impression that something was being done as a response to the crisis.

Though the AEC treaty talks about "accountability," "economic justice," "popular participation," "protection of human rights in accordance with the provisions of the African Charter on Human and Peoples' Rights," and raising the "standard of living of African peoples," there is no evidence in the vast majority of African countries that the leaders who ratified the treaty take these declarations seriously. The suffocation of civil society continues; students, labor leaders, intellectuals and their organizations are still harassed. In Nigeria, several students, pro–democracy and human rights activists, and social critics are still languishing in detention for daring to challenge the corrupt and repressive practices of the military junta.[52] The situation in Zaire and Kenya is no different. Further, many African leaders are still playing games with opposition parties and pro–democracy movements in the hope of dividing the opposition and remaining in power. No African country has shown any respect for the African Charter of Human and Peoples' Rights since it was drawn up in 1981. At the middle of 1991, Cote d'Ivoire, Djibouti, Ethiopia, Kenya, Lesotho, Madagascar, Mauritius, Namibia, The Seychelles, and Swaziland had not ratified the Charter.[53] With the increasing delegitimization of the state, declining resources, and direct challenges to the custodians of state power in Africa, there is no reason to expect them to take their adoption of provisions, which address issues of human rights and social justice, seriously. Given the horrible record of the majority of African leaders, no one really takes them seriously on issues of popular participation, accountability, and economic justice. These are leaders who have established legendary reputations for corruption and abuse of power and office, who have looted their treasuries dry, and who have piled up huge foreign debts that they are unable to service. These are leaders who have, through misplaced priorities, mismanagement, and a lack of vision precipitated gross inequalities, the repression of minorities, the neglect of the rural majority, women, and the vulnerable, and who have put in place policies which deepen and consolidate inequalities and exploitation in their respective nations. Finally, these are leaders who do not believe in accountability, while their governments are dominated by their concubines, relatives, friends, clansmen, and sycophants who sing their praises on a regular basis. Merely including these nice–sounding intentions in the treaty is no evidence of serious commitment to the enactment of policies to transform the nature of African political economies. Since 1991 when the treaty was ratified, no African nation has made significant strides in the direction of economic justice, popular participation, and accountability.

As well, though the AEC treaty talks of "self–reliance," "cultural development," "environmental protection," "economic stability," "mobilization," and "development," the situation in the majority of African countries leaves much to be desired as to the commitment of the respective governments in these areas. Self–reliance dictates the initiation, adoption, and implementation of policies and programs that will promote growth, development, and accumulation, reduce dependence, and challenge foreign domination and exploitation. African regimes are generally not moving in these directions. If anything, economic policies adopted in the last decade have tended to deepen the region's dependence and vulnerability to external penetration and manipulation. In a country like Nigeria, all the economic gains of the 1960s and '70s, through the nationalistic economic policies have been eliminated for an open door policy, which has not increased the inflow of foreign investors and has succeeded in marginalizing indigenous producers.[54] Self–reliance is not a program that can be implemented in the context of an open economy, privatization, and commercialization of parastatals in a way that enables outsiders to buy up the commanding heights of the economy and fully integrate the distorted and weak African economy into an unequal and exploitative global economy. The truth is that self–reliance presupposes the replacement of patterns and structures of vulnerability and dependence with new modes and relations of production and exchange that are informed by increased productivity, competition, and a high degree of autonomy in the formulation and implementation of policies. No African nation can be said to be in the process of building self–reliance at the moment.

The talk about "cultural development" is equally suspect. OAU members seem to conveniently forget that in July 1976 they adopted a "Cultural Charter for Africa" in Port Louis, Mauritius where they pledged to "liberate African peoples from socio–cultural conditions which impede their development in order to recreate and maintain the sense and will for progress, the sense and will for development."[55] What has happened since 1976 is there for all to see. Countries like Nigeria, Benin Republic, Congo, Guinea, and Guinea Bissau have become dumping grounds for dangerous toxic wastes from the West. Yet, the same leaders who have been unable to come up with any credible environmental policies have adopted a treaty which calls for "environmental protection." The truth is that corruption, inefficiency, ignorance, poverty, and poor leadership have made it impossible for the vast majority of African states to develop credible environmental policies since political independence. In 1988, over 10,000 tons of dangerous toxic wastes, imported from Italy by a Nigerian company, was dumped in Koko village. The off–loading was approved by government agents and security forces and no Nigerian was ever arrested or punished for colluding with some Italians to import the waste.[56]

It is widely known that one of the major problems of integration in Africa is the proliferation of integration schemes. As mentioned earlier, they not only task the loyalties and resources of the poverty–stricken nations; integrated nations also compete for foreign resources and impose trade restrictions on one another. As the World Bank has noted, "proliferation and duplication of functions give rise, at the regional level, to conflicts over mandates and to divided loyalty among governments. At the government level, they impose heavy financial and administrative burdens. Even countries such as Nigeria and Cote d'Ivoire are finding it increasingly difficult to meet their financial obligations...Proliferation also creates an unmanageable problem of coordination."[57] The competition between ECOWAS and CEAO before the latter was dissolved is typical in this regard. Francophone leaders who do not attend ECOWAS meetings or pay their dues regularly, attended CEAO meetings dutifully and paid their dues regularly. Yet, the OAU, in its 1991 treaty, plans to strengthen existing schemes, create new ones, and in tune with the old discredited trickle–down theory, build a regionwide community through existing organizations. The only way to demonstrate a new dawn and a seriousness of purpose is to dismantle the existing powerful organizations and mobilize total support and resources to the new initiative. There is a clear contradiction in talking about Pan Africanism, unity, and regional growth and development on the one hand, while strengthening divisive organizations and tendencies on the other. Though the OAU talks of a new agenda which will

> enhance the long–term viability of our economies;...free the imagination and enterprise of all segments of our people on the urgent task of self–development; to emplace a framework for rational incentives; to stress human resources development; to eliminate the distortions in our economies and promote our competitiveness; to employ prudent state–craft anchored on social justice and the notion that the state should be a facilitator of people's efforts,[58]

the required zeal, determination, sacrifices, and restructurings that will make these possible are evidently not in place and certainly not contained in the AEC treaty. The World Bank is quite definite on what should be the realistic path for Africa as far as existing regional organizations are concerned: "As an urgent first step regional organizations need to be rationalized. They should be reformed and consolidated into lean and efficient institutions with a clear mandate and capacity for making decisions. These institutions could then spearhead the creation of a physical, technical, and legal infrastructure that would support regional exchanges in goods, services, labor, and capital."[59]

Without doubt, the hope for a Pan–African Parliament and the "election of members by continental universal suffrage" is welcome and reflects some concessions to the ongoing struggles for democracy.

Virtually all African leaders have been unable to open up "political processes to accommodate freedom of opinions, tolerate differences, accept consensus on issues as well as ensure the effective participation of the people and their organizations and associations."[60] Is it possible for repressive, undemocratic, desperate political and state structures at the national levels to create and nurture a continent–wide democratic culture and tradition? African regimes are currently trying to perform an unprecedented miracle of using the very structures of exploitation, repression, marginalization, brutalization, and human rights abuses—the very structures that were employed in the brutal imposition of orthodox adjustment programs—to establish and nurture a democratic culture. Of course the treaty is silent on *internal* deficiencies and contradictions, which have militated against previous efforts and which make it impossible to generate and extract the required surpluses with which to finance and operate regional schemes. Again, given the very ingenious and complex ways in which African leaders and governments have domesticated the popular will, intimidated the opposition, proscribed trade and students' unions, suffocated civil society, and closed all outlets for democratic empowerment of the people and their communities, it is difficult to see how they can establish a political culture and platform that will lead to the democratic election of an African parliament. Their record thus far in the ongoing struggles against authoritarianism and varieties of despotic regimes gives very little hope that the leaders, old and new, can be relied upon to democratize the continent. Even in Zambia, Frederick Chiluba has harassed those who plan to run against him for the presidency of the country within the ruling Movement for Multiparty Democracy (MMD). In Nigeria, Chief M.K. O. Abiola was jailed for winning an open election and trying to reclaim his popular mandate from a corrupt military junta.

Finally, as has been the tradition in Africa since political independence, the treaty is simply alien to African peoples. It is an affair of donors, international organizations, ministers, presidents, and bureaucrats. Yet, the policies are bound to affect the lives of the people. The treaty is not available to the public and no public education programs have been mounted to mobilize support for the initiative. As Adebayo Adedeji notes, the preparatory process up to the ratification of the treaty at Abuja has "been a governmental affair. There is very little known about it or very little involvement by the people, the grassroots, the non–governmental organizations, the economic operators who really get things done."[61] Such patterns of marginalizing the vast majority makes it impossible to build a body of opinion, the required support, and to get the masses prepared for inevitable shocks and setbacks that follow the implementation of new programs. It also shows that African leaders have not learnt much from past experiences in which the people, their communities, and organizations simply reject elite–dominated and formulated programs with which they cannot identify. This was exactly the way in which IMF and World Bank orthodox adjustment programs were imposed on the people, culminating in political opposition, riots, and instability. The majority of African leaders seem not to appreciate the fact that "recovery and transformation mean self–development through commitment, sacrifices and determination of each individual and all social groups,"[62] and that the starting point for the region must be the encouragement of popular participation, accountability, and the creation of an enabling environment. These will in turn "facilitate socioeconomic transformation,...optimum resource mobilization, efficient resource allocation and the effective implementation of policies and programmes."[63]

Conclusion: Beyond Treaties and Charters

It is clear that African leaders never get tired of adopting or ratifying new charters and treaties. The record on implementation has been dismal just like the performance of African economies since political independence. Unfortunately for the continent, it is pursuing such a monumental project at a very difficult time in the world economy. A world economy characterized by increasing protectionism, the creation of new trading blocs, the decline of official and private support, and the redirection of investment, interest and aid away from Africa (see Chapter Seven). Though the OAU is convinced that "African economies did not witness any significant change for the better" in the last decade and that "from all economic indicators, the continent of Africa appeared to have been by–passed by the positive developments in the world system,"[64] the West and the major international financial institutions do not subscribe to such interpretations. Generally, the predicaments of the region are seen as self–inflicted.

Ironically, the current conditions of poverty, instability, uncertainly, political tensions and conflicts, and general impoverishment hold out positive possibilities for Africa. Since the leaders have exhausted all possible options of diversion, repression, intimidation, bribery, ideological containment, and defensive radicalism; since there is no more East–West game to play; and since there is no more foreign aid to squander on prestige projects, African leaders must now face harsh realities. African peoples and their organizations are asking new questions. They are demanding the democratization of society, increased popular participation, accountability, and social justice. They are increasingly organizing beyond ethnic, regional, and religious lines and are making a bid for state power through their respective organizations. Economic and political crises are forcing more Africans, including professionals, to move beyond national boundaries. This is creating a new awareness (see Chapter Six). The new reality is that the outside world cannot be relied upon to lead Africa out of its current predicament. The problems of Africa have to be resolved by Africans on their own terms and they must be prepared to take full responsibility for the outcomes of their actions. As Michel Camdessus of the IMF has noted recently, "much of Africa will clearly need to rely heavily in the period ahead on domestic sources of finance."[65] Adebayo Adedeji explains the importance of an inward looking approach thus:

> Governments alone cannot and will not be able to generate resources required for recovery and development in Africa. The declining resource flows to Africa under complaints of aid fatigue, the diverting of such flows to Eastern Europe and the increasing marginalization of Africa, all demand increased efforts at internal resource mobilization in African countries. This requires the pooling of the scattered resources of savings, tax payments, voluntary contributions, talents and initiatives of the millions of our people into a huge resource base for Africa's rapid transformation. This demands determination, seriousness, tenacity of purpose and effective partnership between our governments and people.[66]

If this is the way to recovery and the pre–requisite for successful integration, then, Africa still has a long way to go. Other than the limitations arising from the global system, which are not new, the increasing gulf between African governments and their peoples imply that mobilizing the required resources from them will be virtually impossible. The implementation of painful orthodox adjustment programs in most countries has increased hatred, opposition, and distrust for governments; almost wiped out local producers; impoverished the middle classes; marginalized the elites, youths, women, and intellectuals; dehumanized the poor and increased crime, drug abuse and trafficking, prostitution, and cynicism and disillusionment. Under such conditions, mobilization and resource generation cannot take place.

Though the World Bank and the ECA have fully endorsed regionalism as a credible response to the deepening crisis, it is clear that the AEC treaty provides very little hope for the future. African economies are still debt–ridden, crisis–ridden, poor and marginalized in the international division of labor. It is indeed an irony, that in a continent with abundant resources, Africans are living is worse conditions today than was the case at independence over three decades ago. Governments are increasingly unstable and repressive. The elites are facing unprecedented challenges and are desperate in their desire to hold on to state power. The new political elites, are so opportunistic and so hungry for raw power that they easily sacrifice principles and commitment for a piece of power and the opportunity to exploit and loot the treasury.[67]

Though the *African Charter for Popular Participation* calls on all Africans to "support strongly and participate in the efforts to promote effective subregional and regional economic cooperation and integration and intra–African trade,"[68] the governments have made this impossible by dominating the integration process and suffocating civil society. As Babcar Ndiaye, President of the African Development Bank (ADB) noted during the 1991 review of UNPAAERD, "Prospects for the democratic process throughout the continent will no doubt ensure good governance and accountability, promote a market–oriented economy, help improve intra–African trade and favour the development of the African Economic Community."[69] These are expectations, as well as undemonstrated assumptions that there is a direct relationship between democracy and development. Yet, it is clear that Africa needs first, a credible, viable, and fundamental transformation of the *national orders*, then, it will be possible to transform the continent through a continent–wide integration scheme. The large size of the underground or informal trade in Africa is clear evidence that a lot of trade is already taking place across national boundaries. What is missing is the environment in which those involved in this underground trade will develop enough confidence in the state, its custodians and institutions, as well as in the "open" market to want to participate in it. Official trade among African states is a mere $4 billion in a total trade figure of $65 billion. This is just 6 percent of the total trade, the rest is mostly unofficial trade.[70] The benefits of trade within a sub–region as a result of integration is quite evident in the recent increase in trade within the North American Free Trade Area (NAFTA). Since May 1994, "US exports to Mexico have been averaging $1 billion per week. U.S. exports to Canada average over $2 billion per week. U.S. companies are selling more high value products—such as automobiles and computers—than they have in the past" largely because NAFTA has reduced tariff and non–tariff barriers at the borders.[71] As Yoweri Museveni noted at the 1991 Kampala Forum,

> The key word in our development should be cooperation. If the more developed countries of the world see the need for coming together by establishing common markets and by aiming at political union, then we, in Africa, should take a leaf

from the developed world and embark seriously on our own political and economic union....When we have our economic community, we should look ahead to the rationalisation of our economic activities. Abuja (African Economic Treaty) gives us the opportunity to benefit from economies of scale which a continent–wide market can create; it gives us the opportunity to pool our small resources to finance big projects, to prevent wastage and duplication of effort. The community will enhance the establishment of socio–economic infrastructures across the continent. The experts tell us that it will take 34 years to get where the European Community will get next year. We have a duty to prove the experts wrong by moving faster than the Europeans have done since they signed the treaty of Rome in 1958 towards complete economic union.[72]

Along with required political changes, the challenge for Africa is to construct a viable agenda to achieve the goals outlined by Museveni above. Any other approach will amount to avoiding the reality and not preparing to take advantage of the changing global order.

Endnotes

1. Economic Commission for Africa (ECA), *African Alternative Framework to Structural Adjustment Programmes for Socio-Economic Recovery and Transformation* (Addis Ababa: ECA, 1989), p.14.

2. Adebayo Adedeji, quoted in Ernest Harsch, "Africa Seeks Economic Unity," *Africa Recovery* (June 1991), p.12.

3. Economic Commission for Africa, *African Charter for Popular Participation in Development and Transformation* (Addis Ababa: ECA, 1990), p.17.

4. Barber Conable, "Foreword" to World Bank, *Sub-Saharan Africa: From Crisis to Sustainable Growth-A Long-Term Perspective Study* (Washington, D.C.: World Bank, 1989), p.xii.

5. World Bank, *World Development Report 1995: Workers in an Integrating World* (New York: Oxford University Press for the World Bank, 1995), p.52.

6. See Organization of African Unity, *African Priority Programme for Economic Recovery 1986-1990 (APPER)*, (Addis Ababa: OAU Secretariat, 1986).

7. Organization for African Unity, *"Africa's Special Submission to the Special Session of the UN on Africa's Economic and Social Crisis* (Addis Ababa, March 1986. E/ECA/ECM 1/1), p. 12.

8. "Redefining the Future," *Newswatch* (Lagos), (June 10, 1991), p.18.

9. Ibid, p.19.

10. Ibrahim Babangida, Address at the 46th Session of the UN General Assembly, New York, October 4, 1992, p.5.

11. Ibrahim Babangida, "Major Contemporary Issues Facing Nigeria, Africa and the Rest of the World," *The Sunday Magazine* (Lagos) (June 9, 1991), pp.30 and 31.

12. Salim Lone, "Africa Focuses in Internal Weaknesses," *Africa Recovery* (December 1992–February 1993), p. 22.

13. Economic Commission for Africa, *African Alternative Framework to Structural Adjustment Programmes* op. cit, p.13.

14. Victor Chesnault, "Que Faire de l'Afrique Noire?" *Le Monde* (February 28, 1990), p.2.

15. See Julius O. Ihonvbere, "Africa and the New World Order," *The Iranian Journal of International Affairs* Vol. IV, (3–4), (December 1992); "Africa in a New World Order," *Review of African Political Economy* (50) (March 1991); and David S. Wiley, "Academic Analysis and U.S. Policy-Making on Africa: Reflections and Conclusions," *Issue: A Journal of Opinion* Vol. XIX (2) (1991), pp.38–48.

16. Eboe Hutchful, "Eastern Europe: Consequences for Africa," *Review of African Political Economy* (50) (March 1991), p.59. See also Julius O. Ihonvbere, "The Changes in Eastern Europe and Their Implications for Africa's International Economic Relations," *The Nigerian Journal of International Affairs* Vol. 16 (2) (1990), pp.24–41.

17. Adotey Bing, "Salim A. Salim on the OAU and the African Agenda," *Review of African Political Economy* (50) (March 1991), p.61.

18. See Opoku Agyeman, "Pan Africanist Federalism." Mimeo, Montclair State University, 1992.

19. See Africa Leadership Forum, "Report on the Brainstorming Meeting: Conference on Security, Stability, Development and Co-operation in Africa," in Olusegun Obasanjo and Felix G.N. Mosha, (eds.), *Africa: Rise to Challenge*, (New York: AFL, 1991).

20. See ECA, *Economic Report on Africa 1990* (Addis Ababa: ECA, April 1990).

21. Julius O. Ihonvbere, "The Economic Crisis in Sub-Saharan Africa: Depth, Dimensions and Prospects for Recovery," *The Journal of International Studies* (27) (July 1991), pp.41–70.

22. Omar Ali Juma, "Closing Address" in Institute for African Alternatives, *Alternative Development Strategies for Africa*, (London: IFAA, 1989), p.6.

23. Africa Leadership Forum, "Issues Paper for the Security Committee of the Kampala Forum: Collective Continental Security for Stability and Sustained Socio-Economic Transformation in Africa," in Obasanjo and Mosha, (eds.), *Africa: Rise to Challenge*, op. cit., pp. 216 and 218.

24. "UN Secretary-General Urges Fresh Approaches for African Development," *Africa Recovery* (December 1992–February 1993), p. 3. This call was made in 1993 though African leaders had ratified the African Economic Treaty as far back as 1991.

25. Oliver S. Knowles, "ECOWAS: Problems and Potential," in Julius E. Okolo and Stephen Wright, (eds.), *West African Regional Cooperation and Development*, (Boulder: Westview, 1990), p. 149. At the ECOWAS Secretariat in Lagos, Knowles reports that it has "been working in conditions verging on the impossible. Office accommodation has been cramped. Power failures have frequently immobilized all electric office equipment, including typewriters, interpretation booths and air conditioning. Housing has been in short supply and the cost of living is high. Security is poor, and post and telephone communications to other ECOWAS countries have also been poor or nonexistent. The poor working conditions and lack of housing have in turn aggravated recruitment problems, particularly for francophone staff, in a situation where a system of national quotas already limits the scope of recruitment from the relatively limited number of qualified bilingual candidates available," pp. 149-150. In fact, there was time in the 1980s when cheques from the ECOWAS secretariat were bouncing because of insufficient funds in its accounts!

26. World Bank, *Sub-Saharan Africa*, op. cit., p. 148.

27. Ibid, p. 149. The Bank also identifies "the noncompetitiveness of member states compared with third-country suppliers, the high cost of doing business, the shortage of foreign exchange and credit because of distortions in macroeconomic policy, the limited complimentarity of outputs, and the restrictions on food trade" as additional problems with cooperation and integration in Africa, p. 151.

28. Victor Omuabor, "What Has ECOWAS Done?" *African Concord* (15 July 1991), p.39.

29. Ibid.

30. See "When a Giant Limps," *African Concord* (27 August 1990); "A Giant Blunders," Ibid; "Peace by War: ECOMOG Forces Move into Offensive to Contain Rebels," *African Guardian* (1 October 1990); "ECOMOG: Nigeria's Toll– the Unsung Tragedy," *African Concord* (21 January 1991).

31. World Bank, *Sub-Saharan Africa*, op. cit., p.149.

32. "Little Progress on ECOWAS Action Plan," *Africa Recovery* (October 1993), p. 30. In May 1991, ECOWAS had set up a Committee of Eminent Persons under the Chairmanship of General (rtd) Yakubu Gowon of Nigeria to revise the ECOWAS Treaty. The new treaty was designed to facilitate the implementation of programs, and for the organization to take more binding decisions. It also proposed to raise $100–160 million based on one percent levy on each member country's import from third countries to finance the integration process. So far, adherence has remained weak.

33. "ECOWAS: Renewed Drive for Economic Union," *Africa Recovery* (November 1992), p. 35.

34. Ibid.

35. "Little Progress on ECOWAS...," op. cit., pp. 30–31

36. Ibrahim Babangida, Address to the 24th Summit of Heads of State and Government of ECOWAS, Abuja, Nigeria, July 1990.

37. The predecessor of SADC, the SADCC, had relied on an incremental, project-based approach to avoid the failings of other integration schemes in Africa. The emphasis was thus on specific projects rather than market expansion. It was also easier to get donors and lenders to fund or support particular projects rather than broad programs for program harmonization and market expansion. Though it

was also designed to reduce the dependence of its members on the South African economy, the end of apartheid and the admission of South Africa into the OAU has eliminated that portion of its objectives.

38. "Southern Africa Moves Towards Close Ties," *Africa Recovery* (November 1992), p. 35.

39. Ibid.

40. Ernest Harsch, "Africa Seeks Economic Unity," *Africa Recovery* (June 1991), p.13.

41. Ibid.

42. World Bank, *Sub–Saharan Africa*, op. cit., pp. 149–150.

43. Ibid, p. 153.

44. "The African Economic Community Treaty," *United Bank for Africa: Monthly Business and Economic Digest* Vol. 14 (7) (July 1991), p.1.

45. Economic Commission for Africa, *African Charter for Popular Participation in Development*, op. cit., p.18.

46. ECA, *African Alternative Framework...A Popular Version*, (Addis Ababa: ECA, April 1991), p.10.

47. "Abuja Summit Reflects New African Priorities," *Africa Recovery* (September 1991), p.7.

48. "Timetable Towards Unity," *Africa Recovery* (June 1991), p.12.

49. This summary of Article 6 of the AEC Treaty is taken from Ibid.

50. Adebayo Adedeji quoted in Ernest Harsch, "Africa Seeks Economic Unity," op. cit., p.12.

51. Makonnen Haile and Ernest Harsch, "ECA Ministers Call for New International Agenda for Africa," *Africa Recovery* (June 1991), p.28.

52. See Civil Liberties Organization of Nigeria(CLO), "Human Rights Call from CLO: An Alarming Spate of Police Killings–A Call for Intervention," *ZAST* (11–12) (1991), pp.62–69; Julius O. Ihonvbere, "Economic Crisis and Human Rights Abuses in Nigeria, 1985–1991," mimeo, The University of Texas at Austin, (Austin, Texas, December, 1991). See also the numerous publications of the National Association of Democratic Lawyers(NADL), The Committee for the Defense of Human Rights(CDHR), The Committee for Justice in Nigeria(CJN) and the Constitutional Rights Project(CRP).

53. *A Guide to the African Charter on Human and Peoples' Rights* (London: Amnesty International, 1991), p.8.

54. See "Investment in Nigeria: Open Door Policy," *West Africa* (3–9 December 1990) and Julius O. Ihonvbere, "Economic Crisis, Structural Adjustment and Social Crisis in Nigeria," *World Development* Vol. 21, (1) (1993).

55. Organization of African Unity, *Cultural Charter for Africa* (Addis Ababa: OAU, 1976), p.4.

56. See Julius O. Ihonvbere, "Environmental Degradation and Community Response: A Study of Environmental Consciousness in Koko, Nigeria." Paper presented at the Workshops on "Whose Knowledge Counts: Relations Between Formal and Informal Institutions and Resource Users in Africa" co–hosted by CODESRIA and the SSRC (New York), Dakar, Senegal, January 18–21, 1992.

57. World Bank, *Sub–Saharan Africa*, op. cit., p. 152.

58. Chu Okongwu, Minister for Budget and Planning, Federal Republic of Nigeria, speaking on behalf of the OAU at the two–week review of UNPAAERD, New York, 3–13 September, 1991.

59. World Bank, *Sub–Saharan Africa: From Crisis to Sustainable Growth*, op. cit., p. 153.

60. ECA, *African Charter for Popular Participation*, op. cit., p.19.

61. Adebayo Adedeji quoted in Ernest Harsch., "Africa Seeks Economic Unity," op. cit., p.32.

62. Adebayo Adedeji, *The African Alternative: Putting the People First*, (Addis Ababa: ECA, 1990), p.27.

63. Ibid, p.22.

64. Chu Okongwu for the OAU at the 1991 review of UNPAAERD in *Africa Recovery* (December 1991), p.24.

65. Roy Laishley, "Tough Times Ahead for Africa," *Africa Recovery* (June 1991), p.22.

66. Adebayo Adedeji, *The African Alternative: Putting the People First*, op. cit., p.40.

67. A typical case is Nigeria, where leading prodemocracy activists and *democratically elected* politicians joined the military in November 1994, to abolish democracy, dismantle the third republic, and remilitarize the political landscape. Two of such politicians included the elected president of the Senate, Dr. Iyorchia Ayu, and the vice-presidential candidate of the Social Democratic Party, which won the annulled election, Alhaji Baba Kingibe.

68. ECA, *African Charter for Popular Participation in Development* op. cit., p.25.

69. "UNPAAERD Speeches Debate Issues of Debt, Governance, and Aid flows," *Africa Recovery* (December 1991), p.25.

70. World Bank, *Sub-Saharan Africa*, op. cit., p. 158.

71. "Exports to Mexico Reach an Average of $1 Billion Weekly: NAFTA Is Working," *Business Update* (July 1995). In the first six months of 1995, the U.S. has exported goods worth $120 billion within NAFTA, while exports to Mexico and Canada have grown faster than its exports to the rest of the world.

72. Yoweri Kaguta Museveni, Statement to the Kampala Forum, Kampala, Uganda, 19 May 1991. Reproduced in Obasanjo and Mosha, (eds.), *Africa: Rise to Challenge*, op. cit., pp.265–270.

Chapter Six

The Crisis of Democratic Transitions in Africa

...in many African countries the institutions of civil society and democratic governance are weaker today than they were in the immediate postindependence period, making the transition to democracy a daunting challenge.[1]

Most (transitions in Africa) have turned out to be false starts; the democratization has often been shallow...But the pressures for democratization are so strong that for most of Africa it is no longer a question of whether there will be a democratic transition but when.[2]

The current wave of political liberalization in Africa has witnessed unprecedented and monumental changes. Fed up with the suffocation of civil society, repression, corruption, and economic mismanagement, workers, students, women, rural and urban associations, even sections of the military have joined in the agitation for political liberalization and a return to democratic politics and governance.[3] Of course, the results have varied from country to country and from experience to experience. Generally, there is today no nation in Africa that is isolated from the wave of protests, organization for change, demonstrations, and popular enthusiasm for democratic rule.[4] All African states have witnessed the emergence of new pro-democracy movements, leaders, political parties, and issues on the political agenda.

In Ghana, Jerry Rawlings, who initially expressed a disdain for democratic rule, was forced to respect opposition demands, and today he is president of a democratic Ghana. In Kenya, Daniel arap Moi who had argued that democracy would breed violence, ethnic parochialism, and national disintegration was forced by donors and local opposition to conduct multiparty elections in 1992. Today, the opposition, in spite of numerous problems, maintains a visible presence in the Kenyan parliament. In Malawi, president-for-life Hastings Kamuzu Banda, who ruled the country for three decades and tolerated no opposition whatsoever, promised to feed opposition activists to crocodiles in the Shire river. Following pressures from donors and local opposition movements as well as the churches, Banda not only agreed to multiparty elections but was voted out of power in 1994. For the very first time in its postcolonial history, Malawi today enjoys a vibrant, even if problematic, multiparty democratic arrangement. Zambia was no different. Kenneth Kaunda's 27-year rule crumbled as his United National Independence Party (UNIP) was routed by the populist Movement for Multiparty Democracy (MMD) in the

November 1991 elections. Even apartheid South Africa was forced to toe the line when Mandela was released from jail, the African National Congress (ANC) was unbanned, and multiparty democratic elections were held. Today, for the first time in its history, South Africa is accepted in the global system and a black president leads the country. Countries like Togo, Benin, Mali, Cameroon, Senegal, and Uganda have not been left out of this new wave. So intense and robust is the new wave of liberalization that it is being generally referred to as Africa's "second revolution" or "second liberation!"[5] It is therefore important to look at the factors and forces which gave rise to the new wave, the nature of the contestations, the constraints to democracy, and the future of democracy in Africa.

The Origins of the New Wave

Contrary to some of the postulations in the literature, the developments in Eastern Europe did not give rise to Africa's struggle for democracy. To be sure, it did give impetus to the struggles, as most Africans came to see that no matter how brutal and well armed a regime was, it could be overthrown.[6] However, the struggle for democracy, accountability, popular participation in decision-making, and good governance goes way back to the 1960s and the failure of the nationalist project. As the new elites and nationalists appropriated the powers and privileges of the departing colonial lords, they initiated complex programs of exploitation, discrimination, marginalization, concentration of power and resources in urban areas, and intolerance. They depoliticized the people, sacked opposition parties, instituted brutal one-party states, looted the treasury, and relied on defensive radicalism and diversions to reproduce the political system.[7] Within a few years of political independence, Africa became perceived in the eyes of the world as "a continent of virtually unrelieved tyranny, dictatorship, corruption, economic bankruptcy, administrative incompetence, and violence."[8] In short, *political* independence in the 1960s did not witness any significant improvements in the lives or living conditions of the people. While it is true that "No single African country was a democracy at its independence," and that though "most had a semblance of democratic forms of government, all lacked the content, or even a skeletal framework of a true political democracy,"[9] the postcolonial elites did much to make matters worse. It was at this time that peasants, workers, students, women, the unemployed, the marginalized, professionals, trade unions, students and their unions, began to initiate overt and/or covert modes of resistance against the neocolonial state, its institutions, and custodians. It has been easy for the contemporary politicians and pro-democracy movements to point at the failures of the past, the deteriorating conditions of life, and the betrayal of the nationalist ideals to mobilize the people against contemporary incumbent leaders.

A second important factor is the end of the cold war which witnessed a drastic reduction in military and financial support for Africa's brutal dictators. The era also made many of the dictators irrelevant to the needs of the West. The disintegration of the Soviet Union as a nation and superpower meant that its client states were left high and dry, especially as Boris Yeltsin, presiding over a debt-ridden and almost broke Russia, cut off all aid and looked to the West for its own survival. The United States and other European governments were also preoccupied with internal problems—double-digit inflation, unemployment, crime, bankruptcies, the relocation of major corporations to the developing world, and immigration problems. African leaders could no longer play the East against the West, a strategy which had helped Mobutu in Zaire, Moi in Kenya, Doe in Liberia, Barre in Somalia, Nguema in Equatorial Guinea, Bokassa in Central African Republic (formerly empire!), and Banda in Malawi. Japan, the United States, France and the United Kingdom, as well as the multilateral organizations and credit clubs, imposed new political conditionalities which made it very clear to African leaders that foreign aid, investment, and technical support in the post-cold war era were going to be based on political pluralism, good governance, respect for human rights, and visible efforts at containing corruption. This disappearance of technical, military, and financial support, and the new unwillingness to continue to tolerate or accommodate the irresponsibility and excesses of Africa's breed of dictators, strengthened popular opposition and made the state very vulnerable to mass protests.

The delegitimization of the state, its custodians, and institutions contributed significantly to the democratization process. The African state simply lost its credibility and ability to govern. It could not pay salaries, repair roads, provide drugs in hospitals, and maintain security. Most African capitals were taken over by armed robbers and gangsters—Lagos, Lusaka, Bangui, Yaounde, and Nairobi are typical examples.[10] Debt, debt-servicing, corruption, the legacy of privatizing the public sphere, and decades of insensitivity to the needs of the people further eroded the ability of the state to take charge, redirect national politics, and exercise control. It could not pay local and foreign contractors. Suppliers simply refused to do business with states that were rapidly becoming bankrupt. The state could not conduct national censuses, could not maintain peace and order, lacked a capacity to maintain a rural-urban balance, could not protect the environment. And as corruption and waste spread all over the continent, the state remained helpless. It increasingly became totally "irrelevant" to the people as far their daily lives and survival were concerned: it was a wicked, distant, corrupt, violent, aloof, irresponsible, elite-dominated, and useless state.[11] The people, their communities, and organizations realized this fact and took advantage of the openings to challenge the state. To Nicephore Soglo, the recently defeated president of Benin, "People think that once you have got a democracy, everything is going to be free of charge. The danger is impatience."[12] Maybe he is right. But the real problem has been the failure of the postcolonial state and its custodians to perform, make a difference, or at least, appear to be different from the past in a positive sense.

The deepening economic crisis in Africa was, in several respects, and in spite of the pains it has caused, a blessing in disguise. The UN Economic Commission for Africa declared the 1980s as Africa's lost decade. Layashi Yaker, one-time executive secretary of the ECA, argued in the early 1990s that Africa was the only continent to enter the 1990s decade with a negative on all indicators of development.[13] The World Bank in its 1989 report pointed out that Africans were worse off in the 1990s than they were at the time of political independence! The implication here is that colonialism was much kinder to Africa than political independence had been. Deepening poverty, unemployment, inflation, infrastructural decay, social crisis, urban dislocation, hunger, contracting or expensive social services, and uncertainty alienated the people from the governments and its institutions. By the beginning of the 1990s, the continent had lost all economic credibility and was owing over $300 billion in debt. Africa became not only the most "debt distressed" region of the world, but it also became the most risky to invest in.[14] With governments unable to pay wages and salaries, under pressure from creditors, and totally unable to guarantee basic services, the region's economic crisis delegitimized the state and its custodians, alienated the people and their communities, closed credit lines, devalued the worth of public policies, and redirected support and loyalties to opposition movements. As the state became desperate for survival, it lost touch with reality, moved from error to error, and came to rely more on intimidation and repression to reproduce itself. Such repressive actions simply strengthened the opposition and bought global support for opposition movements. The struggle for survival easily meshed with the struggle for democracy.

The emergence of new leaders, political parties, organizations, and pro-democracy movements also invigorated the struggle for democracy. As international organizations, nongovernmental organizations, Western leaders, lenders, and donors all came to endorse good governance and democracy, local leaders received a boost. The trend was set in 1989 when the World Bank, for the very first time in its history in Africa, openly focused on the *political* dimensions of the African predicament. Advocating good governance, gender equality, decentralization of power, human rights, the need to check corruption and waste, and the empowerment and involvement of the people in decision-making, the Bank abandoned its previous economistic interpretation of the African crisis.[15] The opposition in Africa followed up on this new position which was at par with those of the Organization of African Unity (OAU) and ECA. They were not only able to articulate an alternative agenda to the people, but were also able to mobilize financial, materials, and political support from the outside world. In the context of systemic decay, alienation, and grinding poverty, the new leaders, politicians, and movements were able to organize and mobilize the people in the massive challenge to dictatorship. As Sadig Rasheed has noted, it was the courageous activities of local pro-democracy forces that compelled international donors to "put such a concerted pressure on the ruling regimes" in Africa.[16]

In sum therefore, the new struggles for democracy are the result of internal and external factors and forces. To the sure, the unpopularity of military rule, willingness by some elites to salvage whatever was left of the control they exercised over the state, and the desire of hitherto suppressed communities and political interests to assert themselves were just as important. How did African leaders respond to these demands?

Responses to the Calls for Democracy

Many African leaders were indeed taken aback by the spread of the demands and by the constituencies they were coming from. In Ghana, Kenya, Nigeria, Malawi, the leaders were taken aback that church leaders, irrespective of denomination, were openly attacking corruption, declaring support for pro-democracy leaders, calling for an end to one-party and one-person rule, and calling for immediate political liberalization. Trade unions, students, rural organizations, workers, women, and NGOs were unanimous in their calls for an end to military rule and forms of dictatorship. In Malawi and Kenya, the church played such a pivotal role that the incumbent dictators had no choice but to dialogue with the opposition. In Benin, civil servants and lawyers were in the forefront. In Senegal, Cote d'Ivoire, Nigeria, and Ghana, students and professionals, many of the latter organized in human rights associations, were in the forefront. The involvement of diverse interests, cutting across ethnic, religious, and regional lines forced the leaders, even hitherto recalcitrant ones like Kerekou in Benin, Banda in Malawi, Babangida in Nigeria, Moi in Kenya, and Eyadema in Togo to make concessions to popular organizations, liberalize the political systems, and introduce multiparty politics.

The responses have, of course, varied according to the strength and unity among the opposition, the degree of enlightenment of the leadership, the extent of external pressures often evidenced in the cutting off of foreign aid, the exit options open to incumbent leaders, and the dynamics of politics within each social formation.[17] The responses have reflected one or a combination of the following: the national conference, open competitive elections, guided liberalization, opposition to pluralism, attempts to divide the opposition through bribery and/or the registration of scores of opposition parties, co-optation, and intimidation. In some instances as in Nigeria, Senegal, and Kenya, the incumbent regimes have descended heavily on the opposition, throwing their leaders into detention or forcing them into exile. In Nigeria, virtually all the leaders of the National Democratic Coalition (NADECO) and the Campaign for Democracy (CD) are either in exile, underground, or in jail. Arap Moi was equally good at this strategy and he boasted that he would crush the opposition "like rats." Banda in Malawi boasted that he would feed the opposition leaders to crocodiles in the Shire river. In other instances, African regimes have tried administrative reforms, cabinet reshuffles, the dramatic sacking of some prominent ministers and advisors, wage increases to striking workers, scholarships to protesting students, the legalization of opposition parties by the dozens, the release of detainees from detention, general amnesty to exiles, and the establishment of scores of panels and task forces to study a range of issues in the hope of keeping the people busy while the regime reconsolidates. Yet still, some leaders have come up with long-drawn-out transition programs, usually between three and five years, in the hopes of tiring out the opposition, stretching their thin resources, and providing room for divisions. Curious forms of constitutional debates and reviews have also been used to lay the foundation for a conservative transition that could be relied upon to result in very limited or no change at all in existing power balances. In some instances, as in Ghana, Rawlings kept the opposition in the dark for a long time and then called a "snap election" in the hope of catching the opposition unawares. Part of this strategy also includes delaying political activities and campaigns for as long as possible while the incumbent government or ruling party continues to organize, mobilize, and campaign openly. Of course, whenever elections have been called, a major strategy has been to rig the elections in spite of the presence of international monitors from several nations.

Irrespective of their adopted strategy, the new political movements have succeeded in compelling military dictators to accept political pluralism (Benin, Babangida's Nigeria, and Ghana); one-party regimes to allow for more parties (Kenya and Zambia); and one-person life-presidential systems to adopt multiparty political systems (Malawi). The national conference has been more of a francophone phenomena which has been utilized in Benin, Congo, Mali, Gabon, and Niger.

Unfortunately, in spite of these monumental changes, Africa's march to democracy seems to be losing its steam midway.[18] In no country has democracy been consolidated. In a few cases like Nigeria, The Gambia, and Niger, the democratic process has been rolled back by the military. In Benin, the elected president, Nicephore Soglo, was voted out of power, and former dictator Matthew Kerekou voted back into power. In Kenya, over thirteen prodemocracy politicians have apologized to Moi, abandoned the opposition, and rejoined the ruling Kenya Africa National Union (KANU). In Zambia, the MMD has lost so much credibility that its initial constituency, the labor movement, is today its greatest adversary. As well, over thirty-four opposition parties have emerged to challenge the MMD, most of these parties formed by founding MMD members, ex-ministers, and leaders. In Nigeria, the running mate to the assumed winner of the June 12 presidential election, the president of the senate, and leading human rights and prodemocracy leaders like Lateef Jakande, Ebenezer Babatope, Olu Onagoruwa and Abubakar Rimi actually joined the Abacha junta and supported the dismantling of democratic institutions and the remilitarization of the political landscape in November 1993. Below, we discuss some of the constraints to democracy in Africa.

Constraints to Liberalization

Most analysts have become rather cautious or pessimistic about the transitions in Africa. As Guy Martin has eloquently noted, "The final outcome of these ongoing processes of democratic transition in Africa is uncertain at best, and experts' analyses and predictions range from guarded optimism to frank pessimism...Any effort to superimpose a specific narrow formula of democracy could lead to mere formal compliance, such as allowing multipartism without "real democracy."[19] "Formal compliance" has been commonplace in the continent but real changes, evidenced in the drastic and fundamental recomposition of the structures, institution, patterns, and goals of politics have been very few and far between. Claude Ake is even more direct in his skepticism about the transitions:

> With a few exceptions the democratization has been shallow; typically, it takes the form of multiparty elections that are really more of a democratic process than a democratic outcome. Authoritarian state structures remain, accountability to the governed is weak, and the rule of law is sometimes nominal. More often than not, people are voting without choosing.[20]

What then are the constraints to the transition, to regime legitimation, and to democratic consolidation?

The first major constraint is that the current struggles for democracy lack an ideological content. In most cases, there is a pathological fixation on aping World Bank and IMF prescriptions. There is very little creativity or originality. The world is conceived and related to through the eyes of lenders, donors, election monitoring agencies, and foreign funders. While many opposition movements and new political parties have capitalized on the economic and social failings of incumbent regimes, they have provided no concrete alternatives to foreign-packaged prescription. The MMD Manifesto, for instance, sounds and reads more like an IMF and World Bank document. It hardly reflects the socioeconomic and political realities and balances of the country, and completely ignores the country's historical experiences and specificities.[21] To be sure, this struggle to design liberal, and rabidly pro-market programs in order to satisfy donors, lenders, international NGOs, election monitors, and Western governments has also set the platform to alienating, exploiting, and marginalizing the people. Hence, it did not take long for new governments in Malawi and Zambia to alienate the people. The lack of originality and creativity has resulted in a generally conservative political style based on diversions, lies, manipulation, bribery, violence, election rigging, and the inability to cultivate and nurture new political constituencies. On this score, African politics has not moved a step away from where it was in the 1960s: it is still an activity of the few and the rich with the masses serving as spectators or objects of manipulation.

Though it is true that "democracy is spreading like bushfire throughout Africa,"[22] at least until recently, the new pro-democracy movements and political parties have tended to exhibit some common traits: corruption, opportunism, the marginalization of women, concentration in specific regions or urban centers, personalization of politics, confusion, fragmentation, excessive ambition and focus on power. The superficial, defensively radical, opportunistic, diversionary, and narrow focus of the organizations, their politics and strategies have eroded their legitimacy, bred confusion, and made it easy for the incumbent governments to penetrate, divide, and out-maneuver them in the competition for power.[23]

There is not a single pro-democracy movement or new political party in Africa that is interested in the dismantling and reconstruction of the unstable, nonhegemonic, violent, exploitative, and inefficient neocolonial state. Rather, the struggle is to penetrate and take charge of the very same state along with its institutions which the people had hated and challenged since the 1960s. How they hope to use the same repressive state that had shot at children, women, students, and protesters yesterday to mobilize the people for justice democracy, accountability, and mobilization today beats the imagination. This is probably the greatest failing of contemporary democratic initiatives, and the reason why the new efforts have inspired so little enthusiasm among nonbourgeois constituencies. The fact that the new actors and their organizations, like the early nationalists, want to maintain the status quo by keeping the repressive neocolonial state intact demonstrates the struggle of limited objectives and a fundamental fraud in the new political balances and arrangements. The new elites simply wish to replace the old dictators with "democratic" oppressors!

The rise of ethnic and social parochialism has become a major constraint to democracy and democratization. While this is not peculiar to Africa—and certainly reflects the emergence of hitherto repressed interests and coalitions—the reality is that ethnicity, statism, regionalism, and religion have combined at various levels to weaken the opposition, divide the transition agenda, and militate against the construction of a common political platform. It is this division, coupled with opportunism (see below), that have made it possible for the incumbent leaders to outsmart the opposition, splinter and manipulate them, make superficial concessions, and succeed in reducing the entire transition program to one of mere elections. In Kenya, Ghana, Togo, Nigeria, and Cameroon, these primordial factors have been the bane of a genuine transition to democracy. In Kenya, the Forum for the Restoration of Democracy (FORD) simply broke into a Kikuyu- and Luo-dominated factions with neither strong enough to unseat Moi from power. Most Kalenjins have come to see Moi as the best guarantor of the privileges they now enjoy over other major ethnic groups and are willing to give him absolute support.[24] Open complaints about Ewe domination of politics and power in Ghana, in spite of their numerically small size, has also served to divide democratic politics in Ghana. In Nigeria, the core of the struggle for the restoration of the "June 12" election mandate, which had been annulled by the military, remains in the South West with putative support from other regions. In Zambia, Kenneth Kaunda's popularity in the Eastern Province could not be shaken by the MMD in spite of its populist rhetoric. In Malawi, Chihana Chakufwa, the leader of the Alliance for the Restoration of Democracy (AFORD) has been most popular in his home region in the North, and his organization could only win parliamentary seats in the same region. The "new parochialism" is more intolerant and violent, as evidenced in The Sudan, Liberia, Cameroon, Togo, Burundi, Malawi, and Nigeria. It is tearing apart whatever bonds of unity and cooperation had been constructed in Africa since the 1960s, and it is effectively mediating possibilities for constructing a national project and building viable democratic processes and institutions.

The proliferation of political parties has been a major constraint to democracy and democratization in contemporary Africa. The continent has never witnessed this sort of deluge in party formation and interest in state power. To be sure, at one level it is evidence of a robust and vibrant civil society. It is evidence that opportunities exist for people and communities to organize and express their views and goals. Yet, it is also evidence of a lack of accommodation, consensus, dialogue, and a willingness to trust each other. It is evidence of political greed and opportunism. It is also evidence of the fact that elites with interests far beyond the restoration of democracy have hijacked the political process. This is even more so when we see the refusal of the leaders of these parties to reach accommodation with each other, form viable coalitions, and present common candidates and platforms. Every dismissed minister, as in Zambia, has formed a political party. African multimillionaires seem to think that wealth must be translated into power as a strategy for total control of the political economy. Hence, in Nigeria, Kenya, Zambia, and other places, they have formed parties, sponsored candidates, and even presented themselves for election to all sorts of political positions. Every political leader sees himself or herself as a potential president. In Ghana, the refusal to make concessions to one another created confusion within the ranks of the opposition and made it easy for Rawlings to win the 1992 elections. The tendency to form new political parties by the day further fragments civil society, confuses the people, encourages bitter politicking, and diverts attention from serious national issues. The situation in Togo was so bad that the *BBC Focus on Africa* concluded that "[i]t is difficult to imagine how it would be possible to make a bigger mess of multiparty elections."[25] Not only did the opposition boycott the elections, thus allowing Gnasingbe Eyadema to run virtually unopposed, but Edem Kodjo and Kokou Koffingo, one-time sworn enemies of the military dictator, abandoned their constituencies and became allies of Eyadema! Edem Kojo, whose Togolese Union for Democracy (UTD) won only seven seats in parliament, betrayed a pact signed with another opposition party, the Action Committee for Renewal (CAR), and accepted the position of prime minister from Eyadema.

In Malawi, Chihana Chakufwa, who during the campaigns referred to the Bakili Muluzi-led United Democratic Front (UDF) as "MCP" and referred to the UDF and Kamuzu Banda-led Malawi Congress Party (MCP) as the parties of "darkness and death", accepted the hurriedly created position of second vice president from the UDF. This was after an initial alliance with the MCP, an action that thoroughly discredited AFORD and its leaders and alienated its supporters. Even before the May 1994 presidential elections, in which the Alliance for Democracy (AFORD) leader performed very badly, he had been accused of "dictatorial tendencies and of driving around in presidential motorcades."[26] In Senegal, many supporters of the opposition movements were shocked when in May 1991 Abdou Diouf "resurrected the post of prime minister and restored to preeminence" Habib Thiam as part of a grand strategy of incorporation and domestication. Amath Dansokho, leader of the radical opposition Parti d'Independence et Travail was also incorporated into Diouf's cabinet. The greatest shock was when Abdoulaye Wade, the leader of the Parti Senegalaise Democratique (PDS), "whose unrelenting attacks on the Diouf administration have led to popular unrest and landed (him) in jail," joined the cabinet as minister of state![27] In Burkina Faso, the ruling Organization for Popular Democracy/Labour Movement (ODP/MT) has had no problems with incorporating leaders of the so-called "Group of 13" opposition. When a new cabinet was announced on 26 July, 1991, members of the opposition were appointed by Blaise Compaore to about half of the thirty-four cabinet positions.[28] The examples can go on endlessly: the "new" democrats have not been reluctant to sell their principles, supporters, platforms, and programs just to become part of an already discredited and desperate regime. Such actions easily expose why they are in the opposition and why they are, at best, only marginally different from the "old buzzards" of African politics.

Equally fascinating is the shameless and opportunistic proliferation of political parties, many with nuisance value and many "sponsored" by beleaguered leaders as a strategy of creating confusion within the opposition and splitting their votes. In the francophone states, it has not been particularly difficult for incumbent leaders to find willing "opposition politicians" and so-called "democrats" to fill the seats at national conferences with the sole purpose of creating confusion and divisions. In his hey days, though beleaguered and under severe pressure, Mobutu Sese Seko actually succeeded in cramming "4,288 false delegates into a conference venue that (sat) 3,500" in Zaire exactly for this purpose.[29] Nigeria once had about 120 presidential candidates during the zigzag march to the now defunct third republic. When the General Babangida junta scuttled independent efforts at political party formation and proceeded to impose his own two parties on Nigeria, the politicians (including the so-called "new breed") did not challenge the general. Rather, in typical opportunistic fashion, they struggled to join the two government-created parties. Though eleven opposition groups came together to form the Co-ordinating Committee of Democratic Forces of Ghana (CCDFG) before the 1992 "elections" in Ghana, they could not maintain the unity against Rawlings. The hunger for power was too strong and individual ambitions were higher than party platforms and the future of the country.[30] After participating in and losing the presidential elections to Rawlings, the opposition (save for two small parties) took the easy way out by boycotting the parliamentary elections, complaining of—among other things, the inaccuracy of the voters register—the same register that had been used for the presidential polls! Algeria at one point had about one hundred and twelve political parties and organizations on the political scene.[31] Guinea had forty-six opposition parties by early 1995; Malawi now has about twelve political parties; Tanzania had twelve registered opposition parties; Benin has over nine opposition parties; Mauritania has twenty political parties; and Mali has fifty-seven opposition parties. When Houphouet-Boigny acceded to multiparty politics and called elections, over twenty registered opposition parties ran against the incumbent Parti Democratique de Cote d'Ivoire (PDCI). They were crushed in the elections, as they split the few votes of the opposition. In the 1995 election in Cote d'Ivoire, Henri Konan Bedie ran against eleven other so-called presidential candidates. By the time of the elections, there were about eighty opposition parties in the country. In Madagascar, there were originally eighteen presidential candidates for the November 1992 elections. The large deposit of twenty-five million Malagasy francs reduced the number to eight. In Burkina Faso, Blaise Compaore is having a field day against a divided opposition of forty parties and over 1000 associations.[32] The 1994 election in Ethiopia witnessed a 90 percent turnout of the registered voters, who were confused because they had to pick 534 candidates from a total of 1,471 representing thirty-nine different parties. In addition to the 1,471 candidates, there were also 937 independents. Yet, none of the main opposition groups took part in the elections.[33] Zimbabwe has eighteen opposition parties and they have failed woefully in shaking the foundations of Mugabe's ZANU-PF. In fact, the only problem with Mugabe's party are internally generated.

In spite of Mobutu's legendary corruption, decadence, violence, and declining popularity, the opposition was unable to unseat him from power until the military force of Laurent Kabila did so in mid-1997. The opposition alliance—the Sacred Front (Union Sacre)—is made up of 129 opposition movements that refused to reach some reasonable accommodation with each other in order to forge a united front. Etienne Tshisekedi, the opposition leader, belongs to Mobutu's generation and "inner clique," having served the "quintessential African despot" in various capacities.[34] His l'Union pour la Democracie et le Progres Social (UDPS) is seen as regionally based, and there have been serious doubts about his leadership abilities. Like Nguza Karl-i-Bond, Tshisekedi is seen as a Mobutu ally who turned "democrat" after he was marginalized in the country's power equation: he was minister for the interior and later minister for justice. He helped to draft the one-party constitution of the country. He was ambassador to Morocco, national secretary of the ruling party, and chair of the party's political division. Such "establishment" democrats hardly have the capacity to fundamentally challenge the status quo. They are too soft and have gotten so used to power and the perquisites of office that their ability to withstand the pains and sacrifices of genuine struggles for empowerment is usually limited. The continuing domination of the "new" political parties and the pro-democracy movements by such "old timers" remains a major obstacle to the success of the struggle against authoritarianism in Africa. In many instances, their role simply leads to the repackaging of old ideas, dictatorial political styles, and too many compromises with a status quo that needs to be dismantled and discarded.[35]

The conduct, profile, and performance of the new-wave democrats leave much to be desired. They are more unreliable, impatient with democracy, corrupt, violent, more manipulative, and openly disinterested in the welfare of the people. To be sure, there are handful of parties, movements, and persons whose patriotism, honesty, vision, and clarity cannot be questioned. Unfortunately, they are not just in the minority, they also lack the resources and control within their organizations to really call the shots. Without exception, it has taken only a few years for the new parties, politicians, and movements to alienate the people and disgrace themselves. The fall of Nicephore Soglo in Benin is directly related to abuse of office, nonperformance, and the unusually high profile of his spouse and family members in power structures. In Zambia, members of the cabinet were openly accused of being involved in drug trafficking, inflation of contracts, nepotism, and land-grabbing. The turnover of ministers in Zambia under Chiluba has been unprecedented. In Nigeria, the short-lived National Assembly was probably the most profligate in the country's history. Within a couple of months, the politicians had squandered the Assembly's budget on accommodation, entertainment, and other frivolous expenses. It was so bad that in May 1993, the Assembly members were locked out of their rooms by the major hotels in Abuja, the nation's new capital, for huge debts.

Finally, the process of political liberalization in Africa has, in spite of widespread expectations, failed to bring about fundamental changes. It was expected that the political upheavals and the political rhetoric of the new political leaders would heighten expectations among hitherto exploited, marginalized, oppressed, and intimidated communities and persons. Promises were made about food, water, shelter, health care, better roads, power supply, good schools, loans to farmers, better wages, inflation control, the termination of crime and prostitution, open governance, accountability, respect for human rights, and the involvement of the people in the political processes and in decision-making. In short, the people were promised a better life. This has not happened in any country. The performance has been so terrible that the "third wave" has turned into a "third wail" and the discredited dictators are beginning to look like saints! This is only way to explain the continuing popularity of Kamuzu Banda, the ex-life president of Malawi; the reelection of Kerekou in Benin; the resilience of Mobutu in Zaire and Eyadema in Togo; the popularity of Kaunda in Zambia; and the fact that the National Democratic Coalition (NADECO), an association of retired generals, ex-governors, ex-ministers, traditional chiefs, and wealthy businessmen and politicians, is today, the most viable opposition movement to the Abacha junta in Nigeria. As we have seen, the new parties and politicians have been unable to hold their communities and constituencies together. In Kenya, "political paralysis, high rates of inflation, and insecurity have become the order of the day since the Moi government stole an election in December 1992."[36] Denis Venter points out that "Malawi has shown that democracy can cure some ills but may worsen others."[37] The removal of Banda's despotism has unleashed a corrupt and careless press, "unprecedented urban crime...a generally deteriorating security situation,...marked increase in, especially, crimes of violence," and worsening economic crisis.[38] One of the earliest moves of the new democratic president of Malawi, Bakili Muluzi was to put his face on the country's currency. Finally, the liberalization of politics has not improved African economies. Rather, corruption, waste, the creation of extralarge cabinets, sinecure political appointments, and perks for parliamentarians have further put pressure on already scare resources. As well, liberalization has not meant more freedom for individuals, the media, scholars, and students. Schools have been closed, unions proscribed, social critics jailed, discredited politicians rehabilitated without apologies, and media houses raided by security agents just as they had been under the dictators. In Ghana, until his recent retirement, the much dreaded Captain (retired) Kojo Tsikata, who had been head of security and the secret services, remained a towering and much feared figure in spite of the so-called transition from the Provisional National Defence Council (PNDC) to a National Democratic Congress (NDC) government. In fact, the political situation in Africa has hardly improved. The politicians have simply become more careful and sophisticated in practicing the usual politics of manipulation, nepotism, corruption, and repression. One can therefore appreciate Adebayo Adedeji's frustrations when he declared that "the idea of a second liberalization in Africa has gone away with the wind, at least temporarily. Even the most timid attempts at democratization have often failed due to self-centeredness of African leaders and their lack of vision."[39] As a leading pro-democracy activist noted a while back, "True, we are doing our best. It will be foolish however to assume that we are making progress. We are attacking the surface issues. The core issues will require a revolution and more selfless leadership."[40]

Conclusion

Democracy has taken a beating in Africa. Today, most Africans are confused as to the real meaning and content of democracy. Its recent reduction to elections, elections certified as having been "free and fair" by election monitors who promptly depart and abandon the people to their misery under the leadership of "democratic dictators," has even made the situation worse. Governments, including democratic governments, have brutalized the people. Leaders like Mobutu, Museveni, Rawlings, and Eyadema, including those who started out well, have come to see power as their birthright. Governments have brutalized their people, including democratic governments. More than ever, Africans are beginning to appreciate the limitations of liberal democracy in crisis-ridden, dislocated, marginalized, and impoverished economies. Democracy has not reduced corruption and the abuse of office. True, it has opened up the political landscape, but it has not wiped out human rights abuses, reduced primordial conflicts, or promoted accountability. In fact, in spite of pluralism, it is clear that unemployment, poverty, crime, prostitution, violence, and general social decay have increased. To make matters worse, investors and donors have not rushed in to support new democratic governments. Africa continues to receive fewer investments than all other regions of the world. The MMD in Zambia was shocked when its conservative agenda did not translate into billions of dollars in foreign aid pouring into Lusaka. What does the future hold for democracy in Africa?

In spite of the problems above and the deepening socioeconomic crisis, the future of democracy is still bright. In spite of the increasing marginalization of Africa, the continent cannot be neglected by the outside world. Yet, the current crisis, elite opportunism, corruption, and political fragmentation have only strengthened the future of democracy. As Celestin Monga has accurately noted, the current phase of liberalization, "New social frontiers are being traced, new networks of solidarity established, new mentalities are taking shape. Values believed to be lost have reappeared, supplanting and replacing the ideologies whose limits have been exposed by thirty years of single-party rule. In this flux, we are witnessing a diversification of political activities: pressure groups emerge from the shadows, lobbies suddenly spring into broad daylight, without anyone really knowing either the main actors or their ambitions, let alone their scope of action.[41] Without doubt, things would never be the same again in the continent. In spite of the continuing dominant role of the "old guard" politicians, many of the new organizations cannot afford to operate in the traditional or pro-status quo fashion.

It is becoming increasingly clear that democracy cannot thrive in Africa if the economic crisis is not addressed. Orthodox prescriptions, in an already devastated economy, will only worsen the situation. Equally, democracy cannot thrive without a reconstruction of the state. The need for an accountable, transparent, democratic, stable, predictable, efficient, and popular national state cannot be overemphasized. Until the current institutions and structures of the state are dismantled, democracy cannot make any progress in Africa. This will include a restructuring of the military, a transformation of the bureaucracy, a revitalization of the judiciary, constitutional engineering, the guarantee of basic rights and liberties, and the protection of minority rights. These issues are already being articulated by the environmental movements, the human rights and pro-democracy associations, and NGOs.

For the pro-democracy movements and new political parties, there needs to be a total restructuring of operations. Internal democracy, the development of viable alternative programs, the increased participation of women, linkages with other associations, and deviation from the traditional patterns of political manipulation and gerrymandering is necessary. The current politics is already exposing opportunists within the movements as they strive to forge alliances with the status quo parties and governments. The next generation of leaders, hopefully, will learn from past mistakes and map out genuine paths to democracy and democratization.

Finally, civil society needs to be strengthened. To be sure, civil society can be the location for negative, intolerant, and violent politics. Yet, the need to strengthen the people, their constituencies, and communities, with the need to involve the people and their organizations in decision-making processes, constitute part of this process of strengthening civil society. This is the only way to check the opportunism, betrayal, corruption, and excesses of the state and political elites and to pay due attention to issues of gender, environment, popular participation, accountability, and responsibility in government. This also is the only way to acknowledge and respect the interests of minorities, contain or mediate primordial conflicts, and open up the political terrain to democratic contestations for power. As Sadig Rasheed has noted, democracy can only flourish "if democratic change is effected and institutions established that actually function as guardians of the democratic process and of the people."[42] At best, the outside world can assist Africa in the process, but cannot, and should not (as is currently the case) dictate the content and context of politics, the patterns of politics, the acceptability or unacceptability of elections, and the choice of leaders to be accepted or rejected. These have to be determined by the people according to internal dynamics of political alignment and realignments.

Endnotes

1. Sahr John Kpundeh, (ed.), *Democratization in Africa: African Views, African Voices - Summary of Three Workshops* (Washington, D.C.: National Academy of Sciences, 1992), p. 13.

2. Claude Ake, *Democracy and Development in Africa* (Washington, D.C.: The Brookings Institution, 1996), p. 136.

3. See Trace L. Brandt, (ed.), *After The Transition: Problems of Newly Democratizing Countries- Summary of a Workshop* (Washington, D.C.: National Research Council, 1992).

4. See Emeka Nwokedi, *Politics of Democratization: Changing Authoritarian Regimes in Sub-Saharan Africa* (Munster, Germany: LIT Verlag, 1995).

5. See Julius O. Ihonvbere and Terisa Turner, "Africa's Second Revolution in the 1990s," *Security Dialogue* Vol. 24, (3) (September 1993): 349–352.

6. For a discussion see Ali Mazrui, "Eastern European Revolutions: African Origins?" *TransAfrica Forum* Vol. 7, (2) (Summer 1990): 3–11.

7. See Claude Ake, *Revolutionary Pressures in Africa* (London: Zed Books, 1978).

8. Colin Legum, "Democracy in Africa: Hope and Trends," in Dov Ronen, (ed.), *Democracy and Pluralism in Africa* (Boulder, CO: Lynne Rienner, 1986), p. 175.

9. Ibid, p. 177.

10. For very graphic discussions of state delegitimization and collapse, see I. William Zartman (ed.), *Collapsed States: The Disintegration and Restoration of Legitimate Authority* (Boulder, CO: Lynne Rienner, 1995); Fantu Cheru, *The Silent Revolution in Africa: Debt, Development and Democracy* (London and Harare: Zed Books and Anvil, 1989); Lance Morrow, "Africa: The Scramble for Existence," *TIME* (7

September 1992); and Robert Kaplan, "The Coming Anarchy," *Atlantic Monthly* (February 1994). The latter was a curiously influential, though ahistorical, sensational, and journalistic piece.

11. See Julius O. Ihonvbere, "The 'Irrelevant' State, Ethnicity and the Quest for Nationhood in Africa," *Ethnic and Racial Studies* Vol. 17, (1) (January 1994): 42–60; and Claude Ake, "The State in Contemporary Africa," in Ake (ed.), *Political Economy of Nigeria* (London and Lagos: Longman, 1985): 1–8.

12. Nicephore Soglo, president of Benin, quoted in *Jeune Afrique* (1632) (16–22 April 1992).

13. See Layashi Yaker, Keynote Address at the International Conference on "Africa in the 1990s: Challenges and Opportunities." The American Graduate School of International Management, Glendale, Arizona, 18–20, February, 1993.

14. See Ellen Johnson Sirleaf, "Some Reflections on Africa and the Global Economy," in William Minter (ed.), *U.S. Foreign Policy: An Africa Agenda* (Washington, D.C.: Africa Policy Information Center, 1994):7–12.

15. See World Bank, *Sub-Saharan Africa: From Crisis to Sustainable Growth-A Long- Term Perspective Study* (Washington, D.C.: The World Bank, 1989).

16. Sadig Rasheed, "The Democratization Process and Popular Participation in Africa: Emerging Realities and the Challenges Ahead," *Development and Change* Vol. 26 (1996), p. 337.

17. For a discussion of these see Michael Bratton and Nicolas van de Walle, "Popular Protest and Political Reform in Africa," *Comparative Politics* Vol. 24, (4) (July 1992): 419–442; and their "Neopatrimonial Regimes and Postcolonial Transitions in Africa," *World Politics* Vol. 46, (4) (July 1994): 453–489.

18. Sadig Rasheed, "Africa at the Doorstep of the Twenty-first Century: Can Crisis Turn to Opportunity" in Adebayo Adedeji, (ed.), *Africa*

Within the World: Beyond Dispossession and Dependence (London and Ijebu-Ode: Zed Books and ACDESS, 1993), p. 47.

19. Guy Martin, "Preface: Democratic Transition in Africa," *Issue: A Journal of Opinion* Vol. XXI, (1–2) (1993), pp. 6 and 7.

20. Claude Ake, *Democracy and Development in Africa*, op. cit., p. 137.

21. See Julius O. Ihonvbere, *Economic Crisis, Civil Society and Democratization* (Lawrenceville, NJ: Africa World Press, 1996).

22. Guy Martin, "Preface: Democratic Transition in Africa," op. cit., p. 6.

23. See Julius O. Ihonvbere, "On the Threshold of Another False Start?: A Critical Evaluation of Prodemocracy Movements in Africa," paper presented at the 11th Annual Meeting of the Council of Nigerian People and Organizations (CONPO), Washington, D.C., September 14–17, 1995. See also Christine Sylvester, "Whither the Opposition in Zimbabwe?" *The Journal of Modern African Studies* Vol. 33, (3) (1995), pp.403–423.

24. See Makau wa Mutua, "Kenya: Young Turks vs. Old Guard," *Africa Report* Vol. 39, (3) (May–June 1994): 34–36; and Githu Muigai, "Kenya's Opposition and the Crisis of Governance," *Issue: A Journal of Opinion* Vol. XXI, (1–2) (1993): 26–34.

25. "Togo: Opposition? What Opposition?" *BBC Focus on Africa* Vol. 4, (4) (October–December, 1993), p. 19.

26. "Malawi: The Old Man and His Chickens," *BBC Focus on Africa* Vol. 4, (4) (October–December 1993), p. 18.

27. Peter Da Costa, "Senegal: Peace for a Province," *Africa Report* Vol.36, (5) (September–October 1991), p. 53.

28. The country's leading opposition movement, the Alliance for Democracy and Federation, led by Hermann Yameogo, withdrew its participation in the cabinet in mid–August of 1991.

29. "National Conferences: Out with the Old Leaders," *Africa Report* Vol. 36, (5) (September–October 1991), p. 5. In Gabon, Omar Bongo has effectively destabilized the opposition by "acceding to a national conference on multi-party democracy, calling snap elections, and quickly declaring a dubious victory at the polls before the befuddled opposition could effectively consolidate their demands." Ibid, p. 5.

30. See "Ghana: Opposition Forces Unite," *Africa Research Bulletin* (August 1st–31st, 1991).

31. "Algeria: Opposition Skepticism," *Africa Research Bulletin* (April 1st–30th, 1995).

32. Margaret Novicki, "Interview: Soumana Sako—Managing the Transition," *Africa Report* Vol. 36, (5), (September–October 1991), p.50; and Burkina Faso—Compaore's Campaign," Ibid, pp. 55–58. The later report noted that "Compaore has outflanked the opposition more often than not—frequently turning concessions into his own initiatives—avoiding a sovereign national conference and its potential to seize control over events."

33. "Ethiopia's Ruling EPRDF Coalition Wins Again," *Africa Report* Vol. 39, (4) (July–August, 1994), p. 8.

34. "National Conferences: Out with the Old Leaders," op. cit., p. 5.

35. Examples include the role of the leaders of the National Democratic Coalition (NADECO) in Nigeria, made up of retired heads of state, first republic politicians, retired military officers, traditional chiefs, and businessmen. Oginga Odinga's leadership of a faction of FORD in Kenya contributed to the factionalization in the opposition and to their rather weak response to the Moi dictatorship. Kenneth Kaunda, who has regained the leadership of the United National Independence Party (UNIP) in Zambia, has no new ideas and cannot lead the party or nation to recovery and development. Adu Boahen is increasingly being challenged in Ghana by younger activists and politicians as he remains stuck to the political styles of the 1950s and 1960s.

36. Makau wa Mutua, "U.S. Foreign Policy Towards Africa," in William Minter, (ed.), *U.S. Foreign Policy: An Africa Agenda*, op. cit., p. 16.

37. Denis Venter, "Malawi: The Transition to Multi-Party Politics," op. cit., p.178.

38. Ibid, p. 181.

39. Adebayo Adedeji, keynote address at the conference on "An African Agenda for Economic and Social Transformation in the New Global Environment," Lincoln University, November 17–18, 1994.

40. Interview with Femi Falana, president, National Association of Democratic Lawyers (NADL), Lagos, Nigeria, December 1994. Mr. Falana is also a leading member of the CD.

41. Celestin Monga, "Civil Society and Democratisation in Francophone Africa," *The Journal of Modern African Studies* Vol. 33 (3) (1995), p. 360.

42. Sadig Rasheed, "Africa at the Doorstep of the Twenty-First Century: Can Crisis Turn to Opportunity," op. cit., p. 47.

Chapter Seven

Towards the Future: Africa and the New Globalization

A great transformation in world history is creating a new economic, social, and political order: Communism's collapse and the embrace of freer markets by much of the developing world are driving huge increases in global commerce and international investment. The Information Revolution is forging strong links between nations, companies, and peoples. Improving education levels are creating a global middle class that shares "similar concepts of citizenship, similar ideas about economic progress, and a similar picture of human rights."[1]

We are not entering a new century. We are entering a new era.[2]

Global problems, such as threats to the environment, mass migration and arms proliferation, demonstrate that individual governments acting alone are no longer capable of protecting their people. The revolutions in technology and economic integration are also helping end the supremacy of the nation state as it now exists.[3]

There is no doubting the fact that the world is currently undergoing unprecedented and monumental changes. The best futurists could not predict most of these drastic changes a decade ago: the reunification of Germany with the collapse of the Berlin Wall; the peace talks between Israel and Palestine; Palestinian police arresting members of Hammas for attacking Israeli soldiers and settlers; the end of apartheid in South Africa and the election of Nelson Mandela as the first black president of that country; the collapse of the Soviet Union as a superpower and nation; the widespread adoption of market reform programs as dictated and supervised by the World Bank and the International Monetary Fund (IMF); and the emergence of the United States as the hegemonic military power in the world. As well, we can add a renewed role for the United Nations, especially in the areas of humanitarian relief, peacekeeping and peacemaking; the widespread struggles for democracy and popular power, especially in the Third World; the preponderance of micronationalism; and efforts by the United States to sell the "American way of life" as the only credible alternative left for the entire world in the face of the assumed victory of the bourgeoisie over communism and totalitarianism.[4] This has received intellectual support and rationalization from scholars like Francis Fukuyama in his "End of History" thesis, and Samuel P. Huntington in his "Clash of Civilization" postulations.[5]

In the view of Fukuyama, the world now needs to celebrate the "unabashed victory of economic and political liberalism," evidenced in the "triumph of the West, of the Western *idea*," and in the "exhaustion of

viable systematic alternatives to Western liberalism." He goes on to point
at

> the ineluctable spread of consumerist Western culture in such diverse contexts as
> peasants' markets and color television sets now omnipresent throughout China,
> the cooperative restaurants and clothing stores opened in the past year in Moscow,
> the Beethoven piped into Japanese department stores, and the rock music enjoyed
> alike in Prague, Rangoon, and Tehran.

> What we may be witnessing is not just the end of the Cold War, or the passing of
> a particular period of postwar history, but the end of history as such: that is, the
> end point of mankind's ideological evolution and the universalization of Western
> liberal democracy as the final form of human government.[6]

For Huntington, with the end of the cold war, the basis of all future
conflicts "in this new world will not be primarily ideological or primarily
economic. The great divisions among humankind and the dominating
source of conflict will be cultural...the principal conflicts of global politics
will occur between nations and groups of different civilizations. The clash
of civilizations will dominate global politics."[7] Huntington identifies
"seven or eight" civilizations among which he reluctantly includes Africa.
Fukuyama pays no attention to Africa. There seems to have been a rush to
celebrate the demise of the Soviet Union, which was interpreted to mean
the end of all alternative ideological consciousness and discourse.
Fukuyama and Huntington have repackaged cold war divisions, relabelling
them with ethnic, racial and religious stereotypes, and have overlooked the
emergence of more viable institutions and processes of conflict resolution
within the developing world. They confuse a consumerist culture with the
acceptance of everything Western and assume that peoples all over the
world are not only dying to accept and adopt Western values, but also that
they have no alternatives. They are not seeking ways to reduce differences
but ways to draw sharper lines and impose the views and perspectives, as
well as interests, of the West—in most cases, the culture of the United
States—on the world. As Rubenstein and Crocker have noted,

> Huntington's thinking remains bounded by the assumptions of political realism,
> the dominant philosophy of the Cold War period...civilizations are essentially
> superstates motivated by the same imperatives of insecurity and self-
> aggrandizement as were their Cold War and historical predecessors....Huntington
> has misunderstood the process of cultural change and value-formation. He seems
> wholly unaware that,..."culture is not some external straight jacket, but rather
> multiple suits of clothes, some of which we can and do discard because they
> impede our movements."[8]

Thus as far as Africa is concerned, both Fukuyama and Huntington have not demonstrated an appreciable understanding of the dynamics of culture, politics, and society which are gradually unfolding and likely to propel, the continent into the next century and beyond. Their stereotypes and pro-Western interpretations of the world have also served to paint a typical picture of stagnation, dormancy, and irrelevance. Yet, they admit that the world is changing rapidly. The fifty-four countries in Africa with over 500 million people remain part of the global system. Whatever changes are occurring in the global system are bound to affect them, be they the clashing of civilizations or the end of history or the emergence of American global dominance.

The changes above, as well as changes in information technology have greatly impacted on the autonomy, capabilities, and spheres of action open to the nation state. Boutros Boutros-Ghali has observed that "[t]he time of absolute and exclusive sovereignty...has passed" and states must "find a balance between the needs of good internal governance and the requirements of an ever more interdependent world."[9] In addition, as is evident in Africa, states are increasingly under pressure and attack. Quite a handful have become stagnant, exhausted or have collapsed out rightly.[10] The increasing interest in human rights at the global level has opened up new debates on the issues of sovereignty and autonomy. As Sharon Pauling notes, the "conflict between human rights and national sovereignty during times of war, or in the absence of democracy, or during economic marginalization, presents major challenge to the international community."[11] Posing some major arguments on this debate, Chester Crocker has written:

> Under what circumstances are territorial borders to be considered sacrosanct and who shall determine the answer? When do "identity groups" (peoples or ethnic fragments) have the right to secession, autonomy or independence? What "sovereign" rights, if any, do governments have to prevent outsiders from telling them how to treat their people, their economies and their environment? And what about the rights of outsiders to come to the aid of peoples victimized by the actions or inactions of local governments—or to create the functional equivalent of government where, as in Somalia, none exists? [12]

These are very important questions that underscore the need for a transnational conceptualization of issues relating to human rights, ethnic rights and autonomy, economic development, environmental protection, democracy and governance within states and at the global level.

These developments have opened the way for articulating global responses to deepening political problems around the world, especially in

Africa. It is equally the reasoning behind a global moral and political responsibility that has encouraged interventions in states like Somalia, sanctions against apartheid, interventions in Liberia, and peacekeeping missions around the world at great financial and other costs. When the UN Security Council adopted Resolution 688, which states that human suffering in any member state is a threat to global peace and security, it also laid the grounds for a global response to domestic conditions that might have political and nonpolitical dimensions. This has, of course, strengthened (?) the UN in its responses to and involvement in local matters, especially now that the Western powers (the United States in particular) need it to rationalize and legitimize their global agendas. Yet there has been a tendency to present the vintage position of the United States and the Western world as reflective of, and representative of, the conditions of poor, dominated, vulnerable and underdeveloped nations. In other words, adequate attention is hardly given to the number of developing nations that are likely to benefit from the changes in the emerging global order. Though it is true that most states seem to be losing power, influence, and some sovereignty as a result of new changes in the global order, it is also true that some are losing these qualities at a more rapid rate than others. Even if the loss of autonomy were uniform, some nations/regions have the potential and capacity to reclaim such autonomy—if and when it becomes necessary—more decisively than others.

In this chapter, we examine the ways in which the features of sovereignty have been watered down with recent developments in the global system. We then narrow the focus to Africa, making a brief review of the state and its rapid delegitimization due to changes at the substructural and superstructural levels. In this section we make a case for a new democratization agenda for Africa. We conclude by examining the responsibility of the global system to Africa and the degree of internal restructuring required to strengthen capacity in the emerging global division of labor.

Contemporary Erosions of Sovereignty

It would appear that scientific, economic, and social factors, rather than political developments, have contributed significantly to the erosion of state sovereignty in recent times. As Dharan Ghai has noted recently, in a study by the United Nations Research Institute for Social Development (UNRISD), "[e]conomic restructuring and technological development have reduced the effectiveness of a whole range of institutions that have served to provide social and economic security in the post-war period. One of the most complex challenges of our times has thus become the provision of a modicum of universal social and economic security in an era of open markets, fierce competition, rapid technological change and instant communications."[13] As the nations of the world come to depend more on each other, as transportation narrows distances, as communications make it possible for people to interact and exchange information and ideas, and as nations become readily permeable to the power of new communications systems, the ability of the state to lay claim to some higher level of authority gradually weakens:

> The quickening pace of change has caught much of the international community unawares. Capital, goods and people are now moving with such speed and complexity that it has become difficult to make predictions for more than a few years ahead. And political maps are being drawn and redrawn as myriad ethnic or political groups emerge to make new claims and stake out new territory. [14]

Of course, since the 1980s, with the crisis in the former Soviet Union, and more so since the emergence of the independent republics, the triumph of the market has not only narrowed ideological positions but has also drawn nations together in the struggle to penetrate markets, attract foreign aid and investments, and attract new technologies: "Already, capitalism is flourishing in regions as diverse as communist Asia and the former dictatorships of Latin America. Affluence is lifting millions out of poverty, giving many the chance to purchase their first Fiats and Toyotas as well as their first Apple computers and Panasonic VCRs. And inflation is brought to heel in even the most wayward economies."[15] This is certainly a somewhat exaggerated version of recent developments in the global system, especially the points about millions being lifted out of poverty and inflation being controlled. Yet, it does give a fair reflection of the triumph of the market. It is instructive, though, that in many such discussions Africa is completely left out. Yet in Africa, unprecedented socioeconomic and political dislocation and deterioration, and grinding poverty, have forced states to accept and adopt not only externally designed economic reform programs but also political prescriptions for reforms.[16] International bankers and donors have over the years come to exercise an unusually large influence over decision-making processes in the continent.[17] Such developments clearly challenge and erode the traditional capacity of the state in Africa, with implications for its ability to claim or exercise sovereignty at the international level.

The complex ways in which the global economy is now connected beyond ideological considerations (China is one of the largest trading partners of the United States, Vietnam is becoming a major trading partner, and Cuba is working hard to normalize relations) seem to have had the greatest impact. It has become very easy to establish, organize and operate businesses and carry out transactions outside the control of the state. There is no doubt that in a world relatively liberated from hard ideological constraints, "new technology is rewriting old concepts of sovereignty and over time will also change national objectives."[18] As the UNRISD has noted, the "computerization of production and communications systems continues to reinvent working relations, destroying many jobs and creating others—and sustaining new power relations within and between countries." [19] These new power relations have far-reaching implications for the recomposition of political spaces and the articulation of new political agendas around the world.

New "space-age" production systems are culminating in drastic cost-cutting for corporations, which are now in better positions to invest in research and development, attract skilled labor across the globe, and support political interests within nations to push policies favorable to capital. For instance, at the level of communications, "between 1970 and 1990,...the cost of a three-minute call between London and New York fell (in constant 1990 dollars) from $31 to $3. And the number of international calls has increased steadily: during the 1980s telecommunications traffic was expanding by 20 per cent per year."[20] According to the World Bank in its 1995 report, "Technological change and continually falling communications and transport costs have been a major factor behind global integration. Cross-border transport and trade are also easier today because of progress in resolving many of the political conflicts that have divided the economic world for decades, such as the cold war, the apartheid system in South Africa, and the volatile situation in the Middle East."[21] In today's global economy, manufacturing equipment are better built; they are faster, more efficient, and less cumbersome. The laptop computer has made it easy for work and communication to take place from virtually any location. Robots are increasingly being used in the production process, resulting in huge savings. In fact, between 1982 and 1992, the world experienced a ten fold increase in the use of robots.

Recent struggles for democracy in developing countries have benefited significantly from the cellular phone and fax machines, which despotic and repressive governments could not control: "Ideas transmitted by satellite broadcasts, fax machines, and Internet ports are prying open even authoritarian regimes." [22] As Walter B. Wriston has noted, the "information revolution is changing our global economy, transforming national political and business institutions and altering national foreign policy objectives and the methods of achieving them." [23] What has been referred to as the "digital age" with "powerful data networks" is drawing developing nations "into the borderless information economy." [24] For most governments, the choice is often clear: join in this borderless economy or be isolated and remain in the dark. No nation has chosen to opt out of this system, not even those under the control of religious and ideological fundamentalists. Medical practices, experiments in science and technology, banking services, academic research, and other new initiatives are being undertaken in cooperation, by persons separated by hundreds of thousands of miles. [25]

The CNN's "World Report" is a typical example of cooperation between journalists, reporters, and newscasters located around the world. There are about 1.2 billion television sets around the world, facilitating not only the spread of information about new products but also a consumerist culture that recognizes no national boundary or ideology. Many programs are deliberately designed to penetrate, manipulate, and restructure the socioeconomic and cultural practices of other nations and regions. The United States "exports more than 120,000 hours of television programming annually to Europe alone, and the global trade in programming is growing at more than 15 per cent per year."[26] It is not unusual to find young people and elites in Nigeria quite up-to-date on developments in America because their televisions are permanently set on the CNN channel. In fact, in most media houses and government offices around the world, television sets are permanently tuned to CNN, while radio sets are tuned to the BBC, VOA, or some other major international network. Getting information quickly, or as events happen, has become a hallmark of the modern era. Clearly, governments no longer exercise absolute control over all "internal" policies. Every action against groups, communities, individuals, dissidents, even coup plotters, comes under the very critical scrutiny of international human rights groups and foreign governments:

> The state may be losing its monopoly as the sole arbiter of justice within its border. Perhaps this will prove a blessing for humanity in the long run....Today, human rights groups such as Amnesty International challenge the state's claim to be the sole dispenser of justice. In some cases, the International Monetary Fund, the World Bank and other UN agencies have cut aid to the very worst human-rights violators. The U.S. has also been increasingly willing to use aid as a lever, particularly in instances where cold war diplomacy no longer requires it to look the other way, to curb the excesses of its allies. [27]

At no time in world history have these nonstate actors wielded more relevance, influence and power than at the moment. The breakdown of ideological orthodoxies and the search for new patterns of socioeconomic and power relations have further reduced the relevance of the state, in favor of less formal and private structures and institutions.

Governments, in spite of their control over their respective central banks, can hardly boast they control the flow of money or other financial transactions within their borders or beyond. Moreover, foreigners are increasingly owning larger proportions of financial outlays, even in the developed economies. Between 1970 and 1988, the share of American government bonds owned by foreigners rose from 7 to 17 percent. In the former West Germany, the share of the national debt owned by foreigners rose from 5 to 34 percent in the same period. Further, between 1980 and 1990, transborder traffic in equities increased from $120 billion to $1.4 trillion.[28] Aside from the clear failure of states, even a powerful nation like the United States, to control the drug traffic and the laundering of drug money, there is also their failure to break the powerful global financial empire linking drug traffickers in Afghanistan, Bolivia, Colombia, India, Iran, Nigeria, Pakistan, Peru, Saudi Arabia, Saudi Arabia, the United States, Zambia, and parts of Europe. The drug business is worth around $500 billion annually. Over $100 billion dollars have been laundered in Europe and the United States in the last decade. In Bolivia, the drug trade accounts for 20 percent of the country's GNP, and no nation has really succeeded in wiping out the business, not to mention controlling the inflow and outflow of drug money.[29] The computer has put within the reach of average citizens the power to execute complex (even if illegal) banking transactions within the confines of their homes. As P. Passel has revealed, in New York a single building houses a computer that moves a trillion dollars, which is more than the money supply of the United States, across the world every business day.[30] Governments simply have no idea as to the huge amounts of money that move around the world every day:

> The world's financial marketplace will never recede to its old traditional borders. Lines on the maps, traditionally the cause of wars, are now porous. Money and ideas move across borders in a manner and at a speed never before seen. Markets are no longer geographical locations, but on a screen transmitted from anywhere in the world. It is difficult to suddenly accept the judgment of thousands of traders who translate politicians' actions into new monetary values, because this situation has arisen so quickly. Nevertheless, it is about as useful to curse the thermometer for recording a heat wave as it is to rail against the values the global market puts on a nation's currency. [31]

The unprecedented "mobility of global capital" has created stronger linkages between economic and financial constituencies around the world and the "destinies of people from all walks of life—Czech steelworkers, U.S. school teachers, Ghanaian cocoa farmers, Argentine restaurateurs— are increasingly interwoven in a dense web of financial transactions whose speed and volume are difficult to comprehend and whose scale threatens the world economy."[32] It is equally true that "globalization is also making crime much more transnational. Criminals are among the first to take advantage of any relaxation of national border controls and advances in transportation and communications."[33]

The flow of information has had a major impact on state sovereignty. Internet connections are expanding by 16 percent every month, fiber optics are transmitting 40 billion bits of data per second, and the United States Army claims that by A.D. 2000 there will be as many computers as persons in the world. The Internet links well over 25 million users across the world. There are over 120 communications satellites beaming regularly televised images to practically every corner of the globe, and all political upheavals, acts of violence, famine, even construction activity, become part of instant global information. Pictures of violence in apartheid South Africa, of the Tiananmen Square massacre, and of street riots in Zambia and Los Angeles were recorded by satellite, without clearance from governments, and broadcast around the world. In the United States alone, over 5 million people have e-mail addresses, and communication takes just seconds:

> These developments have enormous economic and social impacts—transforming working relations, destroying some jobs and creating others. Many companies can, for example, now export labour-intensive data processing jobs overseas: the Philippines has dozens of companies where women work for just $150 per month, keying in 10,000 characters an hour, which are then transmitted instantly back to mainframe computers in the United States. By shrinking effective distances and allowing instant communications, these developments are also helping to create and sustain new power relationships both within and between countries. [34]

Transnational corporations are exploiting the triumph of the market and strengthening their control not only over what is left of the nation-state but also over the global economy. There are about 37,000 transnational corporations in the world with about 200,000 affiliates, and together they control 75 percent of global trade in manufactured goods and services as well as in commodities.[35] Because about one-third of this trade is intrafirm, governments have had very little or no control over the content and direction of the trade. The attraction that nation-states now have for market relations is evident in the renewed expansion of investments. Companies like "General Electric Co. are sinking tens of millions of dollars into building factories and power plants in Mexico and India. Microsoft Corp gets more than 50% of its revenue from international sales. Toyota Motor Corp is powering its way into Southeast Asia as is Volkswagen into China," and Hewlett-Packard has opened a research and development center in Guadalajara.[36] In spite of the uncertainties of Eastern Europe and the conflicts in the various republics, Western business interests are busy setting up branch offices and taking advantage of new tax incentives in the march towards market economies at the expense of national governments:

> Globalization of the economy is also eroding the power of government in the Western world. Today, no nation can control its economic destiny unilaterally. Half of all the products made in the U.S. now have foreign parts. Due to the growing web of corporate alliances, mergers and takeovers, half of all imports and exports are between companies and their foreign affiliates or parents. Corporate intrafirm trading now comprises somewhere in the range of one third of total international trade....State governors and big city mayors, whether they be in the U.S., Europe or China, compete for the business of multinational corporations. U.S. exports now generate one in six U.S. jobs...up from one in eight as recently as 1986. In just 10 years (1970–80) trade as a percentage of gross national product has doubled. [37]

Yet, the move towards a new global political economy is not flawless or without conflict and disappointments. As mentioned earlier, only nations with goods to sell, with the resources to buy raw materials, exploit cheap labor, take advantage of new market opportunities, and exploit other societies are benefiting from these changes: "The integration of the world economy is good news for those countries sufficiently powerful to take advantage of accelerated growth opportunities. But it will also work to the disadvantage of weaker countries and regions that, in the face of stiff competition, are vulnerable to flights of capital, skill and enterprise."[38] Africa is clearly not part of these changes, even if the state is equally under pressure. [39] It is true that the expanding global economy would lead to increased growth. But the question is growth for whom? It is also true that the rapid changes in the world will lead to increased global awareness, the creation of a new global culture and consciousness, better appreciation of the specificities of other societies, and better living conditions for those who are able to participate in the new economy. Yet, it is clear to all that it is the huge who profit and that it is the hegemony—seeking transnational corporations who will reap more benefits. This will make them even stronger than the nation-state and more capable of controlling the fortunes and future of developing social formations. The state in the developing world, particularly in Africa, has been further weakened by neoliberal prescriptions from donors and lenders, while the "processes of fragmentation that have weakened the state have also affected communities: migration, urbanization and mass media exposure to a global consumer culture have undermined local capacity to respond cohesively to changing circumstances."[40]

Besides these, however, more negative impacts of the new non-state-centric order have been raised. Fast growth is causing severe environmental disasters, especially in the developing world. As the state gets weaker, it is increasingly incapable of protecting the environment. Big corporations are taking advantage of the financial crunch of poorer nations to dump dangerous toxic wastes on their territories.[41] Corruption is increasing as corporations compete for hegemony and try to win the support of politicians and the custodians of state power. This erodes efficiency principles and creates complex patronage systems which militate against development and accountability. In spite of these changes, unemployment is increasing as companies opt for automation and shift jobs to developing nations where labor costs are lower. The U.S. dollar has continued to fall, the Japanese economy is stalling, and unemployment in Europe is about 12 percent. Companies like IBM and Lockheed are laying off thousands of skilled workers in an effort to cut costs and maintain a respectable profit margin.[42] Workers in the West are becoming more myopic and insecure as they blame workers in the developing countries as well as immigrants for their problems. They also see the importation of goods and services from developing regions of the world as having a direct impact on their productivity and place in their economies. Of course, many have no information on the global networks of Western corporations.[43] Overall, the restructured power relations are generating profits, expanding markets, and encouraging new investments as well as research and development on the one hand, but creating extensive negative coalitions, contradictions, crises, and conflicts on the other:

> Today, international economic interdependence is once again generating a lot of discord. Nations are engaged in bitter international negotiations over cross-border pollution, intellectual property rights, and differing work-place standards. Worse are the savage wars in Kuwait, the Balkans, Angola, and other hot spots. Military buildups and the spread of nuclear weapons in Asia and elsewhere offer the potential of even larger conflagrations.[44]

Moreover, the new changes in the global system have "been disruptive for many people and communities" and have "forced many more to migrate in search of a better life."[45] People are moving more than ever from rural to urban areas and across national boundaries in search of the perceived and promised benefits of the new globalization. The end of apartheid and the lifting of sanctions have made it possible for thousands of Africans, skilled and unskilled, to seek greener pastures in South Africa. In particular, thousands of Nigerians and Ghanaians have emigrated to South Africa to take advantage of the new economic boom. There were 16 million refugees in the world at the end of 1993, mostly from Africa. In 1993, over 100 million people around the world were resident outside their countries of citizenship. There are about 3 million illegal immigrants in Europe and about 2.6 million in the United States.[46] There are more Nigerians making refugee and political asylum claims in Europe and America today than was the case during the country's civil war of 1967–70. Immigrants are a source of cheap and ready labor. They remit millions of dollars home, and a nation like the Philippines actually promotes the emigration of citizens as a source of foreign exchange. Yet the developed nations have become very restrictive, and in the United States, Germany, and in other European locations there is a new violent backlash against immigrants, who are now blamed for all the ills of their respective societies. As well, the increased movement of persons across boundaries has intensified ethnic, religious, racial, and other forms of suspicions, violence, and tensions.

The new globalization is also creating new forms of inequality between rich and poor nations; between workers in the rich developed nations and those in the poorer nations; between different forms of capitalist growth and accumulation; it is deepening social and cultural peculiarities which are increasingly being politicized and finding expression in religious fundamentalism and ethnic conflicts:

> Many countries have made enormous economic strides, but the benefits have not been evenly distributed: opulence and poverty march side by side...Even in the richer countries, the social fabric has been steadily weakened—unravelled by unemployment, crime and the pernicious effects of narcotic drugs—while at the same time many of the institutions that, historically, have offered some basic level of social welfare are close to collapse. And while some old ideological enmities have been laid to rest, many new ones are now surfacing: in 1993, 42 countries had major armed conflicts and 37 others suffered from some form of political violence.[47]

The new global order is being constructed without incorporating Africa. To be sure, a handful of countries like South Africa, Botswana, and Egypt are mentioned here and there, but for the entire African continent, the ongoing changes seem to be consolidating the region's peripheralization in the global division of labor.

In spite of these and other problems, there is clear evidence that the sovereignty of the nation-state and its ability to independently determine and execute control over its territory have been severely eroded. As UNRISD has concluded, the "world is changing faster than ever before—and on a broader scale."[48] The wear and tear of state power over time, the rise of powerful nonstate actors, developments in science and technology, and the continuing power of primordial loyalties and considerations by individuals and communities within nation-states continue to create outlets for challenging, conditioning, and eroding the influence and power of the state: "Today the velocity of change is so great in all aspects of science, technology, economics and politics that the tectonic plates of national sovereignty and power have begun to shift." [49] How does this all relate to or affect Africa?

Africa: The Delegitimization of the State and the New Global Order

Africa has been a victim of too many negative developments in the global system. Virtually every powerful imperialist group or interest in history has attacked, pillaged, and destroyed institutions and political processes in Africa. From the Arabs to the Europeans, through the experiences of slavery and colonization, to contemporary neocolonial conditions, Africa has never been given the opportunity to develop on its own terms.[50] *Political independence* in the late 1950s and in the 1960s has brought very little improvement to the conditions of living, and institutions have not become more democratic or sensitive to the needs of the people.[51] In the last quarter of 1995, the World Bank concluded that the "plight of the African continent remains the most serious challenge for the emerging world order."[52] This is rather unfortunate, given the region's abundant wealth and the clear choice between the systemic restructuring for growth and development, on the one hand, and the consolidation and reproduction of wasteful, exploitative, and subservient neocolonial relations on the other.[53] Since the end of colonial rule, leaders in the vast majority of African states, have opted for the second option above, since the state structures were fully under the control of elites who relied on depoliticization, ideological containment, and violence to retain control.

The postcolonial state, largely a reproduction of the exploitative and undemocratic colonial state, lacked the capacity to mobilize the people for the challenges of the postcolonial society. Rather than engage in a program for dismantling alien and exploitative relations at political independence, the new elite used state power to establish unequal relations with imperialism and to repress the people. Civil society was suffocated as popular organizations were banned; scholars, students, journalists and political activists were thrown into jail or forced into exile, while the treasury was looted without restraint. In no time, extreme positions emerged on all fronts, coups and countercoups became a pastime, the economies decayed and at best stagnated, debts piled up, civil unrest became commonplace, and investors held back on new capital or simply abandoned the crisis-ridden economy. Unable to service their debts or maintain creditworthiness, the African economies were soon abandoned by donors, creditors, and suppliers. This forced them to adopt prepackaged stabilization and structural adjustment programs. Since they lacked a base in civil society and remained corrupt and repressive, adjustment programs further alienated the people, generated deeper contradictions and conflicts, and deepened the economic crisis. This severely damaged the already weak legitimacy of the state and furthered its delegitimization. Frustrations and anger found expression in religious and ethnic extremism, coups, riots, demonstrations, and a general commitment to cheat, evade, challenge, and destroy the state, which was now seen as the enemy. Claude Ake effectively summarizes the crisis of the postcolonial state in Africa:

> The state in Africa is plagued by a crisis of legitimacy because of its external dependence, the decision of the political class to inherit the colonial socioeconomic system instead of transforming it, the massive use of state violence to de-radicalize the nationalist movement and impose political monolithism in the face of deep-rooted social pluralism, and the use of force to repress a rising tide of resentment against the failures of the nationalist leadership, especially the mismanagement of development, and the impoverishment of the masses....The post-colonial state is also disconnected from society and exists with it in a relationship of mutual hostility....With minor exceptions, the citizens of the state in contemporary Africa are disconnected from it. They conform to its commands as they must, while committing their political loyalties to kinship groups and political formations within it.[54]

Clearly the state has not been constituted and has not operated as a *state* in Africa. It has operated more like a confused structure with no sense of direction and no sense of mission. It has embarked on a project of destruction rather than one of construction: it has squandered rather than generated resources; it has asphyxiated rather than built and reinvigorated civil society; and it has mortgaged rather than liberated the African economy. Ake is of the view that, in the "face of incompetence, abject failure and betrayal of popular aspirations," the custodians of state power have resorted to violence in Africa largely to cover up their dirty tracks and divert attention. Specifically, Ake argues that "[s]ome African states look like a mere occupying force and politics has assumed the character of warfare, a syndrome which has propelled the specialists of violence, the military, into the center of politics."[55] The implications of this reliance on violence, intimidation, and manipulation are quite obvious:

> An obsessive quest for total power, a tendency to disregard the rule of law, a tendency to reduce right to power, legitimizing coerced acquiescence, oppression and brutalization of the subjects of the state sometimes verging on the gratuitous—these are the standard features of political life in Africa which have made the realization of freedom, even bourgeois freedom, all but impossible.[56]

Under the conditions outlined thus far, it is clear that the notion of sovereignty never applied to African states beyond the legal sense: they were from the start dominated by powerful transnational corporations which they could not control; they lacked control in determining the prices of their exports, not to speak of their imports; they were dependent on foreign aid, technology, skills, information, military supplies, and food; they were vulnerable and subject to all sorts of pressures and manipulative dictates from the developed nations; and they had no power in international organizations.

At the *internal* level, the postcolonial African state was virtually useless to its own people: it could not guarantee any form of security; it lacked a connection to the dynamic developments within nonbourgeois communities and constituencies; the state disrespected its own laws, which the people violated at the slightest opportunity; power distribution and resource allocation favored only a tiny fraction of the population; state currencies were practically worthless; the state lacked reliable statistics on everything (trade, population, crime, immigration, foreign debts, etc.); and more often than not, the African state relied on donors and foreign nations for almost everything including the repair of roads! How could such states lay claim to any sovereignty? Even today, they have no projects for citizenship. Among Africans, the patriotic zeal for Africa is great, but for their respective nations it is very low, and the national anthem and national flag are either completely alien to the people or seen as mere symbols of elite interests.

The resort to ethnic, religious, and regional particularities by Africans is a direct result of the failure of the state.[57] Where a state relies on violence to maintain control, these primordial organizations do not. Where the state relies on lies and propaganda to control citizens, these organizations generally do not. And where the state cannot protect the citizens from the vagaries of life, emergencies, domestic and external violence, these organizations can. Thus the relevance and sovereignty of the state have been virtually encapsulated within the orbit and power of these primordial organizations. The prevalence of coups and countercoups is also a direct indictment of the state, its agents and agencies. Its nonhegemonic nature and limited legitimacy, its failure to provide a basis for rational politics, failure to maintain discipline within the ranks of the elites, and failure to meet the basic needs of the majority, all of this has made it possible for sections of the dominant classes to seize power through military coups. As a rule, military interventions have only succeeded in making the African condition worse and the sovereignty of the state compromised.

The changes discussed earlier practically do not concern Africa. Changes in science and technology, the expansion of new markets, investments abroad, and the development of skills to fit the information superhighway and new fiber optic technology have simply bypassed Africa. True, a few individuals in select countries are acquiring these skills. Yet, they make no impact as the entire continent continues to wallow in crisis, disease, violence, uncertainty, neglect, misery, and unprecedented pain and poverty.[58] Unfortunately, in spite of the region's desperate conditions, its extreme and intolerable poverty,[59] the continent is "simply not commanding the kind of attention in the new world order to keep it from dissolving into new world disorder."[60] Investors are not coming into the region, crisis situations are allowed to mature and explode before responses are made, foreign aid has dried up, and though the cold war has ebbed, repressive leaders and military juntas still do business as usual with Western nations, which have now become the champions for political pluralism in the developing world. Though there are hundreds of pro-democracy movements in the region, and a few have actually succeeded in unseating recalcitrant dictators and presidents-for-life, they have not received the sort of support that Russia, Poland, or even Mexico is receiving from the West. At one level, therefore, the region is clearly being abandoned at the very time it requires support to forge ahead with structural transformations through global support for genuine forces of *democratization and liberation.*[61] With this sort of global neglect and deepening internal crisis, it is becoming increasingly clear that only a crossregional and crossnational response to the African predicament would provide the needed leverage for survival in the twenty-first century:

A concept of sovereignty in an interdependent world must not be seen in terms of absolute sovereignty of each state as in the past, but in terms of cooperation and collaboration of states for the overall interests of all. What is the value and meaning of sovereignty for a state that cannot feed its citizens? Sovereignty without responsibility, particularly responsibility to the citizens of a nation, is meaningless.[62]

With the African state badly bruised and delegitimized, and with the elites in disarray and without legitimacy, Africa simply stands very little or no chance of benefiting from the new globalization.

The Social Basis of a New Sovereignty: The Challenge of Democratization in Africa

It is generally agreed that African boundaries are colonial creations. While regimes have gone to war over the borders, the masses of African peoples have had little or no respect for the borders. Hence, most of the transborder trade in Africa goes unrecorded. As well, there is agreement that the state in Africa has failed in terms of serving as a basis for socioeconomic and political development, growth, and stability.[63] As I. William Zartman has argued, the state in Africa, generally speaking, is almost incapable of performing the "basic functions...as analyzed in various theories of the state." Furthermore,

As the decisionmaking center of government, the state is paralyzed and inoperative: laws are not made, order is not preserved, and social cohesion is not enhanced...As a symbol of identity, it has lost its power of conferring a name on its people and a meaning to their social action...As a territory, it is no longer assured security and provisionment by a central sovereign organization...As the authoritative political institution, it has lost its legitimacy, which is therefore up for grabs, and so has lost its right to command and conduct public affairs...As a system of socioeconomic organization, its functional balance of inputs and outputs is destroyed; it no longer receives supports from nor exercises controls over its people, and it no longer is even the target of demands, because its people know that it is incapable of providing supplies. *No longer functioning, with neither traditional nor charismatic nor institutional sources of legitimacy, it has lost the right to rule.* [64]

Rather than focus on purely political and legal aspects of sovereignty, Africans are raising new issues which articulate the basis of socioeconomic and political progress on cooperation, integration, and collective action. As Olusegun Obasanjo has noted, traditional notions of sovereignty are no longer useful when states embark on a project of perpetually intimidating their peoples and wasting scarce resources; when states can no longer guarantee the safety and security of their citizens; when states can no longer promote the project of development and peace; and when the global order requires efficient, effective, relatively stable, and democratic forms of governance.[65] For vulnerable, weak, poor, foreign-dominated, and marginalized nations like those in Africa, therefore, the only way out is to join forces, sacrifice some degree of autonomy, set up joint institutions, and engage in collective action for peace, stability, and development. This is the more important when it is recognized that "many African nations are but one step away from crisis."[66] In a situation in which the "lost decade of the 1980s" has left the region and its peoples "for the most part poorer, less educated, less healthy, and with fewer prospects for better lives than they had almost a generation ago,"[67] these states need to develop a vision of security "which is broader than the conventional narrow focus on military or strategic security. Welfare must condition security rather than warfare. Many of the dangers of African security and survival, population, environment, poverty, disease, and drugs cannot be dealt with through armaments, neither can they be dealt with successfully unilaterally by one nation."[68] This is exactly the basis on which the new sovereignty is being conceptualized: one with a less absolute regard for borders, the supreme authority of governments, but one with a full realization, rather, that the world is changing and that national borders are not only being easily permeated but are crumbling.

The only platform on which this new idea is being articulated, or could be effectively articulated is in the ongoing struggles for democracy, accountability, social justice, popular participation, gender equality, and the empowerment of the people, their constituencies and communities. This project realizes that poverty in Ghana is similar to poverty in Kenya; that the creative abilities of the people have been suppressed for a very long time; and that only the opening up of the political systems, respect for the will of the people, and the promotion of clear patterns of harmony and unity within a holistic democratic agenda can set Africa on the path to recovery. In Liberia, Burundi, Togo, Somalia, the Sudan, Mozambique, and other spots of crisis and conflict in the region, the disintegration or delegitimization of the state as well as the traditional repression of the people, all in the name of national autonomy and security, are directly related to the outbreak of hostilities. Of course, it is equally on record that many of the ongoing conflicts in Africa have been initiated, encouraged or funded by external interests during and since the end of the cold war: "Frequently external policies and involvement contribute to, and exacerbate, local conflicts and crises. When the crisis becomes full blown it is then that the international community perceives its role as 'let's get in there and clean up the mess' as if it bore no responsibility. Conflicts in Africa, in particular, have their roots in international controversies and failed government policies. Overcentralized, repressive regimes are often at the heart of Africa's problems."[69] It is these conditions that have encouraged the struggles for accountability, participation, democracy and social justice all over the continent. Yet, "whatever form our democratic practice takes, if it fails to deliver in enhancing the living standard and condition of the people, socially and economically, people will soon start to doubt why they should embrace democracy."[70] This will be an unfortunate and dangerous development, as it will see a rapid withdrawal into particularistic cocoons. It will give the beleaguered state and its agents room to reestablish their control and domination and reintroduce new patterns of repression and waste.

If our contention is that, in view of the rapid erosion of state sovereignty and the deepening systemic and economic crisis in Africa, democratization is the only way out, what are the features and constraints of this new agenda for reconstructing state power? In the short term, there is very little to hope for. The current agenda for democracy in Africa is largely informed by pressures from external interests and led by political actors who were directly and/or indirectly responsible for the crisis in Africa. In most instances, political liberalization has unleashed a new brand of intolerance, violence, instability, uncertainty, and stalemate.[71] Largely a precipitate of long-standing repression of the popular will, the current state of near-anarchy in most African states is also a reflection of the privatization of the democratic enterprise by opportunistic elites.[72]

In the longer term however, there is hope for Africa. As the current euphoria evaporates and the victories are seen to be very limited and superficial, genuine struggles for democracy will emerge, new leaders will take over the struggle, and a new agenda for mobilization, education, action, and liberation will be articulated. The option of a return to the status quo is inconceivable under current circumstances. Genuine democratization will facilitate the participation of Africa in the global economy. At the internal level it will reduce expenditure on defence and promote dialogue, creativity, and productivity within nations. At the external level, the lack of democracy would no longer be an excuse for denying foreign aid, withholding new investments, and imposing externally designed economic and political programs. A genuine democratic agenda will have as its core the deconstruction and recomposition of the repressive and inefficient neocolonial state. This is largely because such neocolonial states, which parade themselves as democratic (even in the liberal sense), are incapable of decentralizing the bureaucracy, extracting support and legitimacy from the people, carrying out far-reaching reform programs, bridging the rural-urban gap, improving the lot of women and the poor, controlling the influence of transnational corporations, whipping some discipline into the ranks of the dominant elites, and establishing a credible basis for growth, stability, and development. Such state structures remain vulnerable to mass uprisings, the withdrawal of loyalties by regional, religious and ethnic groups, coups and countercoups, and international sanctions. In the final analysis, such state structures have little time—or the desire and the resources—to participate effectively and profitably in the changing global order.

It is clear therefore that Africa is in a serious bind. The traditional notions of sovereignty no longer hold supreme as the borders of nations become porous, and powerful global tendencies, interests, and patterns of interaction are evolving. As nations struggle to exploit the benefits of this changing order, the African continent is neck-deep in disorder, and is engaged in a retrogressive march because the regimes in the past have squandered opportunities for growth and development, while the new movements lack the courage to genuinely transfer power to the people. The new movements also lack the courage and agenda with which to challenge inherited neocolonial relations, dismantle the oppressive state, and allow the people to reach the very highest points of their creative abilities. Yet, painful lessons will be learned from current experiences, and the continent will have to choose between far-reaching restructuring and democratization on the one hand, and stagnation or outright disintegration on the other.[73]

Conclusions: The Global System and Africa

Carol Lancaster has argued that the marginalization of Africa "is not just speculation. Not only are foreign governments closing embassies and cutting back aid flows, but Africa's role in the world economy is also shrinking. African exports and imports as a percentage of total world trade contracted from 4 percent in 1965 to 2 percent in 1992. Sub-Saharan Africa is seen less and less as a credible or useful economic and diplomatic partner and increasingly as a humanitarian problem for the world."[74] Specifically on the United States, Lancaster notes that "Sub-Saharan Africa has never ranked high among U.S. foreign priorities. The United States has relatively little trade with Africa, currently directing only 1 percent of its exports to the region, and this percentage has been declining over the past decade. U.S. investment in sub-Saharan Africa is similarly

Towards the Future 215

small and like its exports, it is concentrated in two countries—Nigeria and South Africa."[75] This situation is getting worse with a Republican majority in the U.S. Congress. The Republican Senate and House have introduced major bills that are bound to further marginalize U.S. interests in Africa and severely cut assistance to African nations, including those that had been encouraged to carry out far-reaching political and economic reforms.[76] This is even more certain with the Clinton Administration's rather unclear and unfocused approach to Africa's numerous needs and problems.

This is interesting, given the historical linkages between America and Africa and the sizable number of African-Americans in the United States. While low foreign aid, neglect, disrespect, and the marginalization of Africa reflect the weaknesses of the region, they also show the weaknesses of African constituencies abroad, especially in the United States.[77] With encouragement and pressure from the West and from the United States in particular, desperate African regimes have undertaken very painful and difficult adjustment programs. These programs had to be imposed and forced on the people through repressive means. Midway into the implementation of adjustment programs, and in the context of the disruptions, coalitions, conflicts, and contradictions they generated within and between classes, donors, and lenders compelled African regimes to initiate political restructuring programs. Countries like Malawi and Kenya actually had their foreign aid withheld until they opened up political spaces and organized multiparty elections. The vast majority have complied, usually to the peril of incumbent regimes, military and civilian. Yet Western nations, investors, donors, and big corporations have not bothered to support the changes in Africa. Compared with the rush to Eastern Europe, the huge loans and other financial and material support for Russia, and general responses to crisis in many parts of the world, the concern for Africa seems not to be in existence.[78] In fact, with the end of the cold war, an era in which the East and the West used African states as pawns, "U.S. strategic interests in Africa—never compelling—have greatly diminished."[79] Boutros Boutros-Ghali has observed that though African states have embarked on political and economic restructuring programs to satisfy donors and lenders, "investment is not materializing."[80] Salim A. Salim, the secretary-general of the Organization of African Unity (OAU), has noted that as a result of "global changes, there is less flow of resources to Africa. In net terms, Africa is giving out more than it gets from the world community."[81] Finally, Ellen J. Sirleaf has lamented that though "many African governments have been putting in place far-reaching private sector development strategies," no new investment has come to the region.[82] Immigration, investment, information-sharing, and the general flow of skills and resources discriminate against Africa. Thus in an increasingly complex and highly competitive global order, the already desperate and beleaguered African state is in no position to talk about autonomy, sovereignty, or peace when it has no capacity to meet the basic or minimal needs of the people or to control the vagaries of the global system which have significant impacts and implications for the region's recovery. It would appear therefore that the new sovereignty has to be internally driven, deriving its power, content, context, and direction from *domestic* sources rather than from the global system. This in no way implies that the West does not owe Africa support, at least for the centuries of brutalization, exploitation, domination, and underdevelopment. Even on the grounds of self-interest, the West should realize that a peaceful and developing Africa will produce fewer wars, fewer refugees, and fewer immigrants who enter North American and European nations legally and illegally and overstretch social and other services. But Africa cannot wait for the developed countries to make up their minds. Further, it is clear that insofar as Africa remains backward, unstable, and dependent, it will not be taken seriously by the developed nations. This means that the nations of Africa must abandon traditional notions of sovereignty, autonomy, territoriality, and so on, pull their resources together, mobilize their people, integrate their economies, and plan a grand strategy for moving the region forward.

Today, virtually all donors and lenders have come to endorse regionalism as the only way out for nations in an increasingly competitive and complex global order.[83] This is even more necessary for poor and underdeveloped nations that have failed to attract sufficient foreign investments and are clearly behind in the new technologies. The developed countries of Europe and America are taking regionalism very seriously, as evidenced in the establishment of the European Union (EU) and the North American Free Trade Area (NAFTA). The states of Western Europe have already given up some state authority and plan to set up a uniform defense force, a single currency, and common policies on the environment and health. Clearly, they are moving rapidly in that direction. Mexico's membership in NAFTA certainly made it easier for President Clinton to arrange a huge loan to support the former's declining currency, the *peso*. In Africa, regionalism has had a very poor record. There is hardly one integration scheme that can be pronounced a success.[84] Given their usually conservative and pro-status quo dispositions, African elites have often seen regionalism as a political struggle between the bourgeois classes and the people. The people have never been mobilized for collective sacrifices, self-reliance, and development. In the final analysis, regional integration schemes have been severely politicized, other Africans have been branded as "illegal aliens" and expelled *en masse* from some African states, and these same foreigners have been blamed for election-rigging, prostitution, armed robbery, pressure on social services, and failings of governments, which are badly in need of scapegoats. Rather than uniting Africans, regional cooperation schemes have created alienation, suspicion, conflict, and disunity. Because African states have been largely undemocratic, they have found it impossible to cooperate on critical regional matters and make concessions to a larger political center in the longer-term interest of the continent.

The argument can be made that it is not enough to adopt stabilization and adjustment programs or to initiate new programs for regional integration as responses to the predicaments of dependence, underdevelopment, and marginalization. Only a democratic political arrangement within African states can guarantee the ability to make concessions to subregional arrangements, mobilize the people, get the masses to accept the pains of economic and political reforms, and facilitate political negotiations that would reduce the power of the nation-state without creating conditions of suspicion and insecurity. If democracy does not become the basis of governance in Africa, recovery from the current socioeconomic and political disorder will be impossible. The need to open up the political system, create popular, and democratic structures and processes, guarantee basic freedoms and liberties, and empower the people and their communities and organizations cannot be overstressed. In fact, without a genuine mass-based democratic agenda, Africans will continue to flee their respective nations for greener and more peaceful pastures; intellectuals and professionals will continue to relocate abroad; the masses will remain alienated from the state; and all qualities of statehood will come under challenge. Under such conditions sovereignty will have no meaning; states will collapse, become dormant, or remain perpetually violent and unstable; and the region will remain a point of sour jokes in the global community, rejected by old foes and friends alike, and an irrelevant actor in the emerging global division of labor and power. Under such conditions, no matter how generous we might want to be, Africa will not and cannot be part of what the World Bank refers to as a "truly global golden age in the twenty-first century."[85]

Endnotes

1. Christopher Farrell, "The Triple Revolution," *Business Week* (1994 Special Bonus Issue) (November 1994) (emphasis added).

2. Shimon Peres, Israeli Foreign Minister, quoted in Ibid.

3. "The End of Sovereignty," in *Great Decisions 1993* (Ithaca, NY: Foreign Policy Association), p. 7 (emphasis added).

4. Professor Olufemi Taiwo of Loyola University has termed this the "Be-Like-Mike Syndrome." See his unpublished paper, "The Be-Like-Mike Syndrome: An Essay on Contemporary Non-Transitions to Democracy."

5. See Francis Fukuyama, "The End of History?" *The National Interest* (16) (1989) and Samuel P. Huntington, "The Clash of Civilizations?" *Foreign Affairs* (Summer 1993).

6. Francis Fukuyama, "The End of History?" pp. 3–4.

7. Samuel Huntington, "The Clash of Civilizations?" op. cit., p. 22.

8. Richard Rubenstein and Jarle Crocker, "Challenging Huntington," *Foreign Policy* (96) (Fall 1994), pp. 115 and 118.

9. Cited in Francis Mading Deng, "State Collapse: The Humanitarian Challenge to the United Nations," in I. William Zartman (ed.), *Collapsed States: The Disintegration and Restoration of Legitimate Authority*, (Boulder: Lynne Rienner, 1995), p. 212.

10. See the case studies, Ibid.. See also Robert Kaplan, "The Coming Anarchy," *Atlantic Monthly* (February 1994) and Steven Holmes, "Africa: From Cold War to Cold Shoulders," *The New York Times* (March 7, 1993).

11. Sharon Pauling, "International Involvement: How Much Is Enough?" *Africa Notes* (Institute for African Studies, Cornell University) (November 1993), p. 4.

12. Cited in Francis M. Deng, "State Collapse: The Humanitarian Challenge...," op. cit., p. 209.

13. Dharan Ghai, "Preface" to United Nations Research Institute for Social Development, *States of Disarray: The Social Effects of Globalization* (Geneva: UNRISD, 1995), p. v.

14. Ibid., p. 8.

15. "Introduction: 21st Century Capitalism," *Business Week* (1994 Special Bonus Edition) (November 1994).

16. See Julius O. Ihonvbere, "The Economic Crisis in Sub-Saharan Africa: Depth, Dimensions and Prospects for Recovery," *The Journal of International Studies* (27) (July 1991).

17. See Carol Lancaster, "Governance in Africa: Should Foreign Aid Be Linked to Political Reform?" in *Africa Governance in the 1990s: Objectives, Resources, and Constraints*, (Atlanta: The Carter Center of Emory University, March 1990).

18. Walter B. Wriston, "Technology and Sovereignty," *Foreign Affairs* (Winter 1988/89), p. 73.

19. UNRISD, *States of Disarray*, op. cit., p. 9.

20. Ibid., pp. 28–29.

21. World Bank, *World Development Report 1995* (New York: Oxford University Press for the World Bank, 1995), pp. 50–51.

22. UNRISD, *States of Disarray*, op. cit., pp. 28–29.

23. Ibid, p. 65.

24. Ibid.

25. Without doubt, one of the strengths of the U.S. economy is its receptability and adaptability to new ideas and new technologies. This has made production and information dissemination easier and more dynamic. When Gorbachev assumed office as Secretary General of the Communist Party in the former USSR, the country had only 50,000 computers as compared to about 30 million in the U.S. We can understand why the latter was easily ahead of the former in several areas.

26. UNRISD, *States of Disarray*, op. cit., p. 29.

27. "The End of Sovereignty," op. cit., p. 7.

28. See *The Economist* (19 September 1992), and UNRISD, *States of Disarray*, op. cit., pp. 32–33.

29. See UNRISD, *States of Disarray* op. cit.

30. P. Passel, "Fast Money," *New York Times Magazine* (18 October 1992), p. 42.

31. Walter B. Wriston, "Technology and Sovereignty," op. cit., p. 72.

32. UNRISD, *States of Disarray* op. cit., p. 27.

33. Ibid, p. 12.

34. Ibid, p. 29.

35. See E. Kolodner, *Transnational Corporations: Impediments or Catalysts of Social Development?* (Geneva: UNRISD, Occasional Paper No. 5, November 1994), p. 1.

36. Christopher Farrell, "The Triple Revolution," op. cit.

37. "The End of Sovereignty," op. cit., p. 7.

38. UNRISD, *States of Disarray*, op. cit., p. 28.

39. See Julius O. Ihonvbere, "Surviving at the Margins: Africa and the New Global Order," *Current World Leaders* Vol. 35, (6) (December 1992) and Olufemi Vaughn, "The Politics of Global Marginalization," *Journal of African and Asian Studies* Vol. XXIX (3–4) (1994).

40. UNRISD, *States of Disarray*, p. 17.

41. See Julius O. Ihonvbere, "The State and Environmental Degradation in Nigeria: A Study of the 1988 Toxic Waste Dump in Koko," *Journal of Environmental Systems* Vol. 23 (3) (1994–95).

42. Even the United States government plans to lay off between 500,000 and 750,000 defense industry workers in the next five years. According to the National Commission for Economic Conversion and Disarmament, the closure of 78 military bases will cost 78,000 jobs. Since 1990, the US has lost about 800,000 defense-related jobs, and in 1994, 145,00 workers were laid off. Defense contractors laid off 77,000 workers directly in 1994 while sub-contractors and suppliers laid off 68,000 workers. In 1995, it is expected that the defense industry will lay off 48,000 workers directly, while 93,000 jobs will be lost indirectly. In 1994, California "suffered 22 per cent of all defence job losses, with Connecticut and Massachusetts accounting for 15 percent and Texas 9 percent." Bernard Gray, "Half-Million US Defence Jobs to Go," *Financial Times* (July 15–16, 1995).

43. The deepening crisis of the U.S. economy is not unrelated to the crisis of capitalist production and accumulation. Bankruptcies, inflation, idle plants, and the increasing costs of labor and living are precipitates of the indebtedness of the state and the increasing reliance on technology and the shifting of production plants to developing nations where laws are ineffective or nonexistent and labor costs are much lower. At the end of 1993, the US owed investors within and outside its border about $2.7 trillion. This excludes about $1 trillion owed by US agencies. The American state pays out about $200 billion in interest payments annually.

44. Christopher Farrell, "The Triple Revolution," op. cit.

45. UNRISD, *States of Disarray*, op. cit., p. 11.

46. Ibid, pp. 11–12.

47. Ibid, p. 23.

48. Ibid, p. 23.

49. Walter B. Wriston, "Technology and Sovereignty," op. cit., p. 75.

50. See Walter Rodney, *How Europe Underdeveloped Africa* (Washington, D.C.: Howard University Press, 1981); Ali Mazrui, *The Africans* (London: BBC Publications, 1986); and George B. Ayittey, *Africa Betrayed* (New York: St. Martins Press, 1992).

51. See George Ayittey, *Africa Betrayed*, op. cit., p. 8.

52. World Bank, *World Development Report 1995*, op. cit., p. 122.

53. For a catalogue of Africa's abundant natural resources see Organization of African Unity, *The Lagos Plan of Action for the Economic Development of Africa 1980–2000*, (Geneva: Institute for Labour Studies, 1981). It is unfortunate that this document is poorly circulated within the African continent.

54. Claude Ake, "Academic Freedom and Material Base," in Mahmood Mamdani and Mamadou Diouf (eds.), *Academic Freedom in Africa* (Dakar: CODESRIA, 1994), p. 19. See also Claude Ake, "The State in Contemporary Africa," in Ake (ed.), *Political Economy of Nigeria* (London: Longman, 1985).

55. Ibid.

56. Ibid.

57. See Julius O. Ihonvbere, "The 'Irrelevant' State, Ethnicity and the Quest for Nationhood in Africa," *Ethnic and Racial Studies* Vol. 17 (1) (January 1994).

58. See Julius O. Ihonvbere, "Why African Economies Will Not Recover," *Iranian Journal of International Affairs* (Spring–Summer 1994); Adebayo Adedeji, "Economic Progress: What Africa Needs," *TransAfrica Forum* Vol. 7 (2) (Summer 1990); and Marguerite Michaels, "Retreat From Africa," *Foreign Affairs* Vol. 72 (1) (1993).

59. Salim A. Salim, "Africa Emergent." Address at the White House Conference on Africa, Washington, D.C., June 26, 1994.

60. Marguerite Michaels, "Retreat from Africa," op. cit., p. 95.

61. See Michael Clough, *Free at Last? U.S. Policy toward Africa and the End of the Cold War* (New York: Council on Foreign Relations, 1992); Jeffrey Herbst, *U.S. Economic Policy toward Africa* (New York: Council on Foreign Relations, 1993); and Carol Lancaster, *United States and Africa: Into The Twenty-first Century* (Washington, D.C.: Overseas Development Council, Policy Essay No. 7, 1993).

62. Olusegun Obasanjo, "Prospects for Peace," in William Minter (ed.), *U.S. Foreign Policy: An Africa Agenda* (Washington D.C.: Africa Policy Information Center, 1994), p. 20.

63. There is an argument to be made that the state in Africa has not failed. It was never set up to promote development. As a continuation of the repressive and exploitative colonial state, it has served the interests of imperialism and its local agents successfully. Under inherited neo-colonial relations, with a dependent and unproductive elite, and operating on the margins of the global capitalist order, the state in Africa could not have performed otherwise. See Julius O. Ihonvbere, *Nigeria: The Politics of Adjustment and Democracy*, (New Brunswick, NJ: Transaction Publishers, 1994).

64. I. William Zartman, "Introduction: Posing the Problem of State Collapse," in Zartman (ed.), *Collapsed State*, op. cit., p. 5 (emphasis added).

65. See Olusegun Obasanjo, "Prospects for Peace," in William Minter (ed.), *U.S. Foreign Policy: An Africa Agenda* (Washington, D.C.: Africa Policy Information Center, 1994).

66. Anthony Lake, "Afro-Realism vs. Afro-Pessimism," *CSIS Africa Notes* (168) (January 1985), p. 3.

67. Ibid.

68. Olusegun Obasanjo, "Prospects for Peace," op. cit., p. 21.

69. Sharon Pauling, "International Involvement: How Much Is Enough?" op. cit., p. 4.

70. Ibid.

71. See Guy Martin, "Preface: Democratic Transition in Africa," *Issue: A Journal of Opinion* Vol. XXI (1–2) (1993).

72. See Stephen Ellis, "Democracy in Africa: Achievements and Prospects," in Douglas Rimmer, (ed.), *Action in Africa* (London: Heinemann and James Currey, 1993).

73. See Claude Ake, *Revolutionary Pressures in Africa* (London: Zed Books, 1978). Ake actually argues that the choice for Africa is between "socialism" and "barbarism," p. 107.

74. Carol Lancaster, *United States and Africa*...op. cit., p. 19.

75. Ibid, p. 6.

76. See Deborah A. Green, "U.S. Foreign Policy toward Africa and the New Republican Majority," *Program of African Studies News and Current Affairs* (Northwestern University) Vol. 5 (3) (Spring 1995).

77. See Michael Clough, *Free at Last?*... op. cit. and Salim A. Salim, "Africa in Transition," in William Minter (ed.), *U.S. Foreign Policy: An Africa Agenda*, op. cit.

78. It is true that the Clinton administration sent Anthony Lake (National Security Adviser) to nine African countries in December 1994. Since then nothing concrete has happened and the administration has been unable to take decisive actions against military regimes that terminated democratic programs. In fact, by mid-1997, the administration was actually adopting a softer line towards the dictators in Africa.

79. Carol Lancaster, *United States and Africa*, op. cit., p. 6.

80. Boutros Boutros-Ghali, "New Concepts for Development Action in Africa," New York, Africa Recovery Unit of the Department of Public Information, the UN, March 1993.

81. Salim A. Salim, "Africa in Transition," op. cit., p. 3.

82. Ellen Johnson Sirleaf, "Some Reflections on Africa and the Global Economy," in William Minter, (ed.), *U.S. Foreign Policy: An Africa Agenda* (Washington, D.C. : Africa Policy Information Center, 1994), p. 9 (emphasis in original). Sirleaf provides data to support her assertion and concludes that "in the case of Africa today, foreign direct investment flow of the appropriate caliber is either absent or inadequate" and that this seems to be militating against possibilities for growth, development, and recovery.

83. See the contributions on regionalism, security, and development in Olusegun Obasanjo and Felix G. N. Mosha, (eds.), *Africa: Rise to Challenge* (New York: Africa Leadership Forum, 1993). See in particular the contributions by Bade Onimode, P. Anyang'nyongo, Wilfred Ndongko, and Yoweri Museveni. For a critique of the current state of regionalism in Africa see Julius O. Ihonvbere, "The African Crisis, Regionalism and Prospects for Recovery in the 1990s," in Bruce Berman and Piotor Dutkiewicz, (eds.), *Africa and Eastern Europe: Crisis and Transformations* (Kingston, Ontario: Queen's University, 1993).

84. We can compare this to Europe, where referenda were held to determine membership in the European Union, or to the case of the North American Free Trade Area (NAFTA) where there was an extensive debate in the media and President Bill Clinton had to convince

the representatives of the people as to the importance of the project before it passed through Congress. In Africa, regional integration schemes are never debated; they are simply announced!

85. World Bank, *World Development Report 1995*, op. cit., p. 125.

Select Bibliography

Abdulai, David. "Rawlings 'Wins' Ghana's Presidential Elections: Establishing a New Constitutional Order." *Africa Today* Vol. 39, No. 4, 1992.

Adam, Hussein. "Somalia: Militarism, Warlordism or Democracy?" *Review of African Political Economy*, No. 54, 1992.

————. "Somalia: A Terrible Beauty Being Born?" In edited by I. William Zartman. *Collapsed States*, Boulder, Col.: Lynne Rienner, 1995.

Adedeji, Adebayo. "Economic Progress: What Africa Needs." *TransAfrica Forum* Vol. 7, No. 2, 1990.

————. "Putting the People First." Opening address, International Conference on Popular Participation in the Recovery Process in Africa. Arusha, Tanzania, 12 February 1990.

————. "The Case for Remaking Africa," in Douglas Rimmer, ed., *Action in Africa*. London: James Currey and Heinemann, 1993.

————. ed. *Africa Within the World: Beyond Dispossession and Dependence*. London: Zed Books, 1993.

Adedeji, Adebayo, Sadiq Rasheed and Melody Morrison, eds. *The Human Dimensions of Africa's Persistent Economic Crisis*. London: Hans Zell, 1990.

Adedeji, Adebayo, and Timothy M. Shaw, eds. *Economic Crisis in Africa: African Perspectives on Development Problems and Potentials*. Boulder, Col.: Lynne Rienner, 1985.

Africa Leadership Forum, Organization of African Unity, and Economic Commission for Africa. *Report on the Brain Storming Meeting for a Conference on Security, Stability, Development, and Cooperation in Africa*. Addis Ababa, 1718 November 1990.

Africa Watch. *Zambia: Model for Democracy Declares State of Emergency*. New York: Africa Watch, Volume 5, Issue 8, June 10, 1993.

Ake, Claude. "Explaining Political Instability in New States." *Journal of Modern African Studies* Vol. 11, (3) (1973).

―――. "The African Context of Human Rights," *Africa Today* Vol. 34, (1987).

―――. "The Case for Democracy." In Carter Center at Emory University. *African Governance in the 1990s.* Atlanta, Ga.: Emory University, African Governance Program, 1990.

―――. "As Africa Democratizes." *Africa Forum* Vol. 1, (2) (1991).

―――. "Rethinking African Democracy." *Journal of Democracy* Vol. 2, (1) (1991).

―――. "Devaluing Democracy." *Journal of Democracy* Vol. 3, (3) (1992).

―――. "Is Africa Democratizing?" 1993 Guardian Lecture, Nigerian Institute of International Affairs, Lagos, Nigeria, 11 December 1993.

―――. "Academic Freedom and Material Base." In edited by Mahmood Mamdani and Mamadou Diouf. *Academic Freedom in Africa.* Dakar: CODESRIA, 1994.

Allen, C. "Restructuring an Authoritarian State: Democratic Renewal in Benin." *Review of African Political Economy* No.54, July 1992.

Carolyn Baylies, and Morris Szeftel, "Surviving Democracy?" *Review of African Political Economy* No. 54, 1992.
Amihere, K. B. and Baffour Ankomah. "Ghana: Easy Victory Brings Trouble." *New African* No. 305, February 1993.

Amin, Samir. "Democracy and National Strategy in the Periphery." *Third World Quarterly* Vol. 9, No. 4, 1987.

Anglin, Douglas G. "Confrontation in South Africa: Zambia and Portugal." *International Journal* Vol. 25, No. 3, 1970.

AnNa'im, Abdullahi Ahmed. "Problems of Universal Cultural Legitimacy for Human Rights." In edited by Abdullahi Ahmed AnNa'im and Francis

M. Deng, eds. *Human Rights in Africa: CrossCultural Perspectives.* Washington, D.C.: The Brookings Institution, 1990.

────── and Francis M. Deng, eds. *Human Rights in Africa: CrossCultural Perspectives.* Washington, D.C.: The Brookings Institution, 1990.

Anyang'Nyongo, Peter. *Popular Struggles for Democracy in Africa.* London: Zed Press, 1987.

──────. "Political Instability and the Prospects for Democracy in Africa." *Africa Development* Vol. XIII (1) (1988).

──────. "Democratization Processes in Africa." *CODESRIA Bulletin* (2) (1991).

──────. "Africa: The Failure of OneParty Rule." *Journal of Democracy* Vol. 3, (1) (January 1992).

──────. "Regional Integration, Security and Development in Africa." In edited by Olusegun Obasanjo and Felix G. N. Mosha. *Africa: Rise to Challenge.* New York: Africa Leadership Forum, 1993.

Armah, Ayi Kwei. *The Beautyful Ones Are Not Yet Born.* Boston: Houghton Miflin, 1968.

Askin, Steve and Carole Collins. "External Collusion with Kleptocracy: Can Zaire Recapture its Stolen Wealth." *Review of African Political Economy* No. 57, 1993.

Assimeng, J. M. "Sectarian Allegiance and Political Authority: The Watch Tower Society in Zambia, 19071935." *The Journal of Modern African Studies* Vol. 8, No. 1, 1970.

Atwood, Brian. "The U.S. Agenda for International Development." *International Politics and Society* No. 1, (1995).

Ayisi, R. A. "Mozambique: Back to the Stone Age." *Africa Report* Vol. 36 (1) (1991).

Bakary, Tessy D. "An Ambiguous Adventure: Transition From Authoritarian Rule and Economic Reforms." In *Economic Reform in*

Africa's New Era of Political Liberalization: Proceedings of a Workshop for SPA Donors. Washington, D.C.: USAID, 1993.

Bangura, Yusuf and Peter Gibbon, "Adjustment, Authoritarianism and Democracy in SubSaharan Africa: An Introduction to Some Conceptual and Empirical Issues." In Peter Gibbon et al eds. *Authoritarianism, Democracy and Adjustment.* Uppsala: SIAS, 1992.

Bates, Robert H. "Input Structures, Output Functions and Systems Capacity: A Study of Mineworkers' Union of Zambia." *Journal of Politics* Vol. 32, (4) (November 1970).

Bauzon, Kenneth E., ed. *Development and Democratization in the Third World: Myths, Hopes, and Realities.* Washington, D.C.: Crane Russak, 1992.

Baylies, C. and M. Szeftel. "The Rise of a Zambian Capitalist Class in the 1970s." *Journal of Southern African Affairs* Vol. 8, (2) (1982).

—————. the Rise and Fall of Multiparty Politics in Zambia." *Review of African Political Economy* No. 54 (July 1992).

Beckman, Bjorn. "State Capitalism and Public Enterprise in Africa." In Ghai, Y. ed. *Law in the Political Economy of Public Enterprise: African Perspectives.* Uppsala: Scandinavian Institute for African Studies, 1977.

—————. "Imperialism and the National Bourgeoisie." *Review of African Political Economy* No. 22 (1981).

—————. "When Does Democracy Make Sense? Problems of Theory and Practice in the Study of Democratization in Africa and the Third World." Paper to AKUT Conference on Democracy, Uppsala, October 1988.

—————. "Whose Democracy? Bourgeois Versus Popular Democracy." *Review of African Political Economy* Nos. 4546 (1989).

—————. "Empowerment or Repression? The World Bank and the Politics of African Adjustment." In Peter Gibbon, Yusuf Bangura and Arve Osftad, eds. *Authoritarianism, Democracy and Adjustment: The Politics of Economic Reform in Africa.* Uppsala: The Scandinavian Institute of African Studies, 1992.

————. "Comments on Economic Reform and National Disintegration." In *Economic Reform in Africa's New Era of Political Liberalization: Proceedings of a Workshop for SPA Donors*. Washington, D.C.: USAID, 1993.

Berger, Peter E. "The Uncertain Triumph of Democratic Capitalism." *Journal of Democracy* Vol. 3, No. 3, July 1992.

Berkeley, Bill. "Liberia: Between Repression and Slaughter." *Atlantic Monthly* December 1992.

Beveridge, A.A. "Varieties of African Businessmen in Emerging Zambian Stratification System." Paper at the 16th Annual Meeting of the African Studies Association, Syracuse, New York, 1973.

————. "Economic Independence, Indigenization, and the African Businessman: Some Effects of Zambia's Economic Reforms." *African Studies Review* Vol. 17, (3) (1974).

Bhagwati, Jagdish. "Democracy and Development." *Journal of Democracy* Vol. 3, (3) (July 1992).

Biermann, Werner. "The Development of Underdevelopment: The Historical Perspective." In Ben Turok, ed. *Development in Zambia*. London: Zed Press, 1979.

Bing, Adotey. "Salim A. Salim on the OAU and the African Agenda," *Review of African Political Economy* (50) (March 1991).

Binsbergen, Wim van. "Aspects of Democracy and Democratisation in Zambia and Botswana." *Journal of Contemporary African Studies* Vol. 13, (1) (January 1995).

Bjornlund, E., M. Bratton, and C. Gibson. "Observing Multiparty Elections in Africa: Lessons from Zambia." *African Affairs* Vol. 91, (364) (July 1992).

Boahen, Adu. "Military Rule and MultiParty Democracy: The Case of Ghana." *Africa Demos* Vol. 1, (2) (January 1991).

————. "Governance and Conflict Management in Ghana Since Independence." In I. William Zartman, ed. *Conflict Management in West Africa*. Washington, D.C.: The Brookings Institution, 1994.

Bobbio, N. "Gramsci and the Concept of Civil Society." In J. Keane, ed. *Civil Society and the State*. London: Verso, 1988.

BoutrosGhali, Boutros. *An Agenda for Peace: Preventive Diplomacy, Peacemaking and Peacekeeping*. New York: United Nations, 1992.

————. *An Agenda for Peace* (Second Edition with The New Supplement and Related UN Documents). New York: United Nations, 1995.

————. *An Agenda for Development*. New York: United Nations, 1995.

Boyle, P. "Beyond SelfProtection to Prophecy: The Catholic Church and Political Change in Zaire." *Africa Today* Vol. 39, No. 3, 1992.

Bratton, Michael. *The Local Politics of Rural Development: Peasant and Party State in Zambia*. Hanover: University of New England Press, 1980.

————. "Beyond the State: Civil Society and Associational Life in Africa." *World Politics* Vol. XLI (3) (1989).

————. "The Politics of GovernmentNG0 Relations in Africa." *World Development,* (April 1989).

————. "NonGovernmental Organizations in Africa." *Development and Change,* Vol. 21 (1) (January 1990).

————. "Zambia Starts Over." *Journal of Democracy*, Vol. 3, No. 2, April 1992.

————. "Political Liberalization in Africa in the 1990s: Advances and Setbacks," in *Economic Reform in Africa's New Era of Political Liberalization: Proceedings of a Workshop for SPA Donors*. Washington, D.C.: USAID, 1993.

————. "Economic Crisis and Political Realignment in Zambia," in Jennifer Widner, ed. *Economic Change and Political Liberalization in SubSaharan Africa*. Baltimore, Md: The Johns Hopkins Press, 1994.

Bratton, Michael and Nicholas van de Walle. "Popular Protest and Political Reform in Africa." In Goran Hyden and Michael Bratton, eds. *Governance and Politics in Africa*. Boulder: Lynne Rienner, 1991.

————. "Popular Protest and Political Reform in Africa." *Comparative Politics*, Vol. 24, No. 4, July 1992.

Brett, E. A. "Rebuilding Survival Strategies for the Poor: Organizational Options for Reconstruction in the 1990s." In Holger Bernt Hansen and Michael Twaddle, eds., *Changing Uganda: The Dilemmas of Structural Adjustment and Revolutionary Change*. London: James Currey, 1991.

Browne, Robert S. "Africa: Time for a New Development Strategy." In M. Martin and T. Randal, eds. *Development and Change in the Modern World*. New York: Oxford University Press, 1989.

————. "The Continuing Debate on African Development." *TransAfrica Forum*, Vol. 7, No. 2, Summer 1990.

Burawoy, M. "Zambianisation: A Study of the Localisation of a Labour Force." Mimeo, University of Zambia, 1971.

Callaghy, Thomas. "Lost Between State and Market: The Politics of Economic Adjustment in Ghana, Zambia and Nigeria." In Joan M. Nelson, ed., *Economic Crisis and Policy Choice: The Politics of Economic Adjustment in the Third World*. Princeton: Princeton University Press, 1990.

————. "Political Liberalization and Economic Policy Reform in Africa." In *Economic Reform in Africa's New Era of Political Liberalization: Proceedings of a Workshop for SPA Donors*. Washington, D.C.,: USAID, 1993.

Camdessus, Michel. "The IMF: Facing New Challenges." *Finance and Development* No. 25 (June 1988).

————. "The IMF and the Global Economy: Three Addresses." Washington, D.C.: International Monetary Fund, 1989.

————. "Good News Out of Africa." *Finance and Development* No. 28 (December 1991).

Campbell, Bonnie and John Loxley, eds.. *Structural Adjustment in Africa*. New York: St. Martins Press, 1989.

Campbell, Horace. "Angolan Woman and the Electoral Process in Angola, 1992," *Africa Development*, Vol. XVIII (2) (1993).

————. and Howard Stein, eds. *Tanzania and the IMF: The Dynamics of Liberalization*. Boulder, Co.: Westview Press, 1992.

Carter Center of Emory University. *Beyond Autocracy in Africa*. Atlanta, Ga.: Africa Governance Program, 1989.

————. *Perestroika Without Glasnost in Africa*. Atlanta, Ga.: Conference Report Series Vol. 2, No. 1, 1989.

————. *African Governance in the 1990s*. Atlanta, Ga.: African Governance Program, 1990.

Chabal, Patrick, ed. *Political Domination in Africa: Reflections on the Limits of Power*. Cambridge: Cambridge University Press, 1986.

Chalker, Lynda. "The Proper Role of Government." In Douglas Rimmer, ed., *Action in Africa*. London: James Currey and Heinemann, 1993.

Chazan, Naomi. "The New Politics of Participation in Tropical Africa." *Comparative Politics* Vol. 14 (1982).

————. "Planning Democracy in Africa: a Comparative Perspective on Nigeria and Ghana." *Policy Sciences* (22) (1989).

————. "Africa's Democratic Challenge: Strengthening Civil Society and the State." *World Policy Journal* (Spring 1992).

Chege, Michael. "Remembering Africa." *Foreign Affairs* Vol. 71, (1) (199192).

Cheru, Fantu. "The Politics of Desperation: Mozambique and Nkomati." *TransAfrica Forum* (Spring 1986).

————. *The Silent Revolution in Africa: Debt, Development and Democracy*. London and Harare: Zed Books and Anvil, 1989.

Chikulo, Bornwell C.. "Elections in a OneParty Participatory Democracy." In Ben Turok ed., *Development in Zambia*. London: Zed Press, 1979.

Chiluba, Frederick. Address to the Nation on the Eve of Local Government Elections. n.d. Typescript.

————. "Inauguration Speech to the Nation." Lusaka: Government Printer, November 2, 1991.

————. "Marching Towards a Common Market." Opening Statement on the Occasion of the Opening Ceremony of the 10th P.T.A. Summit, Mulungushi Conference Centre, Lusaka, Zambia, 30 January, 1992.

————. Speech on the Occasion of the Official Launching of the "Community Awareness Week" on the Problem of Vandalism in Institutions of Learning on Both Radio and Television, Lusaka, 15th June, 1992.

Chitala, Derrick. "Towards Accountability in a Democracy: The Case of Zambia." Paper presented to Workshop on Civil Society and Consolidation of Democracy in Zambia, February 27, 1992.

Chomsky, Noam. "The Struggle for Democracy in a Changed World," *Review of African Political Economy* (50) (March 1991).

Clark, J. *Democratizing Development: The Role of Voluntary Organizations*. West Hartford, Conn: Kumarian Press, 1991.

———— and Caroline Allison. *Debt and Poverty: A Case Study of Zambia*. Oxford: Oxfam, 1987.

Cliffe, Lionel and David Seddon. "Africa in a New World Order." *Review of African Political Economy*, No. 50 (March 1991).

Clough, Michael. "Beyond Constructive Engagement." *Foreign Policy*, No. 61 (Winter 198586).

————. "Africa in the 1990s." *CSIS Africa Notes*, No. 107 (1990).

————. "The United States and Africa: The Policy of Cynical Disengagement." *Current History*, Vol. 91, (May 1992).

———. "Africa Finds Reasons to Hope for Democracy's Future." *The New York Times*, 22 March 1992.

———. *Free at Last? U.S. Policy Toward Africa and the End of the Cold War*. New York: Council on Foreign Relations, 1992.

Colborne, Desmond. "Recolonizing Africa: The Right to Intervene?" *South Africa International*, Vol. 23, No. 4, 1993.

Colclough, Christopher. "Zambian Adjustment Strategy: With and Without the IMF." *IDS Bulletin*, Vol. 19, (1) (January 1988).

———. "The Labor Market and Economic Stabilization in Zambia." Washington, D.C.: World Bank PPR Working Paper No. 272, November 1989.

———. "Zambian Adjustment Strategy: With and Without the IMF." *IDS Bulletin*, Vol. 19, (1) (January 1988).

———. "The Labour Market and Economic Stabilization in Zambia." Washington, D.C.: World Bank PPR Working Paper No. 272, November 1989.

Colletta, Nat and Nicole Ball. "War to Peace Transition in Uganda." *Finance and Development*, Vol. 30, No. 2, 1993.

Commander, Simon, ed. *Structural Adjustment and Agriculture: Theory and Practice in Africa and Latin America*. London: Overseas Development Institute, 1989.

Cooper, Laurie A., Fred M. Hayward, and Anthony W. J. Lee. *Ghana: A PreElection Assessment Report, June 1, 1992*. Washington, D.C.: International Foundation for Electoral Systems, 1992.

Copans, Jean. "No Short Cuts to Democracy: The Long March Towards Modernity." *Review of African Political Economy* No. 50 (March 1991).

Copeland, D. S. "Structural Adjustment in Africa." *International Perspectives* Vol. 18, (2) (MarchApril 1989).

Cornia, Giovanni Andrea, Richard Jolly, and Frances Stewart, eds. *Adjustment With a Human Face: Protecting the Vulnerable and Promoting Growth.* Oxford: Clarendon Press, 1987.

Coulon, C. "Senegal: The Development and Fragility of Semidemocracy." In L. Diamond et al., eds., *Democracy in Developing Countries: Africa.* Boulder, Col.: Lynne Rienner, 1988.

Crook, R. E. "State, Society and Political Institutions in Cote d'Ivoire and Ghana." *IDS Bulletin*, Vol. 21 (4) (1990).

Cowan, L. Gray. "Zambia Tests Democracy." *CSIS Africa Notes*, No. 141 (October 1992).

Dahl, Robert A. "Why Free Markets Are Not Enough." *Journal of Democracy*, Vol. 3, (3) (July 1992).

Daniel, Philip. "Zambia: Structural Adjustment or Downward Spiral?" *IDS Bulletin*, Vol. 16, (3) (1985).

Decalo, Samuel. "Regionalism, Political Decay and Civil Strife in Chad." *Journal of Modern African Studies*, Vol. 18 (1980).

———. "The Process, Prospects and Constraints of Democratization in Africa." *African Affairs*, Vol. 91 (362) (January 1992).

Deng, Francis. "Africa and the New World DisOrder." *Brookings Review*, (Spring 1993).

———. "State Collapse: The Humanitarian Challenge to the United Nations." In I. William Zartman, ed., *Collapsed States: The Disintegration and Restoration of Legitimate Authority.* Boulder, Co.: Lynne Rienner, 1995.

Diamond, Larry. "Nigeria's Search for a New Political Order." *Journal of Democracy*, Vol. 2, (2) (Spring 1991).

———. *An American Foreign Policy for Democracy.* Washington, D.C.: Progressive Policy Institute, Policy Report No. 11, July 1991.

———. "Promoting Democracy." *Foreign Policy*, (87) (1992).

Diamond, Larry; Juan J. Linz, and Seymour Martin Lipset, eds., *Democracy in Developing Countries: Africa*. Boulder, Co.: Lynne Rienner, 1988.

Doornbos, Martin. "The African State in Academic Debate: Retrospect and Prospect." *Journal of Modern African Studies*, Vol. 28, No. 2, 1990.

Economic Commission for Africa. *The African Charter for Popular Participation in Development and Transformation*. Addis Ababa: ECA, 1990.

EkweEkwe, Herbert. *Conflict and Intervention in Africa*. London: Macmillan, 1990.

Ellis, Stephen. "Democracy in Africa: Achievements and Prospects." In Douglas Rimmer, ed., *Action in Africa*. London: James Currey and Heinemann, 1993.

Ergas, Zakis, ed., *The African State in Transition*. New York: St. Martins Press, 1987.

Evans, Peter. *Dependent Development: The Alliance of Multinationals, State and Local Capital in Brazil*. Princeton: Princeton University Press, 1979.

————. "Predatory, Developmental and Other Apparatuses: A Comparative Political Economy Perspective on the Third World State." *Sociological Forum*, Vol. 4 (4) (1989).

Fatton, Robert. "Liberal Democracy in Africa." *Political Science Quarterly*, Vol. 105, No. 3, 1990.

————. *Predatory Rule: State and Civil Society in Africa*. Boulder, Co.: Lynne Rienner, 1992.

Foltz, William J. "Chad's Third Republic: Strengths, Problems, and Prospects." *CSIS Africa Notes*, No. 77, October 30, 1987.

Forrest, Joshua. "The Quest for 'Hardness' in Africa." *Comparative Politics*, Vol. 20, No. 4, 1988.

Fundanga, Caleb. "Impact of IMF/World Bank Policies on the Peoples of Africa: The Case of Zambia." In Bade Onimode, ed., *The IMF. The World Bank and the African Debt: The Economic Impact.* London: Institute for African Alternatives and Zed Press, 1989.

Gambari, Ibrahim. *Political and Comparative Dimensions of Regional Integration: The Case of ECOWAS.* Atlantic Highlands, N.J.: Humanities Press, 1991.

————. "The Role of Foreign Intervention in African Reconstruction." In I. William Zartman, ed., *Collapsed States.* Boulder, Co.: Lynne Rienner, 1995.

Garba, Joe. *Fractured History: Elite Shifts and Policy Changes in Nigeria.* Princeton, N.J.: Sungai Book, 1995.

Gibbon, Peter, Yusuf Bangura and Arve Ofstad. *Authoritarianism. Democracy and Adjustment: The Politics of Economic Reform in Africa.* Uppsala: Scandinavian Institute of African Studies, 1992.

Global Coalition for Africa,. *African Social and Economic Trends: The 1992 Annual Report.* Washington, D.C.: The GCA, 1992.

Godsell, Bobby. "Six Strategies for African Development." In Douglas Rimmer, ed., *Action in Africa.* London: James Currey and Heinemann, 1993.

Goulbourne, Harry. "The State, Development, and the Need for Participatory Democracy in Africa." In Peter Anyang'Nyongo, ed., *Popular Struggles for Democracy in Africa.* London: Zed Press, 1987.

Graham, Carol. "Zambia's Democratic Transition: The Beginning of the End of the One Party State in Africa?" *Brookings Review,* (Spring 1992).

————. *Safety Nets, Politics and the Poor: Transitions to Market Economies.* Washington, D.C.: The Brookings Institution, 1994.

Hamalengwa, Munyonzwe. "The Political Economy of Human Rights in Africa." *Philosophy and Social Action,* Vol. IX, (3) (JulySeptember 1983).

———. "The Legal System of Zambia." In Peter Sack, Carl Wellman and Mitsukuni Yasaki, eds., *Monistic or Pluralistic Legal Culture? Anthropological and Ethnological Foundations of Traditional and Modern Legal Systems*. Berlin: Dunker and Humbolt, 1991.

———. "Economic Crisis, Human Rights Violations and Prospects for Democratization in Africa: The Case of Zambia." Paper presented at the Conference on Structural Adjustment, Peace and Prospects for Security in Africa, Park Plaza Hotel, Toronto, Canada, October 1990.

———. *Thoughts Are Free: Prison Experience and Reflections on Law and Politics in General*. Toronto: Africa in Canada Press, 1991.

———. *Class Struggles in Zambia 18891989 and the Fall of Kenneth Kaunda 19901991*. Lanham, MD: University Press of America, 1992.

Hatch, John. *Africa Emergent: Africa's Problems Since Independence*. Chicago: Henry Regnery, 1974.

Herbst, Jeffrey. *The Politics of Reform in Ghana, 19821991*. Berkeley: University of California Press, 1993.

———. *U.S. Economic Policy Towards Africa*. New York: Council on Foreign Relations, 1993.

Holman, Michael. "Fresh Start for Africa's Newest Democracy." *Financial Times*, 17 December, 1992.

Hull, Galen. "The French Connection in Africa: Zaire and South Africa." *Journal of Southern African Studies*, Vol. 5, No. 2, 1979.

Huntington, Samuel P. "Political Development and Political Decay." *World Politics*, Vol. 17, No. 3, 1965.

———. "Democracy's Third Wave." *Journal of Democracy*, Vol. 2, No. 2, Spring 1991.

———. *The Third Wave: Democratization in the Late Twentieth Century*. Norman, OK.: Oklahoma University Press, 1992.

————. "Clash of Civilizations?" *Foreign Affairs*, Vol. 72, No. 3, Summer 1993.

Hyden, Goran. "Problems and Prospects of State Coherence." In Donald Rothchild and Victor Olorunsola, eds., *States Versus Ethnic Claims: African Policy Dilemmas*. Boulder, CO: Westview, 1983.

————. "Governance and the Study of Politics." In Goran Hyden and Michael Bratton, eds., *Governance and Politics in Africa*. Boulder, CO: Lynne Rienner, 1992.

Ihonvbere, Julius, O.. "Contradictions of MultiParty Democracy in Peripheral Formations: The Rise and Demise of Nigeria's Second Republic, 197983." In Peter Meyens and Dani Wadada Nabudere eds., *Democracy and the OneParty State in Africa*. Hamburg: Institute for African Studies, 1988.

————. "The African Crisis in Historical and Contemporary Perspective." In Julius O. Ihonvbere, ed., *The Political Economy of Crisis and Underdevelopment in Africa: Selected Works of Claude Ake*. Lagos: JAD Publishers, 1989.

————. "Structural Adjustment in Nigeria." In Ben Turok, ed., *Alternative Development Strategies for Africa Vol. 3Debt and Democracy*. London: Institute for African Alternatives, 1991.

————. "The Economic Crisis in SubSaharan Africa: Depth, Dimensions and Prospects for Recovery." *Journal of International Studies*, No. 27 (July 1991).

————. "Economic Crisis in SubSaharan Africa: Constraints and Prospects for Recovery." *Pakistan Horizon*, Vol. 44, (4) (October 1991).

————. "The African Crisis, The Popular Charter and Prospects for Recovery in the 1990s." *Zeitschtift fur Afrikastudien (ZAST)*, (1112) (1991).

————. "Surviving at the Margins: Africa and the New Global Order." *Current World Leaders*, Vol. 35, (6) (December 1992).

————. "Africa and the New World Order: Prospects for the 1990s." *Iranian Journal of International Affairs*, Vol. IV, (34) (FallWinter 1992).

————. "Is Democracy Possible in Africa? The Elites, The People and Civil Society." *OUEST: Philosophical Discussions* Vol. VI, (2) (December 1992).

————. "The Persian Gulf Crisis and Africa: Implications for the 1990s." *International Studies*, Vol. 29, (3) (1992).

————. The Third World and the New World Order." *Futures* Vol. 24, (10) (December 1992).

————. "Changes in Eastern Europe and Africa's Role in the World Political Economy." In Chronis Polychroniou ed., *Perspectives and Issues in International Political Economy*. Westport, Conn.: Praeger, 1992.

————. "The 'Irrelevant' State, Ethnicity and the Quest for Nationhood in Africa." *Ethnic and Racial Studies*, Vol. 17, (1) (January 1994).

————. "Why African Economies Will Not Recover." *Iranian Journal of International Studies*, (Spring Summer 1994).

————. "Between Debt and Disaster: The Politics of Africa's Debt Crisis." *In Depth: A Journal of Values and Public Policy*, Vol. 4, (1) (Winter 1994).

————. *Nigeria: The Politics of Adjustment and Democracy*. New Brunswick, N.J.: Transaction Publishers, 1994.

"From Movement to Government: The Movement for Multiparty Democracy and the Crisis of Democratic Consolidation in Zambia." *Canadian Journal of African Studies*, (1) (1995).

————. "Government and Opposition Politics in Africa: A Study of the 'Zero Option' Controversy in Zambia." *Afrika Spectrum*, (1) (1995).

————. "Threats to Democratization in SubSaharan Africa: The Case of Zambia." *Asian and African Studies: Journal of the Israeli Oriental Society*, Vol. 28, (1) (1995).

———. "Where is the Third Wave? A Critical Evaluation of Africa's NonTransition to Democracy." *Africa Today* Vol. 43, (4) (1996).

———. "Evolving Sovereignty in an Interdependent World: The Challenge of Democratization in SubSaharan Africa." *International Politics* No. 33 (1996).

———. "From Despotism to Democracy: The Rise of Multiparty Politics in Malawi." *Third World Quarterly* Vol. 18, (2) (1997).

InterAction Council. *Bring Africa Back into the Mainstream of the International System.* New York: InterAction Council, 1993.

International Forum for Democratic Studies. *Nigeria's Political Crisis: Which Way Forward?.* (Conference Report) Washington, D.C.: IFDS, 1995.

Jackson, Robert H. and Carl G. Rosberg. *Personal Rule in Black Africa.* Berkeley: University of California Press, 1982.

———. "The Marginality of the African State." In Gwendolyn M. Carter and Patrick O'Meara eds., *African Independence: The First TwentyFive Years.* Bloomington: Indiana University Press, 1986.

———. "Why Africa's Weak States Persist: The Empirical and the Juridical in Statehood." In Athul Kholi, ed., *The State and Development.* Princeton: Princeton University Press, 1986.

Jaycox, Edward V. K. *The Challenges of African Development.* Washington, D.C.: The World Bank, 1991

———. "Structural Adjustment Spurs African Development." *Africa News*, Vol. 38, Nos. 23, March 821, 1993.

Jeffries, Richard. "The State, Structural Adjustment and Good Government in Africa." *Journal of Commonwealth and Comparative Politics*, Vol. 31, No. 1, 1993.

Joseph, Richard "Africa: The Rebirth of Political Freedom." *Journal of Democracy*, Vol. 2, (4) (1991).

Kansteiner, Walter, H. "U.S. Interests in Africa Revisited,." *CSIS Africa Notes*, No. 157 (February 1994).

Kaplan, Robert D. "The Coming Anarchy." *Atlantic Monthly*, February 1994.

Kasfir, Nelson. "The Ugandan Elections of 1989: Power, Populism, and Democratization." In Holger Bernt Hansen and Michael Twaddle, eds., *Changing Uganda: The Dilemmas of Structural Adjustment and Revolutionary Change*. London: James Currey, 1991.

————. "Popular Sovereignty and Popular Participation: Mixed Constitutional Democracy in the Third World." *Third World Quarterly*, Vol. 13, No. 4, 1993.

KayizziMugerwa, Steve. "External Shocks and Adjustment in a Mineral Dependent Economy: A ShortRun Model for Zambia." *World Development*, (19), (July 1991).

———— and Arne Bigsten. "On Structural Adjustment in Uganda." *Canadian Journal of Development*, Vol. 13, No. 1, 1992.

Keane, J. *Democracy and Civil Society*. London: Verso, 1988.

Kelly, Michael, A. "Democracy and Economic Liberalism: The Foundations of Hope for Africa." *The Midsouth Political Science Journal*, Vol. 13 (Spring 1992).

Klein, Martin, A. "Back To Democracy." Presidential Address to the 1991 Annual Meeting of the African Studies Association, St, Louis, Missouri, November, 1991.

Kolakowski, Leszek. "Uncertainties of a Democratic Age." *Journal of Democracy*, Vol. 1, (1) (Winter 1990).

Kraus, Jon. "The Political Economy of Stabilization and Structural Adjustment in Ghana." In Donald Rothchild, ed., *Ghana: The Political Economy of Recovery*. Boulder, CO.: Lynne Rienner, 1991.

Lancaster, Carol. "Economic Reform in Africa: Is it Working?" *The Washington Quarterly*, (13) (Winter 1990).

———. "Governance in Africa: Should Foreign Aid Be Linked to Political Reform?" In The Carter Center, *African Governance in the 1990s*. Atlanta: Governance Program, Emory University, 1990.

———. "The New Politics of U.S. Aid to Africa." *CSIS Africa Notes*, No. 120 (1991).

———. "Democracy in Africa." *Foreign Policy*, No. 85, Winter 1991/92.

———. *African Economic Reform: The External Dimension*. Washington, D.C. Institute for International Economics, 1991.

———. *United States and Africa: Into the Twentyfirst Century*. Policy Essay No. 7. Washington, D.C.: Overseas Development Council, 1993.

———. "Governance and Development: The Views From Washington." *IDS Bulletin*, Vol. 24, No. 1, January 1993.

——— and John Williamson, eds., *African Debt and Financing*. Washington, D.C.: Institute for International Economics, 1986.

Lawyers Committee for Human Rights. *Zaire: Repression as Policy*. Washington, D.C.: Lawyers Committee for Human Rights, 1990.

Lemarchand, Rene. "African Transitions to Democracy: An Interim (and Mostly Pessimistic) Assessment." *Africa Insight*, Vol. 22, (3) (1992).

———. "Uncivil State and Civil Societies: How Illusion Became Reality." *The Journal of Modern African Studies*, Vol. 31, No. 2, 1992.

Linz, Juan. "Transitions to Democracy." *The Washington Quarterly*, (Summer 1990).

———. "The Perils of Presidentialism." *Journal of Democracy* Vol. 1, (1) (Winter 1990).

Lipset, Seymour Martin. "Some Social Requisites for Democracy: Economic Development and Political Legitimacy." *American Political Science Review*, Vol. 53, (1) (1959).

Loxley, J. "Structural Adjustment Programmes in Africa: Ghana and Zambia." *Review of African Political Economy*, No. 47, 1991.

Lyons, Terrence. "The Transition in Ethiopia." *CSIS Africa Notes*, No. 127, August 1991.

Mamdani, Mahmood. "Uganda: Contradictions of the IMF Program and Perspective." *Development and Change*, No. 21, 1990.

————. "The Social Basis of Constitutionalism in Africa." *The Journal of Modern African Studies*, Vol. 28, No. 3, 1990.

Mandazza, Ibbo. "The State and Democracy in Southern Africa: Towards a Conceptual Framework." In Eghosa Osaghae, ed., *Between State and Civil Society in Africa*. Dakar: CODESRIA, 1994.

Markakis, John and Robert L. Curry. "The Global Economy's Impact on Recent Budgetary Politics in Zambia." *Journal of African Studies*, Vol. 3, (4) (Winter 197677).

Martin, Guy. "Preface: Democratic Transitions in Africa." *Issue* Vol. XXI, (12) (1993).

Martin, M. *The Crumbling Facade of Africa's Debt Negotiations: No Winners*. London: Macmillan, 1991.

————. "Neither Phoenix nor Icarus: Negotiating Economic Reform in Ghana and Zambia, 198388." In T. Callaghy and J. Ravenhill, eds., *Hemmed In: Responses to Africa's Economic Dilemma*. New York: Columbia University Press, 1994.

Mazrui, Ali. "Between Development and Decay: Anarchy, Tyranny, and Progress under Idi Amin." *Third World Quarterly*, Vol. 11, No. 1, 1980.

————. "Is Africa Decaying? The View From Uganda." In Holger Bernt Hansen and Michael Twaddle, eds., *Uganda Now: Between Decay and Development*. London: James Currey, 1988.

————. "Eastern European Revolutions: African Origins." *TransAfrica Forum*, Vol. 7, No. 2, Summer 1990.

Meyns, Peter and Dani Wadada Nabudere, eds., *Democracy and the OneParty State in Africa*. Hamburg: Institute for African Studies, 1989.

Michaels, Marguerite. "Retreat From Africa." *Foreign Affairs*, Vol. 72, (1) (1993).

Minter, William, ed., *U.S. Foreign Policy: An Africa Agenda*. Washington, D.C.: Africa Policy Information Center, 1994.

Monga, Celestin. "Civil Society and Democratisation in Francophone Africa." *The Journal of Modern African Studies*, Vol. 33, (3) (1995).

Moore Jr., Barrington. *Social Origins of Dictatorship and Democracy: Lord and Peasant in the Making of the Modern World*. Boston: Beacon Press, 1966.

Mortimer, Robert. "Algeria: The Clash Between Islam, Democracy, and the Military." *Current History*, Vol. 92, (570) (January 1993).

Muigai, Githu. "Kenya's Opposition and the Crisis of Governance." *Issue*, Vol. XXI, (12) (1993).

Mutua, Makau wa. "U.S. Foreign Policy Towards Africa: Building Democracy Through Popular Participation." In William Minter, ed., *U.S. Foreign Policy: An Africa Agenda*. Washington, D.C.: Africa Policy Information Center, 1994.

Museveni, Yoweri Kaguta. *What is Africa's Problem?* Kampala: NRM Publications, 1992.

———. "Statement at the Kampala Forum." In Olusegun Obasanjo and Felix Mosha, eds., *Africa: Rise to Challenge*. New York: Africa Leadership Forum, 1993.

New Patriotic Party. *The Stolen Verdict: Ghana, November 1992 Presidential Election*. Accra: New Patriotic Party, 1993.

Ng'ethe, Njuguna. "Strongmen, State Formation, Collapse, and Reconstruction in Africa." In I. William Zartman, ed., *Collapsed States*. Boulder, CO: Lynne Rienner, 1995.

Nolutshungu, Samuel. "Fragments of a Democracy: Reflections on Class and Politics in Nigeria." *Third World Quarterly*, Vol. 12, No. 1, January 1990.

———. "Africa in a World of Democracies: Interpretation and Retrieval." *Journal of Commonwealth and Comparative Politics*, Vol. 30, No. 3, 1992.

Novicki, Margaret A. "Zambia: Lesson in Democracy." *Africa Report*, (JanuaryFebruary 1992).

———. "Frederick Chiluba: Champion of Zambia's Democracy." (Interview) *Africa Report*, (JanuaryFebruary 1993).

Nzomo, Maria. "Women, Democracy and Development in Africa." In Walter O. Oyugi et. al., eds., *Democratic Theory and Practice in Africa*. London: Heinemann and James Currey, 1988.

Oakley, Robert and John Hirsch. *Somalia and Operation Restore Hope: Reflections on Peacekeeping*. Washington, D.C.: United States Institute of Peace, 1995.

Obasanjo, Olusegun. "Statement at the Kampala Forum." In Olusegun Obasanjo and Felix Mosha, eds., *Africa: Rise to Challenge*. New York: Africa Leadership Forum, 1991.

———. "Africa in the 21st Century." *Security Dialogue*, Vol. 24, No. 1, 1993.

———. "Prospects for Peace." In William Minter, ed., *U.S. Foreign Policy: An Africa Agenda*. Washington, D.C.: Africa Policy Information Center, 1994.

Ohlson, Thomas and Stephen J. Stedman. *The New Is Not Yet Born: Conflict Resolution in South Africa*. Washington, D.C.: The Brookings Institution, 1994.

OmaraOtunnu, Amii. "The Struggle for Democracy in Uganda." *Journal of Modern African Studies*, Vol. 30, No. 3, 1992.

Organization of African Unity(OAU). *The Lagos Plan of Action for the Economic Development of Africa 19802000.* Geneva: International Institute for Labour Studies, 1982.

————. *Africa's Priority Programme for Economic Recovery, 19861990.* Addis Ababa: OAU Secretariat, 1986.

————. "Africa's Submission to the Special Session of the United Nations General Assembly on Africa's Economic and Social Crisis." Addis Ababa: OAU Secretariat, 13 May 1986.

————. "External Debt Crisis of Africa: Summary of Information, Statistical Data, and Proposed Actions." Addis Ababa: OAU Secretariat, 2021 November 1987.

Osaghae, Eghosa, ed., *Between State and Civil Society in Africa.* Dakar: CODESRIA, 1994.

Ottaway, Marina, "Should Elections Be the Criterion of Democratization in Africa?" *CSIS Africa Notes,* No. 145, February 1993.

————. "Democratization in Collapsed States." In I. William Zartman, ed., *Collapsed States: The Disintegration and Restoration of Legitimate Authority.* Boulder, CO.: Lynne Rienner, 1995.

Oyugi, Walter, E.S. Atieno Odhiambo, Michael Chege and Afrifa K. Gitonga, eds., *Democratic Theory and Practice in Africa.* London: James Currey, 1988.

Parfitt, Trevor W. "Lies, Damned Lies and Statistics: The World Bank/ECA Structural Adjustment Controversy." *Review of African Political Economy,* No. 47 (Spring 1990).

———— and Stephen P. Riley. *The African Debt Crisis.* London: Routeledge, 1989.

Ransdell, Eric. "In Zaire, a Big Man Still Rules the Roost." *U.S. News and World Report,* August 10, 1992.

Ranger, Terrence and Olufemi Vaughn, eds., *Legitimacy and the State in Twentieth Century Africa: Essays in Honour of A. H. M. KirkGreene.* London: Macmillan, 1993.

Rasheed, Sadig. "The Democratization Process and Popular Participation in Africa: Emerging Realities and the Challenges Ahead." *Development and Change* Vol. 26, (1995).

Ravenhill John, ed., *Africa in Economic Crisis.* London: Macmillan, 1986.

Rostow, Dankwart. "Transitions to Democracy: Toward a Dynamic Model." *Comparative Politics* Vol. 2, (3) (1970.)

────── and Kenneth P. Erickson, eds., *Comparative Political Dynamics: Global Research Perspectives.* New York: Harper Collins, 1991.

Rothchild, Donald. "Rawlings and the Engineering of Legitimacy in Ghana." In I. William Zartman, ed., *Collapsed States.* Boulder, CO: Lynne Rienner, 1995.

Rothchild, Donald and Michael W, Foley. "African States and the Politics of Inclusive Coalitions." In D. Rothchild and N. Chazan eds., *The Precarious Balance: State and Society in Africa.* Boulder, CO: Westview Press, 1988.

Salih, Kamal Osman. "The Sudan 198598: The Fading Democracy." In Peter Woodward, ed., *The Sudan After Nimeiri.* London: Routeledge, 1991.

Salim, Salim A.. "Africa in Transition." In William Minter, ed., *U.SD. Foreign Policy: An Africa Agenda.* Washington, D.C.: Africa Policy Information Center, 1994.

Sandbrook, Richard. "Liberal Democracy in Africa: A Socialist Revisionist Perspective." *Canadian Journal of African Studies*, Vol. 22, (1988).

──────. *The Politics of Africa's Economic Stagnation.* Cambridge: Cambridge University Press, 1985.

————. *The Politics of Africa's Economic Recovery.* London: Cambridge University Press, 1993.

———— and Mohamed Halfani, eds., *Empowering PeopleBuilding Community. Civil Associations and Legality in Africa.* Toronto: Center for Urban and Community Studies, University of Toronto, 1993.

Shaw, Timothy. M. "The Foreign Policy of Zambian Interests and Ideology." *Journal of Modern African Studies,* Vol. 13, (1) (1976).

————. "The Political Economy of Energy in Southern Africa: Oil, the OAU and the Multinationals." *Africa Today,* Vol. 23, (1) (1976).

————. "Africa in the 1990s: From Economic Crisis to Structural Adjustment." *Dalhousie Review,* Vol. 68 (12) (1988).

————. "Structural Readjustment: New Framework." *Africa Recovery,* Vol. 2, (4) (December 1988).

————. "Africa's Conjuncture: From Structural Adjustment to SelfReliance." In *Third World Affairs 1988,* London: Third World Foundation, 1988.

————. "Africa in the 1990s: Beyond Continental Crisis to Sustainable Development?" World University Service of Canada (WUSC), Background Series in International Development, Annual Assembly 1990 Edition.

————. "Reformism, Revisionism, and Radicalism in African Political Economy During the 1990s." *Journal of Modern African Studies,* Vol. 27 (1) (March 1991).

———— and A. Mugombe. "The Political Economy of Regional Detente: Zambia and Southern Africa." *Journal of African Studies,* Vol. 4, (4) (197778).

Shezi, Sipho. "South Africa: State Transition and the Management of Collapse." In I. William Zartman, ed., *Collapsed States.* Boulder, CO: Lynne Rienner, 1995.

Shivji, Issa. *Fight My Beloved Continent: New Democracy in Africa.* Harare: SAPES Trust, 1988.

————. *The Concept of Human Rights in Africa.* Dakar: CODESRIA Books, 1989.

————. "The Pitfalls of the Debate on Democracy." *IFDA Dossier* (79) (OctoberDecember 1990).

Sirleaf, Ellen Johnson. "Some Reflections on Africa and the Global Economy." In William Minter, ed., *U.S. Foreign Policy: An Africa Agenda.* Washington, D.C.: Africa Policy Information Center, 1994.

Sithole, Masipula. "Is Zimbabwe Poised on a Liberal Path? The State and Prospects of the Parties." *Issue* Vol. XXI, (12) (1993).

Stadler, Alf. "Strong States Make for a Strong Civil Society." *Theoria* (79) (May 1992).

Sylvester, Christine. "Whither Opposition in Zimbabwe?" *The Journal of Modern African Studies*, Vol. 33, (3) (1995).

Tordoff, William. "Democracy and the OneParty State." *Government and Opposition*, Vol. 2, (4) (JulyOctober, 1967).

Tomkys, Roger. "Implementing Africa's Second Revolution." In Douglas Rimmer, ed., *Action in Africa.* London: James Currey and Heinemann, 1993.

United Nations Economic Commission for Africa (UNECA). *Report of the UN/ECA/FAO Economic Survey Mission on the Economic Development of Zambia.* (The Seers Report) Ndola, Zambia: Falcon Press, 1963.

Van Binsbergen, Wim. "Aspects of Democracy and Democratisation in Zambia and Botswana." *Journal of Contemporary African Studies*, Vol. 13, (1) (January 1995).

Van de Walle, Nicolas. "The Politics of NonReform in Cameroon,." In Thomas Callaghy and John Ravenhill, eds., *Hemmed In: Responses to Africa's Economic Decline.* New York: Columbia University Press, 1993.

————. "Political Liberation and Economic Policy Reform in Africa." *World Development*, Vol. 22, No. 4, 1994.

Vaughn, Olufemi. "The Politics of Global Marginalization." *Journal of African and Asian Studies*, Vol. XXIX, (34) (1994).

Volman, Daniel. "Africa and the New World Order." *The Journal of Modern African Studies*, Vol. 31, (1993).

Wanjohi, N. Gatheru. "The Relationship Between Economic Progress and Democracy in Kenya and Tanzania." In Walter O. Oyugi, et. al., eds., *Democratic Theory and Practice in Africa*. London: Heinemann and James Currey, 1988.

West, Tina. "The Politics of the Implementation of Structural Adjustment in Zambia, 19851987." In *The Politics of Economic Reform in SubSaharan Africa*. Final Report Prepared by the Center for Strategic and International Studies, Washington, D.C., March 1992.

Wiseman, John, A. *Democracy in Black Africa: Survival and Revival*. New York: Paragon House, 1990.

Woods, Dwayne. "Civil Society in Europe and Africa: Limiting State Power Through the Public Sphere." *African Studies Review*, Vol. 35, No. 2, 1992.

"World Bank Hits Nigeria on Oil Earnings Report." *Platt's Oilgram News*, Vol. 70, (55) (March 19, 1992).

World Bank. *Accelerated Development in SubSaharan Africa: An Agenda for Action*. Washington, D.C.: World Bank, 1981.

————. *Industrial Strategy for Late Starters: The Experience of Kenya Tanzania and Zambia*. Washington, D.C.: World Bank Staff Working Papers No. 457, 1981.

————. *SubSaharan Africa: From Crisis to Sustainable Growth*. Washington, D.C.: World Bank, 1989.

———. *A Framework for Capacity Building in Policy Analysis and Economic Management in SubSaharan Africa*. Washington, D.C.: World Bank, 1990.

World Development Report 1995. New York: Oxford University Press, 1995.

Weiss, Herbert. "Zaire: Collapsed Society, Surviving State, Future Polity." In I. William Zartman, ed., *Collapsed States*. Boulder, CO: Lynne Rienner, 1995.

Yaker, Laiyashi. Keynote Address at the International Conference on "Africa in Transition: Challenges and Opportunities." AGSIM, Glendale, Arizona, 1820 February, 1993.

———. "Preliminary Assessment of the African Economy in 1994 and Prospects for 1995." End of Year Statement, UNECA, Addis Ababa, 15 December 1994.

Young, Crawford. *Ideology and Development in Africa*. New Haven: Yale University Press, 1982.

———. "Patterns of Social Conflict: State, Class and Ethnicity." *Daedalus*, Vol.III, (2) (1982).

———. "Beyond Patrimonial Autocracy: The African Challenge." in The Carter Center, *Beyond Autocracy in Africa*. Atlanta, GA: Emory University, 1989.

Zartman, I. William. "Africa in the Year 2000: Some Key Variables." *CSIS Africa Notes*, No. 161 (June 1994).

———. ed., *Collapsed States: The Disintegration and Restoration of Legitimate Authority*. Boulder, CO: Lynne Rienner, 1995.

Index

SOCIETY AND POLITICS IN AFRICA

Yakubu Saaka, General Editor

This multidisciplinary series publishes monographs and edited volumes that provide innovative approaches to the study and appreciation of contemporary African society. Although we focus mainly on subjects in the social sciences, we will consider manuscripts in the humanities that treat context as a significant aspect of discourse. Within the social sciences, we are looking for not only analytically outstanding studies but, what is more important, ones that may also have significant implications for the formulation and implementation of public policy in Africa. We are especially interested in works that challenge pre-existing hierarchies and paradigms.

For additional information about this series or for the submission of manuscripts, please contact:

Peter Lang Publishing
Acquisitions Department
275 7th Avenue, 28th floor
New York, New York 10001

To order other books in this series, please contact our Customer Service Department:

800-770-LANG (within the U.S.)
(212) 647-7706 (outside the U.S.)
(212) 647-7707 FAX
or browse online by series at:
www.peterlang.com

1709048